KEEPING THE DREAM ALIVE

HAS BEEN PUBLISHED
IN A LIMITED EDITION
OF WHICH THIS IS NUMBER

1613

Signed _____

for Lynda

PUBLISHED IN GREAT BRITAIN BY
COMPREHENSIVE ART SERVICES, MANCHESTER M3 2WZ.
1991

©STEWART W. BECKETT

ISBN 095164971X

PRINTED BY APPLE PRINTING, OLDHAM OL9 7LY

KEEPING THE DREAM ALIVE

A COMPREHENSIVE SEASON BY SEASON ACCOUNT OF OLDHAM ATHLETIC'S SOMETIMES PRECARIOUS STRUGGLE TO RE-GAIN FIRST DIVISION STATUS

1923-1991

DIVISION 1 TONIGHT.

"Keeping the Dream Alive"

HOPE

After the Famous Picture by G.F. Watts

ACKNOWLEDGEMENTS

The compilation of this book has involved two stages, firstly obtaining information and the checking of it using other sources. This process has required the assistance of many reference books, newspapers, organisations and individuals and I thank them all. Particular thanks are due to
THE OLDHAM EVENING CHRONICLE (for supplying many photographs reproduced in this book) · J.W. LEES & CO. (BREWERS) LTD.
OLDHAM ATHLETIC A.F.C. LTD. · THE FOOTBALL LEAGUE
THE MANCHESTER EVENING NEWS · COLORSPORT · THE HULTON PICTURE COMPANY · THE LOCAL INTEREST CENTRE, OLDHAM
BOB YOUNG · MR W. FULTON · MARTIN SMITH · VINCENT BROWN
KEDRICK WHITEHEAD · TONY MILLER · GORDON LAWTON
This publication would not have been possible but for the kind co-operation and assistance of the late Mr Graham Collin of the Oldham Evening Chronicle photographic department.

EDITED BY ERIC KRIEGER

DESIGN, PRODUCTION & PICTURE RESEARCH BY STEWART BECKETT
FOR COMPREHENSIVE ART SERVICES
COURTLETS HOUSE
38 KING STREET WEST
MANCHESTER M3 2WZ
ENGLAND

SETTING BY PINNACLE TYPESETTING · MANCHESTER · ENGLAND
PRINTED BY APPLE PRINTING · OLDHAM · ENGLAND

A.S.M.'S CARTOONS RE-ILLUSTRATED BY STEWART BECKETT

Whilst every effort has been made to ensure the accuracy of the information contained in this book, the author apologises in advance for any omissions and inaccuracies which may occur. However, he has relied for some of the information on the memories of those supporters and players who were connected with Oldham Athletic very many years ago, and it is always possible that you, the reader, have more accurate memories.

FORWARD, BY JOE ROYLE

The 'pinch me' season of '89/90, rich with Cup exploits and League promise, but sadly no tangible rewards, was always going to be a hard act to follow as fans everywhere were asking the same question. Can we really do it this time? Directors are fans, a fact not always realised by the lads on the terrace, and whilst dining out with our wives during the summer, Rod Adams the Latics Ground Director suggested to me that we needed a theme to follow the 'pinch me' season. Whilst driving home later than evening, a background cassette of various artists yielded the the theme that 'we're keeping the dream alive'. The theme was found. There had to be no more hangovers as had happened after our play-off experience four years previously. Rod mentioned his theme to Stewart Beckett who had just finished his excellent book on the Cup exploits, entitled *'The Team from a Town of Chimneys—Revisited.'* We had the theme, all we needed was the season to match it. The publication of this book, proves that we're back in Division One after sixty eight years, and who's to say the dream ends here? There may be cause for another volume Stewart or would the be 'Shooting for the Moon?' Dream on.

Joe Royle (Manager O.A.A.F.C. August 1991)

THE SEA OF TROUBLE ~ or waiting for the turn of the tide

OLDHAM ATHLETIC FIRST ELEVEN · DIVISION ONE · 1922-3
Back, left to right: FREEMAN · BASSINDALE · PILKINGTON · MATTHEWS · NAYLOR · GRUNDY
Front left to right. FERGUSSON · STANIFORTH · JONES (C) · HORROCKS
Photo taken at the Hawthorns—West Bromwich on April 14th 1923

Sixty eight years ago...

When Harry Horrocks scored Athletic's third goal against Cardiff City at Boundary Park on May 5th 1923, few people would have believed that fully 68 years would pass before Athletic scored another goal in First Division football, Earl Barrett making history against Liverpool at Anfield on 17th August 1991.

That 1922/23 season like many others, started full of optimism with the usual pre-season Reds v Stripes practice trials, raising much needed cash for the local Royal Infirmary, £200 in this case, a tidy sum sixty odd years ago.

With a professional staff of 30 players, and new signings Hibbert, Horrocks, Douglas, Cooper, Staniforth, Yarwood and Waddell, Athletic embarked on this campaign with a resounding 4-1 victory over Stoke City at Boundary Park, sparking an early season feeling of hope and enthusiasm. League fixtures in those days saw clubs invariably playing each other twice in consecutive weeks, the return fixture against the Potters finishing a 2-2 draw. It was suggested that the 'Latic Fanatics' of the time should not become over optimistic, the reporter knew that Stoke were considered the weakest side in Division One. His caution proved correct, by Christmas, Athletic had lost on 12 occasions, with only 5 victories, scoring a meagre 23 goals and conceding 41, prompting manager Charlie Roberts to resign, and the club's old friend and manager during the halcyon days, David Ashworth, to return after a very successful spell at Liverpool, taking them to the Division One Championship in 1921-22, and on course for a repeat performance this year. It was therefore a surprise when Athletic's directors induced him to return to Oldham in December 1922.

The team's performances did nothing to enhance Mr. Ashworth's reputation. A rare victory in February '23 over Birmingham City, brought an end to a terrible run of consecutive defeats and by the time they beat Blackburn in March, relegation was virtually assured, Billy Ferguson scoring his first goal in Division One football, in a 1-0 victory.

Saturday, April 28th 1923 saw the first Wembley Cup Final, (West Ham v Bolton), and coincided with Athletic's last away game in the First Division for 68 years, a 2-0 defeat at Cardiff City. So Athletic had been relegated for the first time in their history, and Division One football at Boundary Park would become a dim and distant dream.

Bill Horrocks and Earl Barrett —68 years separated their goals.

ARSENAL v

Arsenal's Bill Blyth heads his team's first goal past the despairing grasp
Arsenal a 2-0 victory. (inset) At

TIC · 1922-23

...letic's goalkeeper Howard Matthews. An own goal by Reg Freeman gave
Adlam clears an Arsenal attack.

MELODRAMA
NOVEMBER 4th 1922 · ATHLETIC 0, ASTON VILLA 2.

The Aston Villan: Sorry, old man, but I must play my part.
The Athletic One (falteringly): The dirty dog! g-good j-job for me it's not the last act.

FULHAM v ATHLETIC · 1923-24
Fulham's outside-left Frank Penn leaves Athletic's Adlam and Pilkington in his wake before crossing the ball. Athletic's defence held out for a 0-0 draw.

With the careful attention of the loyal Jimmy Hanson, trainer since 1906, David Ashworth set about a drastic re-building programme, Tom Heaton and Archie Longmuir signed from Athletic's big rivals, Blackburn Rovers, along with Bill Howson from Bradford City, and Thomas Fleetwood, who in earlier years had won a League Championship medal with Everton, counterbalancing many outgoings, the most notable of which was Reginald Freeman's £4,000 move to Middlesbrough, guided by Athletic's old manager (1914-1921) Herbert Bamlett.

Pre-season saw Athletic's long-serving goalkeeper, Howard Matthews, voted onto the Players Union Management Committee, whose chairman was former Latics favourite from pre-war times, Jimmy Fay.

A vote of confidence in the club's future was shown by the high number of season tickets sold, indicating the club's supporters were hoping for a quick return to Division One. The season opened amid a deep trade depression with a game against Blackpool at Bloomfield Road during Oldham Wakes holidays. What better excuse for a depression-busting break by the seaside. Thousands of Oldhamers travelled to the Fylde to cheer Athletic to a 2-2 draw against one of the Second Division's better sides.

The draws continued, as Athletic got off to moderate start, only one win during their first eight games. On October 6th 1923, during a home fixture with Manchester United, Athletic's Sam Wynne had the unusual experience of scoring two goals for Athletic, and two own goals for United. Latics finally won 3-2, Billy Howson scoring the decisive goal.

January 1924 proved Athletic's best month, four matches won, including an epic cup tie with Sunderland, and only one defeat, at lowly Nelson. This was indicative of the club's up-and-down form this season, one week defeating the Wearsiders, one of the best sides in the country, captained by the great Charlie Buchan, then next week falling to Nelson. This point was underlined as Athletic crashed out of the F.A. Cup 2-0 to an ordinary Swindon Town in round 2.

The team was thankful for the re-emergence of top amateur player Johnny Blair in mid-season. He played his first game of the 1923/24 season on New Year's Day, scoring the only goal in a 1-0 win over Stockport County. In all he played 19 games, scoring 15 goals, easily the best average of any Athletic player since the Great War, prompting former Athletic favourite, Billy Cook, to comment, "If he trained as fine as the average professional, he would be one of the best centre forwards in the country". Sadly Johnny Blair fractured an ankle the following season, and never fully lived up to his potential.

Manager Ashworth was urged to strengthen his side, after Athletic jettisoned a fine chance of promotion, finishing 7th in their first season back in Division Two, but Athletic's directors found supporting the manager difficult as the club were deep in debt, with gates down to below the 10,000 mark. Promising players had to leave, Frank Hargreaves being a prime example. His £750 transfer to Everton was unpopular with supporters, although he returned several times over the next 20 years.

Drifting Away

ATHLETIC'S RESERVES · 1923-24

Sketches from Athletic Camp

A space is reserved in the Board Room for a photograph of the 1923-4 team, but it's not yet decided what to put underneath it—"Winners of English Cup" or "Champions of 2nd Division"

The only way I could get all of Gray in, was to catch him when the manager was giving him a few words of advice.

Gray's head after coming out of the bath.

Gray's head after coming out of the dressing room.

Heaton an 'artistic half-back

Longmuir, the sharpshooter

Horrock's is as perky as ever.

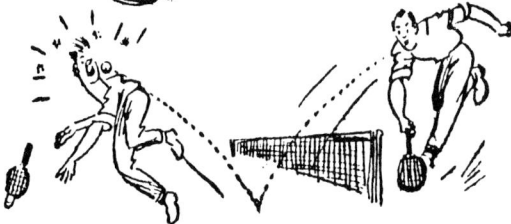

Howard Matthews' service at tennis is nearly as good as his service for the Athletic club.

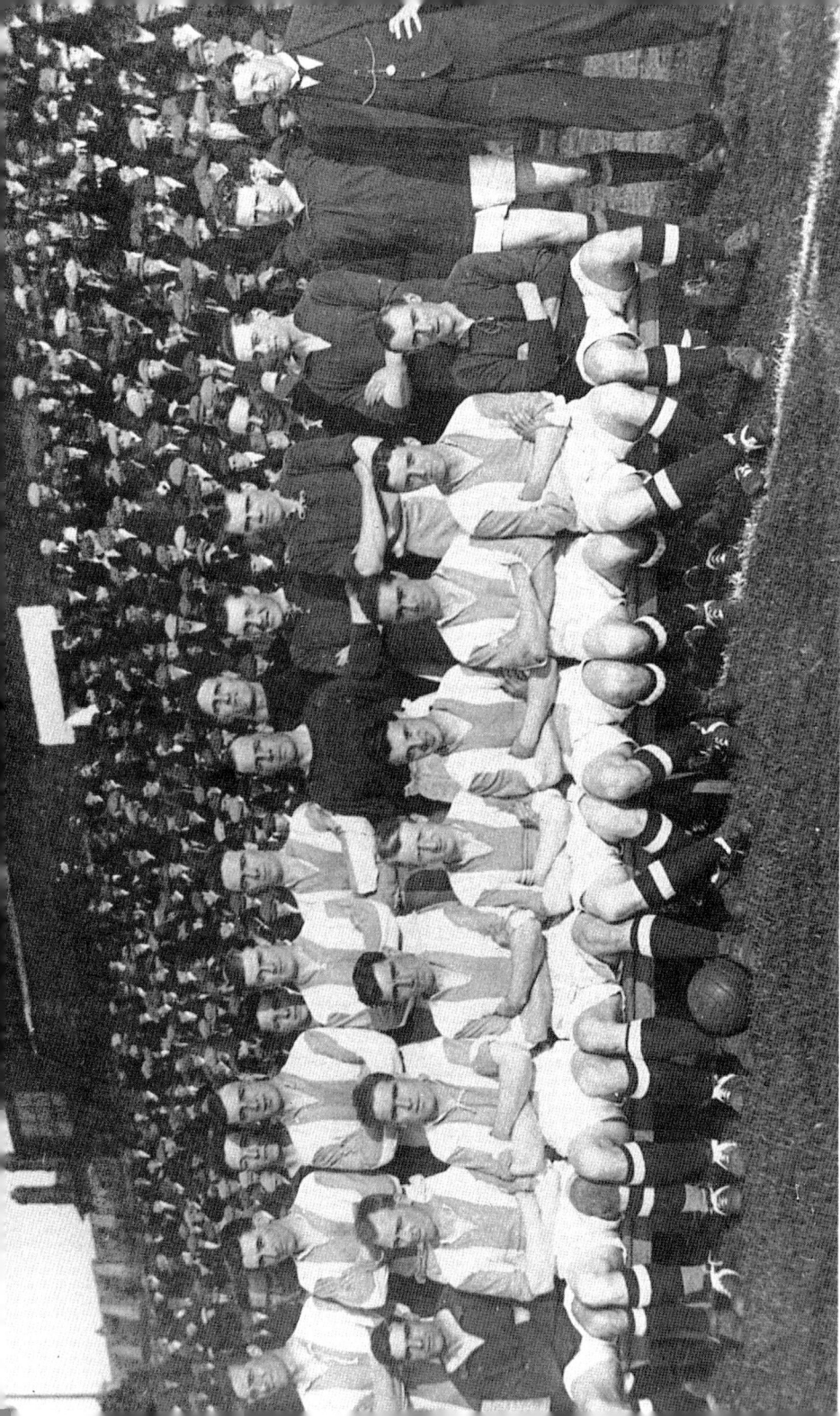

OLDHAM ATHLETIC · 1924-25

Left to right: Back row: BROOME · IVILL · TILLEY · YARWOOD · GILLESPIE · PILKINGTON · ADLAM · MATTHEWS · GRAY · HEATON

WILKINSON · GREGORY · GRICE · WEEDER · HANSON (Trainer)

Front row: MIDDLETON · BLAIR · WYNNE · GRUNDY · BASSINDALE · NAYLOR · DOUGLAS · WATSON · JONES

Although those behind the scenes were aware that negotiations were in progress, the announcement in July 1924 that Athletic's manager, David Ashworth, was to succeed Mr.J.E.Mangnall as manager of Manchester City came as a surprise to the body of Athletic's supporters, and obviously greatly hindered pre-season preparations. Mr. Ashworth had an agreement with the Latics chairman extending over a number of years, but an escape clause allowed him his freedom if a 'better post' became available. During Ashworth's second spell with Athletic, the club's directors had backed their manager to the tune of £3,000 on new players, a tidy sum in those days, especially when one considered Athletic's desperate financial plight. The books showed a 'paper profit' of £504.11.9d, this compared with a loss of £3725 the previous year. The profit was due entirely to outgoing transfers, gate receipts being down by £3,360. The club attributed that figure to the deepening trade recession, and a lack of interest in 2nd Division football.

Athletic's hopes this season were based more on hope than solid foundations. Not having the necessary capital, the directors had to guarantee overdrafts at the bank and find money from their own pockets. "If gates do not improve, something very serious might happen to Athletic," were the comforting words spoken by chairman, L.R. Stanton.

As the 1924-25 season opened,only 19 professionals were on the register. One of these, Jon Yarwood, was unfit to play,and two others, Jimmy Naylor and Isaac Bassendale, were so seriously injured in the practice games as to rule them out of early season.

The economic climate forced Athletic to sign, as a last resort, a number of local amateurs to make up the numbers. "In football it is imperative that possible troubles should be met half way," counselled Athletic's new manager/secretary Mr. Bob Mellor, a long standing servant to his beloved club.

The newcomers pre-season were Ted Ivill, a half-back from Atherton, John Carroll, a forward with Selby, and Albert Broome, an inside-forward from Manchester United. It had been reported in the Glasgow papers that a doctor Fyfe, a prominent centre-forward with the famous amateur club Queens Park, was coming to Oldham to take-up a pre-season trial. Since the rumour began, manager Bob Mellor had made investigations in every direction, but failed to nail the matter down.Inquiries were made in local medical circles, and to the Queens Park club itself without any joy. Doctor Fyfe remains a mystery to this day.

Athletic were still advertising season tickets at 17/- as the season kicked off with a surprise result at Southampton, Latics forcing a 0-0 scoreline, goalkeeper Howard Matthews gaining a standing ovation at the end. No such ovation the following Monday, as Clapton Orient stuck five goals into Matthews' net, with only one in reply. During these two fixtures, both Bob Gillespie and Harry Wilkinson (also a talented cricketer with Oldham and Werneth) were injured, but worse was to follow when goalscorer, Johnny Blair, broke an ankle whilst playing against Clapton Orient at Boundary Park.

This bad luck and below strength staff set the pattern for the best part of this season. The playing squad was quite inadequate without injuries but depletion in this manner was a disaster. It became one long struggle to avoid relegation and

THE GOOD SAMARITAN
(The Oldham Athletic Supporters' Club)

After the famous painting by G.F. Watts, R.A.

it was only a gallant Athletic performance in the last game of the season at Crystal Palace that decided their fate, a John Keedwell goal giving Athletic a 1-0 win, and condemning Palace to the Third Division.

Gates had been gradually dwindling to vanishing point, and it became apparent that unless the public was roused, the club would go under. Athletic shared along with Clapton Orient the doubtful distinction of having the lowest attendances in Division 2. The figures ranging from 25,000 at Old Trafford and Hillsborough, to a paltry 8,000 at Boundary Park. Athletic ended a somewhat strange ban on a supporters' club at Boundary Park, by allowing a club to form in April of 1925, the first meeting being at Whiteheads Cafe, Market Place, with an annual subscription of 1/- a time.

The club's directors could have been forgiven for contemplating a trip to Lourdes for a cure to Athletic's ills, this before a knight in shining armour in the shape of the Green Final sports paper came to the club's assistance, generously opening it's columns for a public appeal. The Athletic directors contributed over £2,000 by giving up debentures to this amount, in addition to a cheque of ten guineas each. The total amount realised exceeded £4,000, and with it, the whole of the tradesmen's accounts of the club were cleared, the balance helping to pay summer wages. From this appeal arose the idea of bazaar, which again raised valuable funds to assist Athletic. In the same month as the bazaar, messrs Barlow and Mellor (Director and Secretary/Manager) reported to the Board that they could sign two promising Durham City players-centre-forward Camsell and goalkeeper Harrison-both for £750. "It was resolved that it be not entertained", recorded Athletic's minutes. Instead, Camsell went to Middlesbrough and his 59 goals saw Boro' to the 1927 Second Division Championship.

CHRISTMAS 1924 · GREAT EXPECTATIONS

The Goose That Must Lay the Golden Eggs

Mother Goose: "Now old friend, it's up to you to lay a few golden eggs, or else we shall have to sell up the dear old home."

"WHERE THE RAINBOW ENDS"

A rainbow appeared over Boundary Park last Saturday, ending at Royton. Later it moved on to Shaw. You can't really blame it!

**BLACKBURN ROVERS 1, ATHLETIC 0
F.A. CUP 1ST ROUND · 1924-25**

Oldham Athletic: "Well, anyway, if I get a thick ear I shall also get a thick purse".

1925-26

Last season's anxieties and fears were a blessing in disguise. They brought home to everyone concerned, in a manner in which nothing else could have done, Athletic's desperate plight. They impressed upon everyone the fact that relegation was not the worst of evils facing the club. Fortunately, the dogged spirit which is claimed to be a characteristic of Oldham folk came to the rescue and turned the tide, creating a new-born enthusiasm and faith in the future, at a time of great hardship, as the countrywide recession bit deeper, culminating in the first great 'General Strike'.

This year, Jimmy Hanson, Athletic's trainer, completed 21 years with Athletic. No club in England had a more conscientious servant. Athletic took the first team squad on a pre-season weekend trip to Southport, where, during a visit to a fairground, full-back Sammy Wynne tried his luck on a football 'shooting range'. "He'll knock that lad out" said one of Sammy's mates, referring to a youthful goalkeeper standing 10 yards away. "He can have 3-1 against" boasted the stall's owner, who later wished he'd kept his mouth shut, as Sammy proceeded to flatten the keeper with a typical thunderbolt, then score a goal with practically every shot. Sammy returned to Southport some months later, when the stall holder was heard to shout, upon seeing the Latics full-back, "Not 3-1 against you sir, it's 3-1 on". Sadly, Sammy Wynne died 18 months later, playing for Bury against Sheffield United, when he collapsed taking a free kick and never recovered.

There were grounds for assuming Athletic's new signings, Goodwin, Hey, Barnes, Goodier, Pynegar, Ormston and the returning Frank Hargreaves from Everton would prove a stronger lot than those who were shown the door. A total of 26 professionals saw training start earlier than usual, due to a very heavy initial list of fixtures. This '25/26 season, incidentally, witnessed the use of a new off-side rule which was felt would prove an advantage to Athletic's style of play.

The season opened in promising fashion with a 2-1 win over Barnsley at Boundary Park before 12,000 people. An excellent attendance considering half of Oldham was enjoying the traditional Wakes holidays. Athletic had a fine record up to Christmas morning, including F.A. Cup ties, Lancashire Cup and League games, they won 14 and drew 5 of their 22 fixtures which was promotion form, but then came a sudden slump. It was a black Christmas-tide as the next 3 League games were lost, Wolves taking maximum points, while Sheffield Wednesday ran rings around Athletic at Hillsborough by 5-1, easily the heaviest defeat of the campaign.

The remainder of the season saw form distinctly patchy, wins draws and defeats being generously intermingled. Taking League matches only, after defeating Barnsley at Oakwell on January 2nd, there were 20 left, of these 7 were won, 3 drawn and 10 lost. Therefore the season divided itself into halves of great contrast:

	P	W	L	D	F	A	POINTS
Before:	18	10	3	5	35	21	25
After:	24	8	13	3	39	41	19

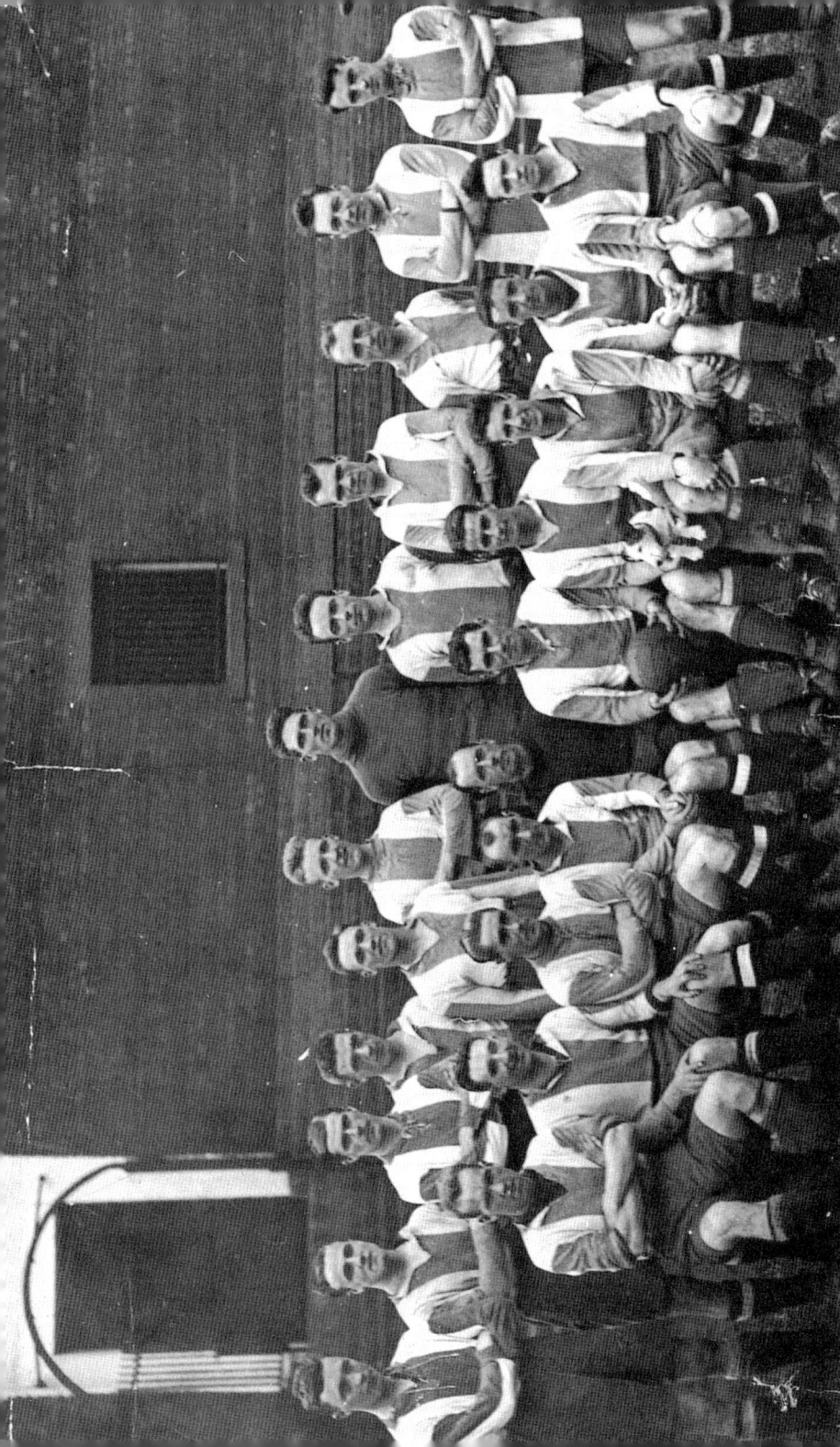

ATHLETIC PHOTO-CALL 1925-26

Back Left-right: BARNES · WHITE · PILKINGTON · TAYLOR · SCHOLES · GOODIER · GRAY · ADLAM · WILKINSON · PYNEGAR · HEATON · NAYLOR
Front Left-right: KEEDWELL · IVILL · DOUGLAS · JONES · MATTHEWS · GRUNDY (Captain, with 'Binky' the club mascot) ORMSTON · HARGREAVES
WATSON · GILLESPIE

For the first time since the Great War, Athletic finished with a credit balance as far as goals were concerned. An increase in both 'for' and 'against' was expected due to the off-side ruling. The 8-3 victory over Nottingham Forest was a record to this date since the club acquired League status in 1907.

Athletic were compelled to play in the preliminary rounds of the F.A. Cup, defeating Lytham in a farcical match at Boundary Park by 10-1, an Oldham club record. In round 2 they had a much harder job than expected, before defeating amateur side Stockton by 6-4. In round 3 Athletic travelled to Millwall, and to everyone's surprise drew 1-1. The metropolitan club won the reply by the only goal. On the plus side, the Athletic 3rd team, formed for the first time this year, won the Lancashire Mid-Week League Championship. However, despite the marked improvement in the club's performances, the attendances at Boundary Park had been disappointing, although there was an upward trend, gates averaging about 10,500. Jimmy Naylor, Latics stylish half-back, completed 36 League and Cup games this season, with Arthur Ormston top scorer with 23 League and Cup goals.

THE START OF A NEW ERA
Mr. Green Final: "And all the best in the New Year, old pal."

DOWN AT THE FIRST HURDLE

F.A. CUP 3RD ROUND, JANUARY 1927

The 'Latic', "And I don't thank you for legging me down, old foggy weather"

STOCKTON v ATHLETIC · F.A. CUP 2ND ROUND, 1925-26
Photo shows the Stockton team defeated 6-4.

To avoid clashing with the Oldham Rugby Charity Match at Watersheddings, Athletic re-arranged their usual pre-season Saturday practice game to Monday, when a pre-match ceremony saw the Mayor of Oldham, Councillor Pollard, declare the new concrete terracing at Boundary Park open. The work had been completed by members of the Athletic Supporters Club, and they were to be complimented on a fine improvement. Had the work been contracted out, it would have cost the club a small fortune.

A team of Athletic footballers visited Crompton for a challenge cricket match the following Saturday. The locals wondered if Sammy Wynne could hit a cricket ball as hard as he did a football-they were'nt disappointed as Sammy proceeded to smash one through the pavilion window.

The Athletic faithfull viewed the club's chances with high hopes this season, as the newly signed players were thought to be of a higher standard than had been the case over the past couple of years. Jack Hacking and Billy Porter arrived from Fleetwood, Ben Brelsford from Barrow, Jack Armitage from Burnley and Norman Crompton from Denbigh. The close season saw the departure of long-serving Howard Matthews to Port Vale, and amateur, Johny Blair, to Arsenal.It was hoped the football-loving public of Oldham would rally round the blue and white flag at Boundary Park in increasing numbers, as the previous season had seen the club distinctly on the upgrade.

Athletic commenced the campaign with 26 professionals, the majority of

THE 'LATICS' SUPPORTER

When his team have won...

... and lost.

OLDHAM ATHLETIC · 1926-27
Left to right: Back row: PYNEGAR · Mr SKIPWORTH (Director) · J. HANSON (Trainer) · ADLAM ·
Front row: KING · SCHOFIELD · WYNNE · HARGREAVES ·

whom had "the asset of height and weight on their side". A difficult programme awaited the team in the first month, but they adapted well. Of the first eleven games, seven were won, one drawn and three lost. With an average Boundary Park attendance approaching 16,000 it was indicative of what a successful team in Oldham would draw. The next dozen matches yielded three wins, three draws and six defeats, and down went the averages. Then came the F.A.Cup tie with Brentford, a 4-2 defeat at Boundary Park, after the original match had been abandoned due to fog, with Athletic leading 2-1. This disappointment some supporters didn't forgive, for a 15,000 gate was never again recorded this season.

From mid-February to early April, seven games were played and only one won, the remainder lost. Many supporters considered the team had 'gone to the dogs', and wherever one went in Oldham, the most uncomplimentary things were overheard about the club. It was the old business of kicking a man when he was down. An end-of-season recovery saw Athletic win five times and draw two of their last seven fixtures, to finish 10th in Division Two on 44 points. Except for the game with Barnsley on New Year's Day, Athletic had scored in every match played. The Boundary Park club missed out on promotion by eleven points, but had slightly improved it's record on last year.

During the season Athletic transferred Bert Gray, the Welsh international goalkeeper to rivals, Manchester City, for £2250, and popular Sammy Wynne to Bury for £2,250, where he sadly died during a game with Sheffield United just four months after his transfer. During the

T (Director) · GRAY · IVILL · PORTER · NAYLOR · ARMITAGE

last game of the season, a Boundary Park fixture against South Shields, both sets of players payed a tribute to Sam Wynne with a minute's silence. The band played Abide With Me. It was an impressive and touching scene. A collection for the player's widow raised £29.18s.1d. Athletic's secretary/ manager Bob Mellor said, "Sammy Wynne was an earnest, lionhearted player. He was as happy as a schoolboy on holiday when playing the game which was just as much his hobby as his life's work. The whole-heartedness of his play was revealed in every game he played".

Athletic transferred Arthur Ormston to Bradford City for £650, £80 going back to the player in lieu of benefit. This season, Jimmy Naylor completed one hundred consecutive first team appearances and Albert Pynegar finished top scorer with 19 League and Cup goals. The team was watched by 256,466 spectators at Boundary Park in the 21 League matches, an increase in the average attendance of only 535. A decorated tramcar carried the Rugby Challenge Cup Winners, Oldham, to a civic reception at the Town Hall as envious glances were cast from Boundary Park.

NEIL HARRIS
Athletic's new centre forward

OLDHAM ATHLETIC · 1927-28 (at Chelsea)

Back row, Left to right: (players only)
ADLAM · MALPASS · HACKING · IVILL · NAYLOR
KING (J) · DYSON · TAYLOR (G) · GRUNDY
PYNEGAR · BRELSFORD

1927-28

In early July 1927, Andrew Wilson was appointed Team Manager of Athletic. The ex-Scottish International and Bristol Rovers manager was delighted at the prospect of returning to a part of Lancashire that saw so much of him during his playing days, and to be connected with a club upon whose ground he had played many First Division games. "There is one game," he recalled, "that will always stand out in my memory, and that was the last time I played on Boundary Park. It was a First Division game, I was captain of Sheffield Wednesday, and my brother David was the Oldham captain. That was Christmas Eve, 1910, and I believe Oldham beat us. For two brothers to face each other and toss for change of ends in a First Division game was surely a rare occurrence". David Wilson, incidentally, spent fourteen seasons at Boundary Park and was now retired and living in Blackpool. "My one aim and object will be to get Oldham Athletic back in the First Division, and in my efforts to do that I shall leave no stone unturned," promised Wilson. The Ladies Committe and Supporters Club arranged a firework display and garden party at Boundary Park to give Athletic's followers the opportunity of meeting the new manager, whose first recruit was Neil Harris, the ex-Newcastle and Scottish International centre-forward. The £400 signing was a member of the Magpies F.A.Cup winning side of 1924. Athletic were banking on the experience, influence and guiding hand of Mr. Wilson to have an overall effect on the club, but many thought there was too much expected of the new manager and his prize-signing Harris.

GETTING TO THE TOP OF THE BILL

"Wish we had a show like this at Watersheddings" / "must see them at Wembley!" / "Look like taking the City by storm" / "Sure to take a big part in the 1st Division Revue!" / "He used to star years ago" / "Please Dad can I be a 'Latic' when I grow up?"

"Latic", the entertainer (sotto voce): And they thought I was no good when I came on!

The club opened the campaign with a playing staff of 30, and the pre-season practice matches indicated active competition for places in the first team. Of last season's players, 22 had been retained, and eight new men signed, including Arden Maddison from Port Vale, Harry Stafford from Heywood St. James', and Cliff Stanton from Altrincham.

Although Athletic had 34 players on the books, it proved impossible to field an eleven capable of making a sustained effort to secure promotion. Things looked promising until the third week in February but then came the slump, the last 14 games yielding only four wins, two draws and eight defeats. But for a hard fought 1-1 draw at Preston North End, and a convincing 5-0 victory over Hull City, it would have been an extremely dismal finish to Wilson's first season in charge, but they finished a respectable 7th on 46 points.

The club did not do particularly well in the F.A.Cup. After a very creditable win over Blackpool at Bloomfield Road by 4-1, the team lost 3-0 at Tottenham, finishing the game with only eight players on the pitch, the depletion due to serious injuries. A bumper crowd of 36,828 paid £2,720 to watch Athletic's walking-wounded.

During this season the roof blew off the Chadderton Road End during construction. It was re-erected, then blew off again, before eventually providing 'happy' shelter for several thousand fans.

From a financial viewpoint, it was gratifying to see an increase in support and a consequent advance in the gross gate receipts. Albert Pynegar was leading scorer again with 19 league goals. Ever-presents were Teddy Ivill and Jimmy Naylor, who achieved this distinction for the third time in five seasons.

TOTTENHAM 3, ATHLETIC 0 · F.A. CUP 4TH ROUND · 1927-28
Athletic's centre-half Jack Armitage gives the Spurs' centre-forward an eyefull as he clears a Tottenham attack. (inset) Armitage clears again!

A thletic were in a much healthier position financially than had been the recent case, but they pointed out to supporters that this did not mean 'bank balance building', but rather an appreciable reduction in debt. The club, therefore, faced this season with only one experienced centre-half, and little top class cover for any position. The 28 professionals included six new men, Peter Floyd from Lancaster Town, Tom Smelt and Cliff Foster from Manchester City, Matt Gray from Atherton, John Lowe from Port Vale, and Alf Brown from local junior football.

Early season injuries had manager, Wilson, struggling to patch a team together, as one draw and four defeats reflected. Things got worse, as the first half of the season witnessed a gradual decline until all seemed lost. Of the first nineteen matches played, only three were won, and two drawn, the team earning censure in the press for their shocking displays which saw only 8 points collected up to Christmas morning. Then came the New Year and the Great Escape, Athletic winning 25 points from 13 games (2 points for a win in these days), to finish 18th in the League on 37 points and escape relegation by three points.

Had the team shown similar form before Christmas, they would undoubtedly have been hob-nobbing with the promotion candidates. It seemed inexplicable that any team of professional footballers should show such varying form from week

THE WINTER OF HIS DISCONTENT
"Blow, blow, thou winter wind. Thou art not so unkind as man's ingratitude".

Oldham Athletic look like "catching a cold" this season.

OLDHAM ATHLETIC · 1928-29
Left to right: Back row:
MADDISON · BROWN · PORTER · NAYLOR
ADLAM · HEY · DYSON
Centre row:
ARMITAGE · KING (J) · TAYLOR · HACKING
GOODIER · FLOYD · JONES (E) · STANTON
Front row:
LOWE · PYNEGAR · HARRIS · GRUNDY · IVILL
WATSON · FOSTER (players only)

The Relegation Bird of Prey

"Not much use me hovering over here, he's gaining strength"

to week. There was no doubt that the resurrection in Athletic's fortunes dated from the time the younger players got their chance-Fred Worrall, Jimmy Dyson, Stewart Littlewood, Matt Gray and Bill Hasson, all with an average age of only 21, would serve Athletic well in future years. "Once we got all our men fit, had a break in the luck, and a few promising youngsters, all was well," said manager Wilson, "we have had nothing but bad luck since the previous January with players being hurt, and our best players at that".

Ted Goodier who had joined Athletic as a squad player three years previously, proved himself a splendid successor to the popular Jimmy Naylor, who reluctantly moved to Huddersfield Town in December '28 for what was understood to be the highest fee received (£3,750) by Athletic to this date. Teddy Ivill was the only professional on the club's books not to miss a match, recording a maximum 44 in League and Cup for the second season running. Centre-forward Stewart Littlewood, a £1,300 signing in January '29 from Port Vale, finished leading scorer with 12 goals. A third round F.A.Cup tie with local rivals, Bolton Wanderers, earned a 2-0 victory for the 'Trotters', in front of a 34,449 crowd at Burnden Park.

1929–1930 REVUE

The "Ball"-et Overture

" "To those supporters of Oldham Athletic who are in their early 20's and who desire to see First Division football before qualifying for a state pension, should make periodical visits to Maine Road"—these were the light-hearted sentiments expressed by the cynical few prior to the season's kick-off.

Athletic started with a comparatively young squad of 26 professionals, with new additions Frank Moss, a goalkeeper signed from Preston North End, Tommy Seymour from Welsh amateurs, Connah's Quay, Billy 'Spud' Murphy from Southampton, Joe Taylor from Blackpool, and Seth King, a £400 capture from Sheffield United, who was appointed club captain.

This turned out to be a season of splendid achievement and promise, turned sour by the final failure to snatch promotion. Athletic were top of the 2nd Division table practically throughout the season, and at the three-quarter stage were five points clear. Then came Easter and the turning point. Injuries hit senior players at a time when Athletic played 3 important games in 4 days, two matches against promotion rivals, Blackpool, and one against Bristol City. One point gained from those fixtures, let promotion slip from their grasp. If four points had been forthcoming, Athletic would have been in the First Division, despite losing their last fixture at Barnsley.

There had been several noteworthy occurrences, such as Stewart Littlewood's record in scoring 28 goals, and the club's record in aggregating 90 goals in the League. Despite end-of-season failures, collecting 20 away points was the best return for many seaons, and Athletic's goal average was among the best in all four divisions. Teddy Ivill, Les Adlam and Seth King all completed a maximum 44 League and Cup appearances.

Keeping the "Wolves" from their "Goal"

Goodier did nothing "goodier" than score the £1000 goal,

which the "Wolves" heard, but never saw.

The boy who took the board round announcing an excursion for the replay looked like committing murder.

REPLAY EXCURSION TO WOLVERHAMPTON

Hacking was there "to be shot at" but not shot past.

The "Wolves" intended to win by hook, or Crook (this is him)

Hasson argued with "The Arm of the Law" (Bellis, the policeman.)

It is usually a bad sign when the crowd leave "Spion Kop" before time;

but in the last minute, they burst into jubilation. (A)

WELL IN HIS STRIDE.
STEWART LITTLEWOOD : Only another three to go. **S'easy.**

Picture of a biased Rugby supporter trying to get down to Boundary Park last Saturday without being recognised.

The Thrilling Cup Tie

(A) ATHLETIC 1, WOLVES 0 · F.A. Cup 3rd Round · 1929-30
(B) ATHLETIC 3, SHEFFIELD WEDNESDAY 4 · F.A. Cup 4th Round · 1929-30

In the F.A. Cup, Athletic gained a fortunate victory over the Wolves, Ted Goodier scoring the only goal on full time. In the 4th round, Seth King and his men went under by 4-3 to Sheffield Wednesday the League Champions, in a heroic and memorable struggle before a Boundary Park record 46,471 spectators. This match was unanimously voted the finest ever seen on the ground. During the F.A. Cup Final of this year between Huddersfield Town and Arsenal, the German Airship Graf Zeppelin decided to put in an impromptu appearance, casting a shadow over the stadium and the rest of the decade. Ex-Athletic player, Jimmy Naylor, now playing for Huddersfield was quoted as saying, ''I did not see this ugly monster of the air until it had turned for Cardington. As I looked up to the stand opposite the Royal Pavilion, the engines roared as though it were scraping the roof of the stand, how can we get on with the game when this thing is upon us.'' The airship soon went with its flock of accompanying aeroplanes, and Huddersfield lost 2-0.

Biffs for the Champion (?)

Oldham Athletic: How am I going on with my sparring? Owt like a champion?
Second: You're gaining on points, but tha'll a to watch them London kids, they're trying to hand
out the K.O.

Everton : Well, you didn't knock me off
my perch.
'Latic : No, but I had a jolly good try.

THE HOPELESS DAWN.

A Happy New Year

King: Don't stand knocking walk right in, a right royal welcome awaits.

Athletic players cup-tie training before Sheffield Wed. match · January 1930.

Out in the Cold

Footballer (bitterly):
God rest ye, merry gentlemen, let nothing you dismay.

Swansea's "Swan-Song"

" WHAT ARE THE WILD WAVES SAYING? "
Athletic look like being at the mercy of
the Blackpool waves. King hopes to
skipper his crew through.

The disappointment of last season tended to blind the eyes of the average supporter to the fact that Athletic had, in the brief space of a season, risen from the depths to a position of respectability. Athletic's squad was still young, and the experiences of the last two seasons would stand them in good stead. ''Young men should improve at their trade, whatever it may be'', said manager Wilson. With new signings, Bert Burridge from Sheffield Wednesday, Tommy Pickersgill from Runcorn, Cliff Stanton from Macclesfield, Fred Fitton from Burnley and John Pears from Accrington Stanley, Athletic kicked off during the Wakes holidays with a 2-0 victory over Bradford P.A., at Boundary Park.

The first seven games yielded five wins and two defeats, with the support fairly satisfactory, although it was evident that the bitter disappointment felt at the team's failure to win promotion the previous year had not been entirely forgotten. The next seven engagements produced one win, one draw, and five defeats, and it was then the treasurer began to feel a draught.

With the exception of reasonable returns from the visits of Bury and Wolves, things went from bad to worse. The F.A. Cup debacle, when Watford visited Boundary Park and knocked the bottom out of Athletic's universe by winning 3-1, was the real focal point as far as support was concerned, turning the season into a financial disaster. Athletic hardly deserved the huge financial decrease. A drop from promotion contenders, to twelvth position in the table was bound to be reflected in gate receipts, but certainly not to the extent of a 35 per cent slump.

The loss of points in away matches, and the inability to score, had been a constant problem for Athletic, only sixteen goals in 21 fixtures. To a certain degree, this season's falling away was due to Stewart Littlewood's marked loss of form. He scored only seven goals in 23 appearances before his £1,550 transfer back to Port Vale in March '31, and there was no doubt that some of the younger players did not make the progress expected.

The Green Final reported, ''It seems the Oldham soccer fans will stay away from Boundary Park unless there is a promotion battle, or football up to or exceeding the Arsenal standard. But just maybe the necessity for saving an ill-be-spared shilling is the real reason.''

Teddy Ivill completed his fourth season without missing a League game, Seth King completed his second, both with 43 League and Cup appearances. Jimmy Dyson finished leading scorer with 16 goals.

ATHLETIC SECOND ELEVEN · 1930-31

OLDHAM ATHLETIC · 1930-3?
Left to right: Back row: STAFFORD (Reserve) · IVILL · HACKING
Front row: WORRALL · DYSON · LITTLEWOOD · KENNE?
Sitting: ADLAM · GRAY

SUNDAY GRAPHIC

SUNDAY, MARCH 22, 1931

Join Our League of Youth To-day. Entry Form Page 11

HOME DEFEAT FOR BURY AGAINST OLDHAM

Oldham scored a great victory in defeating Bury at Gigg-lane by three goals to one. Harrison, the Bury goalkeeper, saved his side from a heavier defeat, and is seen above, making two of his many saves during raids by the Oldham forwards.

Johnstone (Oldham) beats Harrison to score his side's second goal.

Dyson (Oldham) heads for goal.

Moss (Oldham) gathers the ball w... J. R. Smith bearing down upon him.

An action study during the clearing of a corner-kick from the Bury goal area.

J. R. Smith, of Bury, gets highest i a heading duel.

Printed and Published for the DAILY SKETCH AND SUNDAY GRAPHIC, LTD., 200, Gray's Inn-road, London, W.C.1, by ALLIED NEWSPAPERS LIMITED, Withy Grove, Manchester.—SUNDAY, MARCH 22, 1931.

The "Shakers" Shaken at Boundary Park

HOPE soon opened the score for Bury;

then Stanton put the ball on Hasson's head for a goal; that was FAITH;

then Amos found himself alone with the ball so he banged it in - that was CHARITY

Playing the game on the wing Playing the game which is thrilling After a two points win, we get a lot more than a shilling.

Knocking the players about having a rare old time.

I'm not going off, till a quarter to four, For it's my — day — out.

After Fitton had nosed the ball, he reminded one of the late George Formby.

If only he would play the part, what a star! And besides, if he stepped into his shoes what a shot!

Happy Days are Here Again

Gorgeous Bradford made Oldham Wakes bright, and

Dyson's opening goal made it brighter still.

Charlie Pringle, Bradford's captain, plays with his head, as befits the son-in-law of Billy Meredith.

Seth King's hair suggests that Alf the football world's a stage --- and one man in his time plays many parts.

Gerrup! show's started.

First, the babe mewling & puking in his trainer's arms;

then, like the school-boy creeping like a snail, unwillingly to play;

the lover, sighing for the bonus, to the secretary's eye-brows;

...the "old soldier" handling like fury in the goal's mouth;

.... bearded like the bard; and then, the Final - sans hope, sans win, sans "fairy-ann."

On book form, this season's Second Division had an open aspect about it. Athletic's prospects looked just about the same as they were twelve months previous, and it was no secret that during the close season the club had hardly known were the next 'bob' was coming from. Last season's ups and downs led to a number of reserves being given their chance in the senior team, but the final nine games saw a return to a more settled eleven. Four new players were signed, but it was considered unlikely that any of them would immediately be serious contenders for first team duty. They were Austin Trippier from Rochdale, Jimmy Hope from Winsford United, Jack Roscoe from Mossley and Bill Galsthorpe, a local amateur. Latics goalkeeper Frank Moss was rushed to hospital after swallowing his false teeth during a pre-seaon trial game. He fully recovered to join Arsenal for £2,225, the cash breathing much needed life into Athletic's coffers. Moss made a big name for himself in Arsenal's great championship winning sides of the early to mid-1930's.

Athletic upset their supporters by increasing the price of a season ticket from £2.10s to £3.00, and then upset them even more by having a most disappointing season. Except on isolated occasions, the standard of performance had been mediocre. Relegation was dodged only in the last few weeks of the season, when narrow victories over Bradford P.A. and Charlton Athletic at Boundary Park secured Athletic's Second Division future. Sandwiched between those two wins was an appalling performance at Wolverhampton, the home side placing seven goals into Athletic's net, which summed-up the club's season.

PHOTO-CALL 1931-32

The Oldham Athletic Jockey: Wish they'd run a Dublin sweep for us.
(At Boundary Park Stables they feel that the fences should be done away with)

To secure only 24 points out of 42 played for at Boundary Park was more than disappointing. Had the team shown just average form at home, the relegation issue would never have raised it head. Athletic's goals total of 62 was among the lowest returns in the Second Division. They completed the season in 18th place with 36 points. The one ray of sunshine in a gloomy season was provided by the F.A. Cup tie against Huddersfield Town at Boundary Park, when 30,607 spectators, paying gross receipts of £1,903 saw Athletic battle to a 1-1 draw. The replay was won by Huddersfield 6-0.

Athletic's ever present financial problems forced the mid-season departures of Fred Worrall to Portsmouth for £3,000, Ted Goodier and Les Adlam to Q.P.R. for a joint fee of £1,500, and Jimmy Dyson to Grimsby Town for £2,350. These departures drained the club's playing fortunes, and lack of interest caused attendances to drop until in the latter half of the campaign, the gross receipts averaged only a shade over £270. But for the highest League gate of the season, that of 13,817 paying £612 for the Good Friday visit of Plymouth Argyle, the average for the last eight games would have been a miserable £230.

Teddy Ivill and Billy Porter were the teams only ever-presents with 44 League and Cup appearances. John Pears and William Johnstone were joint top goalscorers with eleven each. The club finished bottom of the Northern Mid-Week League, but reached the final of the Lancashire Senior Cup which they last won in 1914. This Boundary Park fixture was won by Manchester City, 1-0.

Manager Andrew Wilson, obviously disillusioned at the way his team had been broken up, without adequate replacement, left Athletic in July '32 to become Stockport County's new manager. Only four of the exciting 1929-30 team built by Wilson remained on the club's books. Teddy Ivill, Billy Porter, Matt Gray and Bill Hasson, the remainder had all been sold. Club Secretary, Bob Mellor, again stepped in to fill the gap, his second stint as Caretaker Manager.

The club opened the season with 27 professionals and the realisation that it would be a tremendous stuggle to keep its head above water. Athletic did invest a small amount of last season's transfer cash, signing Billy Johnston from Manchester United for £300, Alf Agar from Accrington Stanley for £200, George Pateman from Portsmouth, Bill Baldwin from Barrow, Jim Dickenson from Blackpool, Norman Burnskill from Huddersfield Town and Ernest Steele, the well-known Middleton cricketer,

The club directors turned down a potentially lucrative offer to introduce dog racing at Boundary Park, and in doing so pleased local church leaders, who 'did not believe in that form of sport.' The outcome of which was the formation of an Appeals Committee, but the initial response of the Oldham public was slow, money was a rare commodity during these days of depressed trade in the town.

This season turned out to be near calamitous, for not only was the threat of relegation very real, but it was no exaggeration to say that Athletic were in serious danger of absolute extinction. With the bank putting the break on, the

Manchester United's Visit

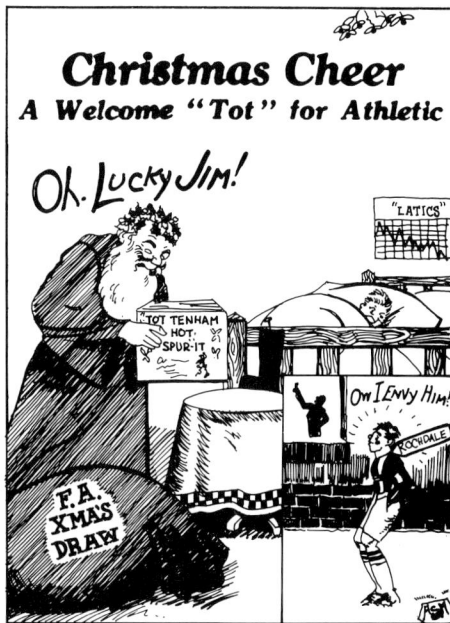

Christmas Cheer
A Welcome "Tot" for Athletic

much-maligned directors had once more to dig deep in order that current expenses could be met. It was touch and go, and a crash was only narrowly averted.

When the gloom was at its deepest, and the treasury empty, Manchester City came to Athletic's aid in a most sporting manner, loaning forward, Harry Rowley, and old favourite, Jimmy Naylor, to Athletic's cause. That was in mid-February, and at the beginning of March, Manchester United followed suit, Tom Reid joining the Boundary Park team.

This proved to be the turning point towards safety as a new spirit seemed to come over the whole team, beginning with a fine win at Lincoln City in early March.

With Jimmy Naylor injured, the experiment of playing Billy Johnston at left-half proved very successful. The left flank, comprising Johnson, Rowley and Pears, developed brilliantly and with Tom Reid leading the line well, the battle to avoid relegation was won.

The last thirteen games saw eight wins, 2 draws, and only three defeats, leaving Athletic in the safety of 16th position in Division Two with 38 points. The dropping of eighteeen points at Boundary Park accounted for the relegation scare and dwindling support, for the securing of fourteen away points was not a bad return. One bitter blow was the home F.A. Cup defeat at the hands of the Spurs, and it didn't ease matters that the final scoreline was 6-0 in favour of the Londoners. As far as League games were concerned, the biggest wins were over Notts County by five clear goals, and Bradford City by 6-1, both these

ATHLETIC'S FIRST ELEVEN · 1932-33
Back, left to right: TUFNELL (Trainer) · PICKERSGILL · PORTER · PEARSON · IVILL · BRUNSKILL · SEYMOUR (res)
Front, left to right: GRAY (M) · HASSON · JOHNSTON (W) · JOHNSTONE (W.G.) · JOHNSON (H) · AGAR

victories secured in the closing weeks of the season, and serving to indicate to what extent the team had improved.

In calling upon 27 players for first team duty, the club used five fewer than the previous season. Matt Gray made most appearances with 43 in League and Cup, and John Pears again topped the scoring charts with 13 League goals. During this season the club parted company with Teddy Ivill, a loyal servant, who had the distinction of playing 224 consecutive League matches for Athletic. He was transferred to Charlton Athletic.

The Boundary Park directors had a meeting following the final match of the season concerning the appointment of a new manager. Chairman, Mr. L. R. Stanton, announced that several applications had been received, including one from James McMullen the Scottish International and Manchester City player. Mr. McMullen was appointed the following day, and he immediately signed goalkeeper Fred Swift, brother of the famous Frank, from Chorley.

WHAT FATE DECREES

ATHLETIC'S 'FASHION CONSCIOUS' RESERVE TEAM · 1933-34

Back Left-right: MURRAY · HARGREAVES (Trainer) · GRICE · LIGHTFOOT · Mr BLOOR (Director) · SWIFT · DICKENSON · Mr FARMER (Director) · WHITEHEAD
Front Left-right: BUCKLEY · FORRESTER · WALSH · JOHNSON · HASSON · GRAY (M)

1933-34

In late July '33, Boundary Park was transformed from a ground usually the scene of a battle for promotion or relegation, to a spectacle of gaiety. The occasion was a garden party organised by the ladies section of the Athletic Appeals Committee, to augment the £5,000 appeals fund on behalf of the club. The Appeals Chairman, Councillor H. Shepherd, sent a message, laying special emphasis on the urgency of raising funds if the club were to obtain any measure of success during the 1933-34 season. An excellent programme of music was supplied by the Werneth Silver Band, and the Cotton Queen was given a rousing reception as she walked to the platform to receive bouquets.

The next week, Athletic followed their custom of holding two public practice games, giving supporters the opportunity of running the rule over some of the newcomers. Along with goalkeeper Swift, came Peter Burke from Prescott Cables, Arthur Bailey from Manchester North End, and in August, Cliff Chadwick from Fleetwood. It was announced that the club's old friend, Frank Hargreaves, had been appointed assistant trainer to Harry Tufnell, Mr. J.W. Clay having left after only one season in the position.

History seemed to have repeated itself, as Athletic were again facing a campaign that was likely to prove critical in the club's history. It was not merely a case of hoping for attendances that would permit a hand to mouth existence, but a marked appreciation in the average receipts necessary to meet the creditors' demands.

Athletic had just cause for slight optimism, as they could field the same team that proved equal to holding its own for the latter end of the previous season, loan signing Harry Rowley joining the club on a permanent basis for £750 just before the season kicked-off. Athletic's professional squad of 25 players could look forward to a derby atmosphere on six occasions, as Manchester United, Bolton Wanderers, Bury, Blackpool, Burnley and Preston North End were all Second Division clubs this season. The last time Blackpool visited Boundary Park 45,120 people paid £2,459 for the privilege, so the club's bank manager was in an optimistic mood.

New Manager, McMullan, was determined to coach his team on the right lines, and the general opinion was that he had a staff of players who were eager and ready to listen to an ex-player of undoubted ability and reputation.

McMullan emphasised that he was entering upon his apprenticeship in management, and it would be a testing time for him. He confessed he was pleased with his Oldham appointment, but realised he had a job of work on hand remembering the club's financial position. "It is when the task is hardest that a man has a chance of making good," he said.

Athletic were able to look back on a season which represented a marked advance on the previous campaign. This time the team finished ninth in Division Two, with a total of 44 points, and even flirted for a fleeting moment with the promotion aspirants. Not only had the 'pointage' increased, but the general standard of play showed a commendable improvement, due to the influence and experience of the new team manager. The only snag from the playing point of view

Special training in Buxton for the Sheffield Wednesday Cup-replay, January 1934

was the few rather impoverished displays at Boundary Park, where as many as 13 points had been sacrificed. When promotion was missed by nine points, the moral was obvious.

Along with the occupation of quite a respectable position in the League, there was an improved run in the F.A. Cup, defeating Reading at Elm Park 2-1, drawing with Sheffield Wednesday 1-1 at Boundary Park before 46,011 spectators, then losing 6-1 in the replay at Hillsborough. Apart from the cup tie receipts, there was only one gate where the gross receipts came to four figures, and that was for the visit of Manchester United early in the season, when the sum of £1,160 was taken from an attendance of 22,520. A gate of £83 gross for the last home game, when Hull City were slammed to the tune of seven clear goals, made a sad comparison. With the team clear of all relegation worries, the last seven home fixtures produced an average of 7,800 spectators, and receipts of £355. These seven games included visits from Bolton, Blackpool, and Preston North End. No wonder it was written that the game was dead in the town.

During the season there were more sales, but no money was made available. Clifton Chadwick went to Middlesbrough for a moderate fee, while John Pears left for Preston North End, also for a modest sum. Jack Hacking departed for Manchester United and Athletic's share was merely a few pounds, but the ex-international goalkeeper played a prominent part in helping the Old Trafford club to escape relegation and Athletic thus made an ample return for the loan of Tom Reid the previous season.

Of the newcomers this season, Peter Burke, Fred Swift, Arthur Bailey and Fred Schofield had all proved their worth, while Bill Walsh, introduced late in the season, did well to score five goals in six outings. The forwards, while recording 72 goals, had been erratic, having nine scoreless games and sixteen which produced no more than a single goal. Centre-forward Tom Reid top scored with 17 goals in League and Cup, and Bill Porter clocked most appearances with 45 League and Cup.

Manager Jimmy McMullan dropped a pre-season bombshell by resigning his position at Athletic after just 12 months in the job. He left Athletic in May 1934 to become Aston Villa's first ever team manager. The club's versatile secretary, Bob Mellor, stepped into the manager's shoes yet again, this time it was to last longer, until February 1935.

Thanks to the much abused directors, the club managed to survive the close season and try another shot at obtaining a living income. Wages during the summer months had come from private pockets, and it seemed the future of Oldham Athletic was again in the lap of the gods, rather than the lap of the public. "From reports, Oldham Athletic seem to be entering upon this new season with gloomy forebodings. A bit of the 'Never say die' spirit and good football might do the trick", wrote the Green Final recorder, "a population of half a million and a good ground warrant a little more optimism."

Our Two Principal Boys

Dick Whittington (Oldham): Why don't you play Dick, so that you could have a turn?
Sinbad (Athletic): How the heck can I, with a wretch like this on my back? I can't shake him off.

The transfer of the popular Bill Hasson to Millwall started the campaign off on the wrong foot, and financial stringency saw that additions to the playing staff had to be closely watched. At the start of the 1934-35 season there were only 23 paid players on the books including six new men, Jack Silcock from Manchester United, George Talbot from Liverpool, Jack Robson from Rochdale, Frank Britton from Blackburn Rovers, Billy Hulton, and Fred Brown from New Mills. It was evident early on that the team was hardly good enough, and it was disastrous that new players could not be signed when they were so badly needed.

Athletic won only five of the first eighteen matches, and then embarked on a terrible run of eight consecutive defeats which effectively sealed their fate. Wins over Manchester United and Bury halted the slide, but six defeats and only two victories in the last eleven games placed Athletic in a final League positions of 21st, and relgation to Division Three. Athetlic were saved the indignity of finishing at the very bottom of the table by Notts County, who where a point worse off, with an inferior goal average.

This was the most calamitous season in Athletic's history so far, the reserve

ATHLETIC'S FIRST ELEVEN · 1934-35

Back Left to right: SHARP (Res) · SCHOFIELD · GRICE · Mr. BLOOR (Dir) · SWIFT · SEYMOUR · BRUNSKILL · TUFNELL (Trainer)
Front Left to right: BURKE · ROBSON · LEEDHAM · REID · GRAY (M) · WALSH

team floundering at the bottom of the Central League, the Northern Mid-Week League team figuring at the bottom of both sections of their competition, and the F.A. Cup seeing Athletic draw Sheffield Wednesday yet again and lose a close fought game at Hillsborough 3-1. Wednesday went on to win the Cup.

Athletic conceded 95 goals, representing the biggest surrender since the club entered the League nearly 30 years before. Not a single victory was achieved on their travels, just three draws, making Athletic the only team in the four divisions of the League that failed to win away from home. During the season the principal outging transfers were those of Harry Rowley and Billy Porter to Manchester United. There were some in-bound deals, but of these only Jack Robson and Fred Leedham, signed in February '35, had been offered new contracts.

Athletic used 26 players for senior action this campaign, Tommy Seymour making most appearances with 43 League and Cup. Billy Walsh finished top scorer with 12 goals in League and Cup. The club was a long way from enjoying a gate of four figures so far as money was concerned, the nearest being the £701 secured from the visit of Manchester United. The only other gates over the £500 mark, were the £678 for the visit of Blackpool, and £618 for that of Bolton Wanderers. The average crowd worked out at 7,332, paying £326 a match.

1935-36

A thletic were on the threshold of a new adventure—the Third Division North, were it was thought that "Owt could happen". Boundary Park was considered locally to be far too good a setting for Northern Section Football, and promotion was thought of as a near certainty at the first attempt. A club spokesman, said, "There is a greater disposition in the Northern Section to make up for a lack of science with a little bit of 'extra vigour'. Well, we are down, and when you are in Rome, you must do as Rome does. We shall have to play them at their own game." Athletic's team past and present had a reputation for doing well against the giants of the League, and frequently descending to the level of the weaker teams. "We must have none of the latter this time," warned Manager Mellor.

Popular goalkeeper Fred Swift left for Bolton Wanderers in a straight exchange for forward, Bill Chambers, who became one of Athletic's fourteen new professionals. The others being Henry Church from Bolton, T. Bottrell from Stockport, Lewis Caunce from Wigan Athletic (Goalkeepers); Bob Eastwood from Bacup, Robert Talbot from Wigan Athletic, Beaumont Ratcliffe from New Brighton (Full-Backs); Tommy Williamson from Northwich, George Milligan from Manchester North End (Half-Backs); Norman Alden from Liverpool, Paddy Robbins from Blackburn, Tommy Davis and Charlie Butler from New Brighton and Arthur Jones from Hyde United (Forwards).

Following an opening 4-1 victory over Rotherham United, who were managed by Latics old friend, Reginald Freeman, Athletic soon realised that there were more good sides in this Division than they had thought, and the early feeling of

ATHLETIC,
Back Left to right: TUFNELL (Trainer) · Mr. T. FARROW & H. SHEPHERD (Director) · J. HAN.
HARGREAVES (Asst. Trainer) · Mr. W. B
2nd row left to right: LEEDHAM · BRUNSKILL · SCHOFIELI
Front, left to right: BUCKLEY · WALSH · ·

optimism soon turned to pessimism, especially when Tranmere Rovers planted thirteen goals into Athletic's net at Prenton Park, on Boxing Day 1935. In a record 13-4 scoreline, Rovers centre-forward 'Bunny' Bell scored nine times. Despite that, the club had not done badly this season, finishing a respectable 7th in the table, but it was made to appear a semi-tragedy because supporters had become obsessed with the idea that Athletic could not help jumping back into Division Two at the first time of asking. Athletic finished fifteen points behind Chesterfield, who galloped away with the championship, after being headed most of the journey by Tranmere Rovers.

The team certainly wound up the season well, with nine out of the last twelve points won, but it was all too late. Athletic defeated Ferryhill Athletic 6-1 in the F.A. Cup 1st round, before losing 4-1 at Bristol Rovers, following a 1-1 draw at Boundary Park.

Of the fourteen new professionals signed pre-season, eight had left the club during the course of the campaign, 27 players figuring in the senior team in all. Only Fred Schofield achieved the maximum 42 League appearances, although Bill Walsh went close with 41. Walsh had a dual distinction by scoring 32 League goals, not only beating Stewart Littlewood's individual scoring record of 28 goals in 1929-30, but made himself the top marksman in the Northern Section.

A great rally in the second half of the season enabled the reserve team to maintain it's place in the Central League. The club didn't enjoy one five-figure gate, the nearest being the 9,780 spectators attracted by Stockport County's visit. On nine occasions the gate was under five thousand.

3LIC TRIAL
) · HILTON · CHURCH · ROBSON · CAUNCE · GRAY · SHAW · Mr. A.M. BARLOW (Dir)
· Mr. R. MELLOR (Secretary/Manager).
· ROBBINS · RATCLIFFE · ALDEN · MILLIGAN · TALBOT
RKE · SEYMOUR · JONES · CHAMBERS

MILLIGAN IS ALWAYS THERE

FIRST TEAM PHOTO-CALL 1936-37
Back Left to right: DAVIS · RATCLIFFE · STAFFORD (2nd XI Trainer) · MILLIGAN · PRICE
Front Left to right: JONES (A) · WILLIAMSON · GRAY (M) · LEEDHAM · BUCKLEY
On ground: HILTON · BRUNSKILL

It was thought imperative that Athletic got off the mark in impressive fashion this season, to give supporters adequate proof that the club was to be among the challengers for the Northern Section title. The club chairman, Mr. Arthur Barlow, was as 'keen as mustard' to put Athletic back on the soccer map, and the players were fully aware of the importance of success. Trainers, Frank Hargreaves and Harry Stafford, were out to prove their worth, the former on his promotion to first team duties, and the pair put Athletic's squad through rigorous sessions in a bid for super fitness.

The club had retained 14 of last season's players and there were eleven newcomers, among them Norman Price, a strong full-back from Stalybridge Celtic, and Percy Downes, an outside-left from Burnley.

The Boundary Park club was certainly among the promotion favourites, and kept well up among the leaders until January '37. When Stockport County came to Oldham in early February, Athletic had a great chance of consolidating their position for the run home. A fine crowd of over 23,000 assembled for this highlight of the season, but the home team lost 0-2. Athletic inexplicably lost confidence, and this result proved the turning point so far as the club's 1936-37 adventure was concerned.

The Boundary Park men finished nine points behind Stockport, who went on to win the championship, six in arrears of Lincoln City, who were neck and neck with the Edgeley Park outfit right up to the last week of the season; Athletic finished fourth on 51 points. Away form was bettered only by Stockport and Lincoln, but too many points were frittered away at Boundary Park.

The F.A. Cup brought some revenge over Tranmere Rovers, but only by 1-0. There followed a splendid 3-2 win at fancied Lincoln City, and visions of a fine Cup run emerged, but Exeter City, who had to apply for re-election to the Southern Section, put an end to those hopes 3-0.

In the main, Athletic had been represented by the following team: Cauce · Hilton · Price · Williamson · Ratcliffe · Milligan · Jones (A) · McCormick · Davis ·Robbins and Downes. Tom Davis' opportunism saw him break the club's individual scoring record previously held by Bill Walsh who totalled 32 only the previous winter; Davis' final bag was 33. Half-back, George Milligan, after missing the first two games, was an ever present for the remainder of the campaign, playing in 43 consecutive matches and he had yet to celebrate his twentieth birthday. Norman Price and Tommy Willimson also completed 43 league and cup matches.

The club awarded the long serving Matt Gray a testimonial in April '37, when a Latics Old Boys eleven played Athletic at Boundary Park. Gray cost nothing more than a £10 signing-on fee in May 1928 and gave many years unstinting service, first as a forward and later as a half-back.

After finishing bottom of the Central League, Athletic reserves failed to be rel-elected, and were demoted to the Lancashire Combination.

OLDHAM ATHLETIC CLUB GROUP · 1937-38

1937-38

This season was preceded with minimal transfer activity, in or out. Only three new professionals had been signed, Henry Brown, a local amateur, Frank Eckersley, formerly of Manchester City, and Andrew Paterson from Wigan Athletic. No blame could be attributed to the club's directors that so few recruits had been signed, they had done their utmost once again to pay summer wages, and the treasure chest was empty. Athletic's expenditure had to be kept to the minimum, so it was impossible to sign on the dozen or so players which the team desperately needed.

The club evolved its team from last season's players, and the remarkable scoring form of Jack 'Legs' Diamond in Athletic's final practice game pleased everyone connected with the club. He started as centre-forward for the reserves and scored a hat-trick in the first 30 minutes. At half time he changed teams and scored another 3 goals for the seniors, yet finished on the losing side. He re-signed professional forms after this game, and starred in the first four matches, scoring 5 times. Diamond's good form continued, and he proved a capable replacement for Tommy Davis who left Athletic in February '38.

The Footballer: Well, thank goodness, the festive season is over. Now I can look forward to the New Year.
The Spirit of Turkey: I wish I could

TOP OF THE LADDER

THE DIZZY HEIGHTS OF FAME

3RD DIVISION

NORTHERN

The ''Latic'' say, Bob, I want that Second Division ladder now. I've got to the top of this one.
Manager Mellor: Well, you'll have to wait there and see—but don't wobble.

The team certainly turned in some enjoyable performances this season, especially at Boundary Park, where they surrendered the best home record in all four divisions at the very last hurdle to Bradford City, who had one of the worst away records. Athletic failed to make any significant progress on the previous year, again finishing in 4th position with the same number of points, five behind champions Tranmere, after one of the most intense struggles the Northern Section had known. Memories of 1930 were stirred by this latest failure to win promotion, as occasionally they topped the table, only slipping away when the end was in sight.

The first real addition to the team came in March when Ronald Ferrier landed at Boundary Park for a four figure fee from Manchester United, but he arrived too late to clinch Athletic's promotion bid. There was another disappointment when Athletic were ousted from the F.A.Cup in the first round by Wrexham, while the club did not cut much ice in the subsidiary cup competitions.

There was a noteworthy increase in support as League gates were up by nearly £3,000, 191,554 people paying a gross receipt total of £8,678 compared with £5,858 the previous year.

So far as the players were concerned, Jack Diamond top scored with 17 League goals, the only other player reaching double figures being Tom Davies with eleven, scored before his transfer to promoted Tranmere. Eight players made more than thirty appearances in the senior side, namely, Caunce, Hilton, Price, Williamson, Ratcliffe, Milligan, Robbins and Diamond. In the reserve eleven, S.F.Gardner with a total of 25, scored more goals than any other reserve player in the post-war period.

OLDHAM'S COTTON WEEK.

JACK 'LEGS' DIAMOND

Do You Remember?—Well, Perhaps You Don't!

LIVERPOOL FOOTBALL UNITY

...many years before a gamble in the 'pools was even thought of

Perhaps you'll remember "Latics" always had their stripes when they gambolled in Sheepfoot Lane (sounds like a spring song doesn't it) That was

Macalister was captain (Oh no! not the one that "cured th', mi lad!")

It's a braw bricht, moonlicht nicht dye ken

Why conna tha speak like an Owdhamer agen

Bet they sign on Meredith

And Bloomer

And Crompton

And Dicky Hat!

I knaw an' hur nobbut a lad at the time

Maybe you remember when Jimmy Hanson first became trainer – but still one can hardly expect you to go as far back as that!

It was the "talk of the town" when Appleyard & Speddie were signed on – for a time, and

then it was!

Remember our Own Dicky At Dixon who went to Scotland came back with a wifie, an' sich all' accent his own brither didn't know him did he heck

ASM

ATHLETIC ALSO HAD FAMOUS MEN

LATICS

Fit, fat and jolly!

Pah! we giv'em away

It must be most pleasing at "B.P." to see a lot of the chickens come home to roost

Land of my Fathers – and Mothers too!

Of course, they should swank about their Jubilee at Watersheddings, and what fine folk they have been – and are: but just hold your hush a mo.

"Latics" have something to swank about too! Somewhere about this time during the last war, they were about top of the FIRST Division.

International "goalies" were as common as owt anything

A good full-back Billy Cook was nearly the best goal kicker of his day.

Donnachie's legs could lick creation, for surely there was never a pair created like them

ASM

All our Evanses & Joneses played for their country, look you! and so did our English men too, yes indeed — after they'd left Oldham. We had Scottish internationals too, McTavish Yreh, if that's no' Scotch – nowt is

Of course if Oldham had been a motor x not a cotton town (& it nearly was) & we could have

joined Lord Nuffield on the Board, when he was nobbut a lad, we could have blown up the Arsenal to smithereens.

1938-39

All clubs were instructed by the Football League to arrange pre-season friendly matches to help bolster a £100,000 Jubilee Benevolent Fund, set up to benefit seriously injured players. Athletic's contribution was a Boundary Park match against local rivals Stockport County, which they lost 6-1. ''Not a confidence boosting preparation for the new season,'' was manager Mellor's understatement of the summer.

Of the fourteen players mostly concerned with first team duties last season, three had left the club. Norman Price had joined Gainsborough Trinity, Paddy Robbins went to Hartlepool United, and George Milligan was transferred to Everton for £3,150. This transfer effectively broke up one of the strongest half back lines in the Northern Section - Williamson, Ratcliffe and Milligan. Joe Taylor, a £200 signing from Stockport was first choice as Milligan's replacement, but he had made his name as an inside-forward. Tom Shipman, a full-back signed from Reading, was the obvious replacement for Norman Price, and there were four new faces in forward positions, Albert Valentine, Bill Vallance, Ernest Wright and David Halford.

Athletic again entered the Northern Mid-Week League, which was to stage a knockout competition, and provide another opportunity for budding talent to show its paces for the Tuesday afternoon fans.

Athletic got off to a flying start in the League this season, five victories and one draw from the first six games. The turning point in this campaign was the home defeat by Rochdale at the end of December. It left Athletic thirteen points behind the leaders, Barnsley, with 2 matches in hand, but to all intents and purposes, out of the hunt.

OLDHAM ATHLETIC FIRST XI · 1938-39

Back, Left to right: HALFORD · ASPINALL · CAUNCE · HARGREAVES (Trainer) · FERRIER · EAVES
Front, Left to right: GRAY (M) · HILTON · RATCLIFFE (Capt) · DIAMOND · SHIPMAN
On ground: PATTERSON · WILLIAMSON

The rank and file of the club's supporters thought so as gates slumped in an alarming fashion, falling by almost 50 per cent, receipts showing a corresponding drop from an average of £425 per game to one of £169. Fancy a club trying to carry on on £169 gates, when it had been officially placed on record that an average return of £500 was required, just to break even. As far as the League was concerned, the best gate was attracted by Southport, 13,108 spectators paying £602. Rock bottom came on a villainous afternoon, 2,708 people paying just £84 for the visit of Hartlepool United. Athletic's last three home gates brought in a meagre £337, just about as much as they took earlier in the season for Stockport's visit on a fog-bound day, when it looked about 10-1 against there being any play at all. The irony of it was that the weather for these last three games was brilliant, and the 3 matches were won by a total margin of 13-2.

The club suffered terrible luck on the injury front, with three senior players sidelined with serious problems for most of the season, and others had been on

Matt Gray · 1939

A GOLDEN OPPORTUNITY.

Mr. BOB MELLOR, the Athletic secretary, is a great success in his new role, " Little Goldilocks !'—clever artists, these Mellors.

the shelf for varying periods. These problems were a big handicap to a club relying on a comparatively short list of professionals, and went some way to explain why Athletic's reserve team has such a moderate season in the Lancashire Combination.

A first round 1-0 F.A.Cup defeat at the hands of Crewe Alexandra was hardly an invitation to the missing supporters to return to Boundary Park on a permanent basis. The first game attracted the biggest crowd of the season, 14,525 people watching Athletic struggle to a 2-2 draw, and lose a lot more than just the tie. The team were knocked out at the first hurdle from the Northern Section Cup and only reached the second round of the Lancashire Senior Cup, Athletic were not cup-minded these days. To summarise, in comparison to the previous season, there was a drop of two in the total points won, a drop of 43,810 spectators, and one of £2,397 in the amount of cash taken at the turnstiles. Goalkeeper Lewis Caunce made most appearances with 43 League and Cup and Ron Ferrier scored a healthy 24 goals in all competitions.

Is it the Break in the Clouds at Last?

FOOTBALL DURING THE LAST WAR

"The Jerries" captured Sergt Bond the old international footballer while he was shaving & proudly announced it over the parapet.

BRADFORD CITY PAID $1,000 FOR DICKY BOND. THIS MORNING YR. GOT HIM FOR NOTHING.

Blimey! 'eres one for oop th' line.

was at Etaples

In a "friendly" Rugby match between England & Australia, there were nearly as many casualties as up the line.

During the Great War one battalion went "over the top" kicking a football.

You can always get your own back on the sergeant at football

Steve Bloomer had to kick old socks, or any old thing, as a prisoner of war for four years at Ruhleben.

Following a season which, owing to the declaration of war with Germany, had been entirely different to anything previously experienced, Athletic emerged as well, if not better than, most other clubs in the country. Never a lavishly supported club at the best of times, the crowds at several matches this season, either of the friendly or newly-instituted regional variety, had been so good that many of the higher grade clubs had been casting envious glances. Athletic could therefore regard the campaign with some satisfaction, considering the extraordinary conditions which existed.

Athletic had no great hopes of promotion when they entered their Third Division North programme on August 26th, having made only a few inexpensive signings in an attempt to strengthen obvious weaknesses in the team. It actually became necessary to recall players who had either been placed on the transfer list, or who had been given free transfers. There were fourteen of the 'old brigade' on call, and five newcomers in E.Chapman from Accrington, T.Hampson, Leeds United, G.Nicholson, Cardiff City, T.West, Stockport and D.Read from Bath City.

On the day which saw Roosevelt's second peace appeal to Hitler and air-raid warnings in Oldham, Athletic kicked off the season in thunderstorm conditions with a 3-1 home victory over Carlisle United, followed by two away defeats at Halifax and Accrington Stanley before the outbreak of war saw the suspension of ordinary football fixtures. Manager, Bob Mellor, had been in touch with the Football League, and was informed that all footballers' contracts were to be terminated as from the week-end of September 3rd 1939. Mr. Mellor had captain Beaumont Ratcliffe and vice-captain Billy Hilton before him, and explained the position. The players realising that such a situation could not be avoided, accepted it philosophically. There was grumbling when the season was suddenly cut short over the fact that some clubs had had two home 'gates' to other clubs one. Bob Mellor pointed this out to Mr. Fred Howarth, the Football League Secretary, who promised to bring the point to the notice of the Management Committee. It was decided that all matches played before the season was terminated should be from the 'gate' standpoint, treated as Cup-ties. The receipts were to be split between the clubs on a 50/50 basis. This was to the Boundary Park club's advantage, as only the Carlisle United game was a home affair, and there were very good gates at both Halifax and Accrington.

There was a cessation of play until September 16th, when the authorities partly lifted the ban against the gathering of big crowds at sporting events, allowing Athletic, and all other clubs to start a series of friendly games pending the arrangement of a new competitive system sponsored by the Football League. Known as Regional Competitions, these were formed in various parts of the country and opened on October 21st '39.

There were to be eight regional areas and Athletic would play in the League North West Region, with an insistance from the authorities that all travelling had to be completed within one day. There were no bonuses for the players, and no more than 14 players from any one team were allowed to be paid the maximum wage of thirty shillings. Gates were divided on a Cup-tie basis, and a maximum attendance of 15,000 was set for each of the regional groups.

The groupings were not all that could be desired as far as Athletic were concerned, but they still had some attractive fixtures, even if the programme allowed only 22 matches. Such clubs as Preston North End, Blackpool, Bolton Wanderers, Burnley, Bury and Blackburn Rovers were included in the fixtures, so Athletic had some of the country's elite teams visiting Boundary Park. This did not mean seeing the best players as the constitution of the teams changed so quickly, players being allowed to turn out for other than their registered clubs. Some clubs felt the effect of the war more than others, notably Bolton Wanderers, who lost their entire first team as a result of enlistments.

In a few weeks the Athletic team composition was completely revolutionised by the return to Boundary Park of old favourites, Billy Porter, Fred Worrall, Tom Butler. Cliff Chadwick, Arthur Buckley, George Milligan and Billy Walsh, who made only two appearances before military duties led to his departure. It was regarded a great compliment to Athletic's management that so many of their old players, who had achieved fame in higher grades of football, should be so willing to help the club which gave them their first chance to make good in the game. Athletic finished fifth in the North West Division of the War Regional League, winning half of their 22 matches.

The Boundary Park club's hopes of making money from the cup competitions were rudely shattered. They had a bye in the first round of the Lancashire Cup, and in round two they fell ingloriouly at Accrington Stanley 7-1. When the Wartime Cup competition started, they suffered a blow by being deprived of the services of their 'borrowed men', Porter, Worrall, Butler, Chadwick and Buckley. This situation led to an almost complete reorganisation of the side, but they managed to draw in the preliminary round at Southport 1-1, and were regarded as likely victors of the replay at Boundary Park, but the seasiders won 1-0 with a goal in extra time.

In May 1940, a strong Blackpool side defeated Athletic 11-2 at Bloomfield Road in a League North West fixture, Pool's Jock Dodds scoring seven times, Ron Ferrier replied with one of Athletic's consolation goals and finished top goalscorer for the club with 19 goals in the regional matches, and 9 in friendly games. Later the same month Athletic entertained Blackburn Rovers before the lowest recorded attendance for a first team fixture at Boundary Park, only 412 people seeing Athletic's 5-2 defeat in the North West League.

AIR RAIDS

In the event of an Air-Raid Warning during the game the match will be abandoned immediately, and all Exit gates opened.

You are asked to disperse quietly and go either to the nearest Shelter, or to your home, if sufficiently close to the ground.

SEASON 1939-40

1	Aug	26	(h)	Carlisle U	W 3-1
2		28	(a)	Halifax T	L 0-2
3	Sep	2	(a)	Accringtons	L 0-2

THESE MATCHES WERE PLAYED IN THE
ABORTIVE DIVISION THREE NORTH

4	Oct	21	(h)	Southport	W 4-3
5		28	(a)	Accrington S	W 2-1
6	Nov	4	(h)	Accrington S	W 3-1
7		11	(h)	Bolton W	D 2-2
8		18	(a)	Preston NE	L 1-6
9		25	(h)	Burnley	W 3-1
10	Dec	2	(a)	Carlisle U	W 2-0
11		9	(a)	Bury	L 0-2
12		23	(h)	Rochdale	L 0-3
13	Jan	6	(a)	Blackburn R	W 3-1
14		13	(a)	Bolton W	L 0-3
15	Feb	10	(a)	Southport	D 0-0
16		17	(h)	Barrow	W 8-2

17	Mar	16	(h)	Preston NE	W 3-2
18		23	(a)	Burnley	L 3-4
19		30	(h)	Carlisle U	W 8-1
20	Apr	6	(h)	Bury	W 3-2
21	May	13	(a)	Blackpool	L 2-11
23		25	(a)	Rochdale	L 1-3
24		28	(h)	Blackburn R	L 2-5
25	Jun	8	(h)	Blackpool	W 4-2

League War Cup

| 1 | Apr | 13 | (a) | Southport | D 1-1 |
| | | 16 | (h) | Southport | L 0-1 |

FINAL LEAGUE POSITION: 5th in the North West Division of War Regional League.

THIRD DIVISION NORTH

	P	W	D	L	F	A	Pts.
Accrington	3	3	0	0	6	1	6
Halifax	3	2	1	0	6	1	5
Darlington	3	2	1	0	5	2	5
Chester	3	2	1	0	5	2	5
Rochdale	3	2	0	1	2	2	4
New Brighton	3	2	0	1	4	5	4
Tranmere	3	1	1	1	6	6	3
Rotherham	3	1	1	1	5	6	3
Wrexham	3	1	1	1	3	2	3
Lincoln	3	1	1	1	6	7	3
Crewe	2	1	1	0	3	0	3
OLDHAM	3	1	0	2	3	5	2
Doncaster	3	1	0	2	4	5	2
Gateshead	3	1	0	2	6	7	2
Southport	3	0	2	1	4	5	2
Hull	2	0	2	0	3	3	2
Hartlepool	3	0	2	1	1	4	2
Barrow	3	0	2	1	4	5	2
Carlisle	2	1	0	1	3	3	2
York	3	0	1	2	3	5	1
Bradford C	3	0	1	2	3	6	1
Stockport	2	0	0	2	0	5	0

NORTH WEST

	P	W	D	L	F	A	Pts.
Bury	22	16	4	2	64	30	34
Preston	22	15	5	2	63	27	32
Blackpool	22	13	3	6	75	36	32
Bolton	22	13	5	4	55	30	30
OLDHAM	22	11	9	2	55	61	24
Burnley	22	9	8	5	48	43	23
Barrow	22	8	10	4	54	57	20
Blackburn	22	7	11	4	37	40	18
Rochdale	22	5	12	5	38	58	15
Southport	22	5	13	4	34	62	14
Carlisle	22	4	4	4	38	68	12
Accrington	22	2	14	6	31	78	10

APPEARANCES:
(In all competitions)

* BRADSHAW G.F.	1
* BUTLER T.	16
BAILEY A.	21
BLACKSHAW H.K.	3
* BUCKLEY A.	19
CAUNCE L.	22
CORNOCK W.B.	3
CHADWICK C.	6
CHAPMAN E.	3
DYSON J.M.	2
FERRIER R.J.	26
HILTON W.A.	13
HAMPSON T.	19
HAYES W.	3
HALFORD D.	3
JONES T.	8
LUDLAM W.	2
* MILLIGAN G.H.	3
NICHOLSON G.	2
NEWTON F.	1
PATERSON A.	12
* PORTER W.	20
RATCLIFFE B.	3
SHIPMAN T.E.R.	26
TAYLOR R.	1
VALENTINE A.F.	2
WILLIAMSON T.	25
* WORRALL F.	18
* WALSH W.	2
WRIGHT E.	10
* WHALLEY H.	2

*Guest Player

GOAL SCORERS: (In all competitions)
FERRIER 19, WORRALL 11, BUCKLEY 7, BAILEY 6, BUTLER 4, VALENTINE 2, WRIGHT 2,
HILTON, HAMPSON, PORTER, WILLIAMSON, CHADWICK, DYSON, WALSH, BLACKSHAW.
ALL ONE GOAL EACH. TOTAL 59

'GAS ATTACK' PRECAUTIONS — BOUNDARY PARK 1941

1940-41

In their second season of wartime football, Athletic had a near fifty percent record for matches won and goals scored for and against. Positions in the North Regional competition were reckoned purely on goal average, as the clubs did not play the same number of games; in fact Blackpool and Bolton did not enter the competition until the second half of the campaign, Hull City dropped out in April, and a number of other clubs were frequently idle. Mr. Bob Mellor, Athletic's secretary/manager was assiduous in his efforts to keep the flag flying at Boundary Park, and was rewarded with a full season's programme.

Athletic's home games were usually well attended, and results on the field regarded as satisfactory, considering all the difficulties in times such as these. Figures released in March '41 showed a total of 28,859 British civilians had been killed in air-raids since the war started, many of these in the Manchester area, and put into true perspective how difficult it was to maintain any form of sporting activity in such dire circumstances. Athletic were fortunate that most of their players were able to turn out in the majority of games, and although disappointments were unavoidable, the constitution of the team was sometimes unknown until a minute or two before kick-off.

Altogether, the club called on 37 players, some of whom made only one or two appearances, and the club were grateful to those local amateurs who turned out, often at short notice, to help the club out of a difficulty. It was fitting for a club which had always been famous for the quality of it's goalkeepers, to have the assistance in the latter half of the season of such a star performer as George Swindin, the Arsenal player, whose arrival added stability to the defence at a time of difficulty. Ron Ferrier again appeared at the head of the goalscoring list with 20.

Apart from the financial viewpoint, this season served to provide another very important function in maintaining an interest in the game generally, and keeping the club and players together. Had there been no football at Boundary Park, the ground would have deteriorated, public interest lost, and when time came to start again, the club would have faced tremendous difficulties. A considerable amount of public interest had been maintained, and wartime football had certainly justified itself.

BILLY HILTON   TOMMY WILLIAMSON

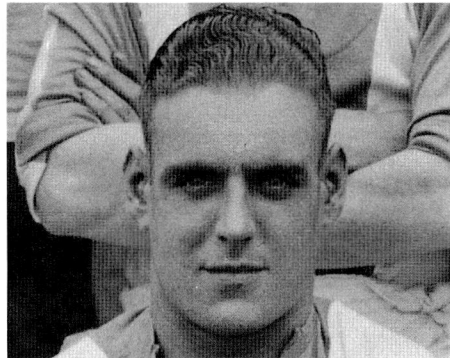

SEASON 1940-41

1	Aug	31	(a)	Bury	D 4-4	21	Jan	18	(h)	Liverpool	L 0-3
2	Sep	7	(h)	Stockport C	W 4-1	22	Feb	1	(a)	Manchester C	L 4-5
3		14	(h)	Manchester U	W 2-1	23		8	(h)	Manchester C	L 2-5
4		21	(a)	Manchester U	W 3-2	24	Mar	1	(h)	Burnley	W 2-0
5		28	(a)	Stockport C	W 5-1	25		8	(a)	Burnley	L 0-4
6	Oct	5	(h)	Bury	L 3-4	26		22	(h)	Manchester U	L 0-1
7		12	(a)	Preston NE	L 0-3	27		29	(h)	Huddersfield T	W 3-1
8		19	(h)	Burnley	W 6-1	28	Apr	5	(a)	Huddersfield T	L 0-1
9		26	(a)	Burnley	L 1-2	29		12	(a)	Preston NE	L 0-4
10	Nov	2	(h)	Preston NE	L 2-6	30		14	(a)	Rochdale	W 4-0
11		9	(h)	Bradford	D 4-4	31		19	(a)	Blackpool	L 2-6
12		16	(h)	Halifax T	L 1-2	32		26	(h)	Bury	W 2-0
13		23	(a)	Halifax T	W 1-0	33	May	3	(a)	Bury	W 3-2
14		30	(h)	Chester	D 0-0	34		10	(h)	Rochdale	W 5-0
15	Dec	7	(a)	Manchester C	W 1-0	35		17	(h)	Everton	D 1-1
16		14	(h)	Blackburn R	W 1-0	36		31	(h)	Bolton W	L 1-3
17		21	(a)	Blackburn R	L 2-3	37	Jun	7	(h)	Bolton W	W 3-1
18		25	(a)	Rochdale	W 3-2		League War Cup				
19	Jan	4	(a)	Bolton W	L 1-2	1	Feb	15	(a)	Blackburn R	L 0-2
20		11	(h)	Bolton W	W 2-1			22	(h)	Blackburn R	L 1-5

FINAL LEAGUE POSITION: 20th in the North Regional League. Matches 19 & 20 were Lancashire Cup games which also counted in the League. Match 20 went into extra-time, Bolton winning 5-3 to progress in the Cup, the score at 90 minutes (2-1) counting for the League.

NORTH	P	W	L	D	F	A	Goal Avge*
Preston	29	18	4	7	81	37	2.189
Chesterfield	35	20	9	6	76	40	1.900
Manchester C	35	18	7	10	104	55	1.890
Barnsley	30	18	8	4	86	49	1.775
Everton	34	19	8	7	85	51	1.666
Blackpool	20	13	4	3	56	34	1.646
Halifax	30	10	7	13	64	51	1.254
Manchester U	35	14	13	8	80	65	1.249
Lincoln	27	13	7	7	65	53	1.226
Newcastle	23	12	11	0	49	41	1.195
Huddersfield	33	11	16	6	69	58	1.189
Middlesbrough	27	16	10	1	84	71	1.183
New Brighton	26	15	10	1	97	82	1.182
Burnley	35	15	17	11	7	62	53	1.169
Leeds	30	13	9	8	62	54	1.148
Liverpool	37	15	16	6	91	82	1.102
Wrexham	29	15	9	5	78	71	1.098
Chester	35	14	15	6	94	89	1.056
Doncaster	32	15	10	7	77	74	1.040
OLDHAM	37	17	16	4	78	77	1.012
Grimsby	27	12	13	2	60	63	.952
Bradford PA	31	9	15	7	64	74	.864
Rotherham	29	12	12	5	48	57	.842
Blackburn	32	9	13	10	49	60	.816
Bury	38	10	19	9	80	100	.800
Bolton	16	6	8	2	31	40	.775
Tranmere	25	9	11	5	67	90	.744
Sheffield U	25	6	13	6	44	60	.733
Bradford C	29	8	18	3	72	99	.727
Rochdale	32	12	15	5	64	92	.695
Southport	28	7	19	2	61	88	.693
York	25	7	14	4	49	71	.690
Hull	23	8	12	3	44	67	.656
Sheffield W	30	9	15	6	50	78	.641
Stockport	29	9	15	5	54	93	.580
Crewe	24	2	19	3	32	84	.380

APPEARANCES:
(In all competitions)

* BUCKLEY A.....................................2
* BUTLER T..4
  BLACKSHAW H.K.............................18
  BAILEY A...32
  BOWDEN J...5
  CAUNCE L...16
  CORNOCK W.B......................................6
* CHADWICK C....................................17
  CHAPMAN E...1
* COUSER H...1
* DOUGLAS C.......................................5
  EATON C...20
  EATON C...2
  FERRIER R.U....................................27
  GLYNN K.T...2
  GRAY M..6
  GOSNELL G..6
  HAMPSON T..32
  HILTON W.A..19
  LEWIS C...1
  LUDLAM W...1
* LOMAX J..1
  MILLWARD A.E......................................1
  NICHOLSON G.......................................3
* PORTER W...20
  READETT H...7
* SWINDIN G.H....................................14
  SHIPMAN T.E.R....................................39
  TAYLOR J.T.......................................28
  THOMAS W.E...6
  VALENTINE A.F......................................1
  WILLIAMSON T.....................................35
  WILKINSON H..1
  WRIGHT E...2
* WORRALL F.......................................27
* WHALLEY H.......................................20
* WALSH W...1

*Guest Player

GOAL SCORERS:
(In all competitions)
FERRIER 20, BAILEY 13, WORRALL 8,
WHALLEY 6, BLACKSHAW 6, CHADWICK 5,
TAYLOR 5, WILLIAMSON 3, GOSNELL 3,
HAMPSON 2, GRAY 2, SHIPMAN, PORTER,
EATON, BUTLER, WALSH ALL ONE GOAL
EACH. 1 OWN GOAL
TOTAL 78

RONALD FERRIER

A thletic completed their third season of wartime football when they visited Blackpool and drew 2-2 before 4,000 spectators. It had not been a very successful season, the second half results being distinctly poor, but the game was the thing in these times, and nobody was in the least depressed at Boundary Park. The League North competition ended at Christmas this season, with Blackpool the winners. Athletic won only 6 of their 18 matches, drawing four, and finishing 21st in the table on 16 points. Athletic's home game with Halifax Town on December 6th '41 saw the second lowest ever attendance on the ground for a first team game; 479 people heard a half-time announcement that the Japanese had attacked Pearl Harbour and changed the course of the war. The 6-2 win for Athletic seemed of little importance.

In the second half of the season the League War Cup competition was instituted with 51 clubs. The top 32 clubs entered the knockout competition after an initial ten matches had been played by each club. Athletic qualified, but progressed no further than the first round proper, the famous Sunderland club defeating Athletic 3-2 at Roker Park, after a 1-1 scoreline at Boundary Park. After they were ousted from the Cup competition, Athletic resumed their League programme, winning only four of their 18 matches and finishing a disappointing 22nd in the Northern League Second competition. After defeating Bradford in the ninth match of their qualifying programme, Athletic found it extremely difficult to collect points and did not in fact win another game, their only consolation being two draws.

During the latter half of the season, the club found it necessary to make more changes than during the first period, and this had probably much to do with the indifferent results. Channel Islander, Sylvester Rabey, who made five appearances for Athletic at outside-left this season, was sadly killed during war training in the summer of '42. He was one of the 34 players called on for first team duty this season. The most consistent being Tommy Williamson with 35 appearances, closely followed by Tom Shipman on 33. Arthur Bailey was top scorer with 17 goals, Fred Worrall had 9, and T.Hampson scored 8.

In the Lancashire Senior Cup, Athletic fell at the first hurdle, Manchester United winning 5-1 at Maine Road, and 2-1 at Boundary Park.

TOM SHIPMAN   BERT EAVES

SEASON 1941-42

1	Aug	30	(a)	Rochdale	L 2-3
2	Sep	6	(h)	Rochdale	W 3-0
3		13	(h)	Preston NE	D 1-1
4		20	(a)	Preston NE	L 0-7
5		27	(a)	Southport	L 3-4
6	Oct	4	(h)	Southport	W 3-1
7		11	(h)	Bury	D 5-5
8		18	(a)	Bury	L 0-5
9		25	(a)	Bolton W	W 5-3
10	Nov	1	(h)	Bolton W	W 2-0
11		8	(h)	Blackburn R	D 2-2
12		15	(a)	Blackburn R	L 1-2
13		22	(a)	Blackpool	L 1-5
14		29	(h)	Blackpool	L 0-3
15	Dec	6	(h)	Halifax T	W 6-2
16		13	(a)	Halifax T	L 0-3
17		20	(h)	Burnley	W 5-2
18		25	(a)	Burnley	D 1-1
19	Dec	27	(a)	Rochdale	L 0-1
20	Jan	3	(h)	Rochdale	W 3-2
21		10	(a)	Manchester U	D 1-1
22		17	(a)	Manchester U	L 1-3
23		31	(h)	Tranmere R	W 6-0
24	Feb	14	(a)	Bradford	L 1-3
25		21	(h)	Everton	W 1-0
26		28	(a)	Everton	L 0-4
27	Mar	14	(h)	Bradford	W 5-2
28		21	(a)	Tranmere R	L 0-1
29		28	(h)	Everton	L 1-2
30	Apr	4	(h)	Sunderland	D 1-1
31		6	(a)	Sunderland	L 2-3
32		11	(h)	Chester	L 2-3
33		25	(a)	Manchester U	L 1-5
34	May	2	(h)	Manchester U	L 1-2
35		9	(h)	Blackpool	L 2-8
36		16	(a)	Blackpool	D 2-2

FINAL LEAGUE POSITION: 21st in League Northern Section, First Competition

FINAL LEAGUE POSITION: 22nd in League Northern, Second Competition

In the Second Competition points were calculated on 23 games and the results also included games played in the League Cup Qualifying, Knock-out competitions and regional cups. Matches 19-28 inclusive were also in the League Cup Qualifying competition . Matches 30 & 31 were also League Cup Knock-out games. Matches 33 & 34 were also Lancashire Cup-ties.

NORTH
Ending 25 December 1941

	P	W	L	D	F	A	Pts
Blackpool	18	14	3	1	75	19	29
Lincoln	18	13	2	3	54	28	29
Preston	18	13	4	1	58	18	27
Manchester U	18	10	2	6	79	27	26
Stoke	18	12	4	2	75	36	26
Everton	18	12	4	2	61	31	26
Blackburn	18	10	2	6	40	24	26
Liverpool	18	11	3	4	66	44	26
Gateshead	18	9	4	5	39	35	23
Sunderland	18	9	5	4	50	30	22
Huddersfield	18	10	7	1	48	33	21
Bradford	18	8	5	5	33	28	21
Grimsby	18	7	5	6	41	31	20
Barnsley	18	8	6	4	39	31	20
Newcastle	18	7	5	6	46	39	20
Sheffield W	18	7	6	5	33	37	19
Manchester C	18	8	7	3	48	54	19
Sheffield U	18	7	7	4	39	38	18
Burnley	18	6	6	6	36	40	18
Halifax	18	7	8	3	29	41	17
OLDHAM	18	6	8	4	40	49	16
Rochdale	18	6	8	4	28	52	16
Chesterfield	18	5	8	5	27	31	15
Chester	18	6	9	3	45	53	15
Middlesbrough	18	6	9	3	44	56	15
Leeds	18	7	10	1	36	46	15
Doncaster	18	6	10	2	39	46	14
Bradford C	18	5	9	4	32	42	14
Rotherham	18	6	10	2	33	47	14
New Brighton	18	4	8	6	39	75	14
Tranmere	18	5	10	3	35	59	13
York	18	4	10	4	41	55	12
Mansfield	18	6	12	0	29	50	12
Bolton	18	3	10	5	35	48	11
Southport	18	5	12	1	33	61	11
Bury	18	3	12	3	37	59	9
Wrexham	18	2	11	5	40	69	9
Stockport	18	2	14	2	34	73	6

APPEARANCES:
(In all competitions)

BLACKSHAW H.K.	6
* BUTLER T.	2
BAILEY H.	34
* BUCKLEY A.	3
CHADWICK T.	10
CHAPMAN E.	14
* CARTER D.F.	1
* DAVIES G.	1
EAVES T.A.	12
EATON C.	1
FERRIER R.J.	7
FURNESS W.	5
GRAY M.	32
* GOSNELL G.L.	1
* HALL J.	1
HOLMES G.	1
HILTON W.A.	28
HURST G.	11
* HOLDCROFT G.H.	1
HAMPSON T.	32
JUMP F.	6
KIBBLE G.	3
KEATING E.	13
* PRICE A.J.W.	1
RATCLIFFE B.	1
RABEY S.K.	5
* SWINDIN G.H.	25
SHIPMAN T.E.R.	33
SMITH G.W.	1
STOKES J.	1
TAYLOR J.T.	35
TAYLOR F.	9
WINDSON J.	1
* WORRAL F.	26

*Guest Player

GOAL SCORERS:
(In all competitions)
BAILEY 18, CHAPMAN 13, WORRALL 8, HAMPSON 8, TAYLOR J.T. 5, KEATING 4, FERRIER 4, GRAY 2, TAYLOR F. 2, BLACKSHAW 2, HILTON, HURST G., SMITH, STOKES, ALL ONE GOAL EACH.
TOTAL 70

LEAGUE CHAMPIONSHIP
27 December 1941 to 30 May 1942

	P	W	L	D	F	A	Pts	Avg*
Manchester U	19	12	3	4	44	25	28	33.89
Blackpool	22	14	4	4	108	34	32	33.45
Northampton	21	14	5	2	70	31	30	32.85
Liverpool	21	14	5	2	57	39	30	32.85
Wolves	20	13	6	1	52	29	27	31.05
Huddersfield	20	9	5	6	42	33	24	27.60
Blackburn	22	10	6	6	40	31	26	27.18
WBA	18	9	6	3	53	43	21	26.83
Grimsby	18	8	5	5	31	22	21	26.83
Sunderland	22	9	6	7	53	42	25	26.13
Cardiff	20	9	7	4	59	38	22	25.30
Preston	19	6	6	7	41	30	19	23.00
Chesterfield	18	8	8	2	32	31	18	23.00
Midd'brough	18	7	7	4	37	36	18	23.00
Everton	23	9	9	5	37	41	23	23.00
Stoke	20	9	9	2	41	49	20	23.00
Leicester	18	6	8	4	38	38	16	20.44
Bradford PA	19	5	8	6	35	40	16	19.36
Halifax	19	8	7	3	30	40	15	18.15
Burnley	19	7	11	1	29	53	15	18.15
Chester	20	6	11	3	34	41	15	17.25
OLDHAM	18	4	11	3	30	43	11	14.05
All above qualified								
Barnsley	15	9	3	3	48	23	21	
Bolton	15	5	6	4	26	33	14	
Bradford C	14	6	7	1	28	25	13	
B'mouth & BA	8	2	4	2	11	21	8	
Bristol C	7	5	3	55	29	21		
Bury	15	6	7	2	46	39	14	
Doncaster	9	2	7	0	10	30	4	
Gateshead	13	4	7	2	23	36	10	
Leeds	17	7	10	0	33	33	14	
Lincoln	13	7	5	1	45	33	15	
Luton	16	4	10	2	20	54	10	
Manchester C	17	9	7	1	33	26	19	
Mansfield	11	1	8	2	15	36	4	
New Brighton	11	5	6	0	23	28	10	
Newcastle	17	5	6	6	33	40	16	
Norwich	12	7	4	1	27	19	15	
Nottingham F	16	8	7	1	32	30	17	
Rochdale	15	5	8	2	33	39	10	
Rotherham	15	6	7	2	32	34	14	
Sheffield U	17	8	5	4	39	33	20	
Sheffield W	15	5	8	2	22	36	12	
Southampton	12	5	5	2	27	32	12	
Southport	16	6	8	2	30	38	14	
Stockport	10	1	6	3	12	38	5	
Swansea	11	6	4	1	39	6		
Tranmere	15	4	8	3	24	55	11	
Walsall	13	4	9	0	14	34	8	
Wrexham	12	4	6	2	26	32	10	
York	15	5	8	2	36	40	12	

Avge — points calculated on 23 matches. Note: only those playing 18 or more qualified for the Championship.

LEAGUE CUP QUALIFYING COMPETITION
27 December 1941 to 28 March 1942

	P	W	L	D	F	A	Pts	Avg*
Northampton	9	7	1	1	27	14	16.66
Blackburn	10	7	1	2	19	7	16.00
Manchester U	10	6	1	3	23	13	15.00
Blackpool	10	6	2	2	45	19	14.00
Barnsley	10	6	2	2	33	16	14.00
Liverpool	10	7	3	0	33	24	14.00
Bristol C	10	5	2	3	29	16	13.00
Nottingham F	9	5	1	15	9	11	12.22
Leicester	9	4	2	3	27	19	11	12.22
Rotherham	9	5	3	1	20	15	11	12.22
Grimsby	9	4	2	3	15	12	11	12.22
Cardiff	10	5	3	2	39	19	12	12.00
Sunderland	10	5	3	2	30	19	12	12.00
Wolves	10	6	4	0	28	19	12	12.00
Huddersfield	10	5	3	2	23	16	12	12.00
Midd'brough	10	4	2	4	24	17	12	12.00
Everton	10	5	3	2	15	16	12	12.00
Liverpool	6	3	2	1	17	11	7	11.66
Lincoln	9	5	4	0	27	21	10	11.11
WBA	9	4	3	2	29	24	10	11.11
Preston	10	6	11	3	34	41	15	11.00
Manchester C	10	5	4	1	21	14	11	11.00
Stoke	10	5	4	1	22	15	11	11.00
Sheffield U	10	4	3	3	23	19	11	11.00
Southampton	10	5	4	1	25	28	11	11.00
Bury	9	4	4	1	33	24	9	10.00
Bradford C	8	4	4	0	14	11	8	10.00
Southport	9	4	4	1	20	19	9	10.00
OLDHAM	10	4	5	1	18	17	9	9.00
Chester	10	4	5	1	19	20	9	9.00
Burnley	10	4	5	1	18	19	9	9.00
Bradford PA	10	3	4	3	22	26	9	9.00
All above qualified								
York	10	2	3	5	22	27	9	9.00
Chesterfield	10	3	4	5	12	9	9	9.00
Wrexham	9	3	4	2	22	23	8	8.88
Bolton	9	3	4	2	16	17	8	8.88
Leeds	10	4	6	0	22	15	8	8.00
Newcastle	10	2	4	4	15	23	8	8.00
New Brighton	10	4	6	0	18	38	8	8.00
B'mouth & BA	8	2	4	2	11	21	6	7.50
Swansea	8	1	3	4	9	21	6	7.50
Halifax	9	2	5	2	11	20	6	6.66
Rochdale	9	3	6	0	13	29	6	6.66
Gateshead	10	2	6	2	15	30	6	6.00
Luton	10	2	6	2	15	30	6	6.00
Tranmere	10	2	6	2	16	42	6	6.00
Doncaster	8	2	6	0	10	27	4	5.00
Stockport	10	1	6	3	12	38	5	5.00
Mansfield	7	1	5	1	10	19	3	4.28
Walsall	10	2	8	0	9	29	4	4.00
Sheffield W	8	1	6	1	8	25	3	3.75

Avge — points calculated on 23 matches

FRED WORRALL

1942-43

It had been a struggle, but Athletic had kept the flag flying at Boundary Park for another season of Regional football. There were times when the directors and their ever diligent secretary/manager Bob Mellor, did not know where the team was coming from only a few minutes before the start of a game, but a side always turned out, enabling the club's supporters to watch some of the leading teams and players in action at Boundary Park

In these austerity seasons when it counted as an achievement to fulfil your fixtures, never mind win them, the actual results were of little importance. Nevertheless, Athletic's record gave some idea of the bad luck which dogged the team on the field. Of the 38 matches played, they won nine, drew six, and lost 23. The team scored 64 goals, and had 105 scored against them. There were 9 games in which Athletic did all the attacking but just could not score, and lost by the odd goal. Most teams had better scoring records than Athletic, but few had been able to say that they fielded as many of their own players as Athletic had throughout the season. Athletic had given encouragement to local junior talent, and in one match, every member of the team except one, was an Athletic player. The exception was Fred Worrall, the only regular guest player in the side, and you could hardly call Worrall a stranger at Boundary Park. Worrall's choosing to play for his old club when he could have played in an all-star winning team was an indication of Athletic's team spirit.

Altogether, Athletic tried 39 players, and Tom Shipman had the distinction of playing in every match. Corporal Waite was leading goalscorer with 18, spread over both halves of the season, Worrall scored 10, six coming in the last 6 games.

The main thing for Athletic supporters at home or overseas, especially the latter, was that League football was alive in Oldham, and that with all the changing conditions and growing difficulties, Athletic were staying the pace with the top-flight clubs.

BEAUMONT RATCLIFFE   ARTHUR BUCKLEY

SEASON 1942-43

1	Aug	29	(a)	Chester	L 1-5
2	Sep	5	(h)	Chester	L 2-3
3		12	(a)	Burnley	L 0-3
4		19	(h)	Burnley	L 1-3
5		26	(a)	Rochdale	L 1-3
6	Oct	3	(h)	Rochdale	W 1-0
7		10	(h)	Halifax T	W 3-0
8		17	(a)	Halifax T	L 1-4
9		24	(a)	Blackburn R	L 1-8
10		31	(h)	Blackburn R	L 0-1
11	Nov	7	(a)	Bury	L 1-4
12		14	(h)	Bury	D 3-3
13		21	(h)	Bolton W	W 3-1
14		28	(a)	Bolton W	D 1-1
15	Dec	5	(a)	Blackpool	L 3-8
16		12	(h)	Blackpool	L 1-4
17		19	(a)	Southport	L 0-3
18		25	(h)	Southport	W 6-0
19	Dec	26	(a)	Rochdale	L 3-4
20	Jan	2	(h)	Rochdale	L 2-3
21		9	(h)	Bolton W	D 3-3
22		16	(a)	Bolton W	L 0-5
23		23	(a)	Halifax T	L 3-4
24		30	(h)	Halifax T	L 0-1
25	Feb	6	(a)	Blackpool	L 0-4
26		13	(h)	Blackpool	D 1-1
27		20	*(a)	Blackburn R	L 1-7
28		27	(h)	Blackburn R	L 1-2
29	Mar	6	(h)	Southport	W 2-1
30		13	(a)	Southport	L 1-2
31		20	(a)	Rochdale*	L 0-1
32		27	(h)	Rochdale*	W 3-1
33	Apr	3	(h)	B/pool Services*	D 3-3
34		10	(a)	B/pool Services*	W 4-1
35		17	(a)	Manchester U*	L 0-3
36		24	(h)	Manchester U*	W 3-1
37		26	(a)	Stockport C	D 1-1
38	May	1	(h)	Bradford	W 4-3

FINAL LEAGUE POSITION: 44th in Football
League North (First Championship)

FINAL LEAGUE POSITION: 48th in Football
League North (Second Championship)

Matches 19-32 inclusive and 35-38 inclusive were in the Football League North Second Competition. Matches 19-28 inclusive were in the League Cup Qualifying Competition as well as counting towards the League. Matches marked thus* were in the Lancashire Cup of which Matches 31, 32, 34 & 35 counted towards the League.

LEAGUE NORTH CUP
QUALIFYING COMPETITION
26 December 1942 to 27 February 1943

	P	W	L	D	F	A	Pts
Manchester C	10	7	1	2	30	15	16
Rochdale	10	7	1	2	31	16	16
Liverpool	10	7	1	2	27	14	16
Lovell's	10	6	1	3	32	10	15
Chesterfield	10	7	2	1	22	12	15
Huddersfield	9	7	2	0	31	14	14
Sheffield W	10	5	1	4	26	16	14
Coventry	10	7	3	0	16	10	14
Stoke	10	6	2	2	24	16	14
York	9	6	2	1	33	17	13
Manchester U	10	5	3	2	27	15	13
Newcastle	9	6	2	1	37	21	13
Blackpool	10	4	1	5	26	16	13
Aston Villa	10	6	4	0	21	13	13
Chester	10	5	3	2	22	14	12
Notts Co	10	5	3	2	22	14	12
Bristol C	10	5	3	2	24	21	12
Leicester	10	6	4	0	27	22	12
Nottingham F	10	5	3	2	20	19	12
Aberaman	10	6	4	0	22	22	12
Halifax	10	5	3	2	20	21	12
Barnsley	10	5	3	2	19	20	12
WBA	10	6	4	0	19	22	12
Bradford PA	9	4	2	3	18	11	11
Wolves	10	4	3	3	23	17	11
Blackburn	10	4	3	3	27	20	11
Bath	10	5	4	1	31	24	11
Bradford C	10	5	4	1	20	17	11

LEAGUE NORTH CUP
Continued

	P	W	L	D	F	A	Pts
Sheffield U	10	4	3	3	26	28	11
Bury	10	4	4	2	29	16	10
Everton	10	5	5	0	34	23	10
Derby	10	4	4	2	22	16	10
All above qualified							
Grimsby	10	3	3	4	22	20	10
Bolton	10	4	4	2	20	24	10
Gateshead	10	5	5	0	25	30	10
Lincoln	10	4	5	1	23	18	9
Sunderland	10	3	4	3	31	26	9
Northampton	10	4	5	1	19	19	9
Birmingham	10	3	6	1	15	17	7
Wrexham	10	2	5	3	16	23	7
Stockport	10	3	6	1	22	46	7
Walsall	10	3	5	2	13	18	6
Doncaster	10	2	6	2	17	35	6
Swansea	10	2	6	2	17	35	6
Tranmere	10	2	6	2	14	30	6
Southport	10	1	6	3	21	37	5
Burnley	10	1	6	3	10	22	5
Crewe	10	1	6	3	8	30	5
Cardiff	10	1	7	2	10	26	4
Leeds	10	1	8	1	16	34	3
Rotherham	10	0	7	3	12	29	3
Mansfield	10	1	8	1	12	41	3
OLDHAM	10	0	8	2	14	34	2
Middlesbrough	10	1	9	0	13	45	2

APPEARANCES:
(In all competitions)

AINSWORTH A	25	HAYES W	4
ASHWORTH J	1	HURST C	17
BIRCH N	1	HURST G	4
BUCKLEY F	5	KEATING R	2
* BUCKLEY A	2	LAWRENCE R	3
BAILEY A	24	* MILLIGAN G.H	3
CHAPMAN A	6	MARTIN R.O	4
* EASTWOOD R	5	MEECHAM W	1
FURNESS W	1	* PERCIVAL J	1
GRAY M	27	PHIPPS J	1
HEROD E	5	RILEY T	1
HILTON W.A	32	RADCLIFFE M	26
HAMPSON T	5		

* READETT H	1	
SHIPMAN T.E.R	38	
SPENCER K	2	
STOKES J	2	
SOUTHERN S.C	1	
SAUNDERS	1	
TAYLOR J.T	35	
TILLING H.K	32	
THOMAS W	1	
WILLIAMS K	4	
WILLIAMSON T	34	
* WORRALL F	23	
WAITE W	28	

GOAL SCORERS: (In all competitions)
WAITE 18, WORRALL 10, BAILEY 8, TILLING 8, HILTON 3, BUCKLEY F. 2, CHAPMAN 2, BUCKLEY A. 2, AINSWORTH 2, HAMPSON 2, TAYLOR J.T. 5, WILLIAMSON, HURST C, HURST G, ONE GOAL EACH. TOTAL 64

GEORGE MILLIGAN

NORTH SECOND CHAMPIONSHIP
26 December 1941 to 1 May 1943

	P	W	L	D	F	A	Pts
Liverpool	20	15	3	2	64	32	32
Lovell's	20	11	4	5	63	32	27
Manchester C	19	11	3	5	43	24	27
Aston Villa	20	13	6	1	44	30	27
Sheffield W	20	9	3	8	43	26	26
Manchester U	19	11	5	3	52	26	25
York	18	11	4	3	52	30	25
Huddersfield	19	11	5	3	48	28	25
Coventry	20	11	6	3	33	21	25
Stoke	20	10	6	4	42	34	24
Notts Co	20	9	5	6	37	34	24
Blackpool	19	8	4	7	49	31	23
Newcastle	19	10	6	3	62	42	23
Blackburn	18	9	5	4	45	35	22
Bristol C	19	8	5	6	41	33	22
Chesterfield	20	9	7	4	35	30	22
Derby	20	8	7	5	41	34	21
Aberaman	18	10	7	1	39	41	21
Sunderland	19	8	7	4	58	40	20
Rochdale	16	9	5	2	39	26	20
Leicester	29	9	9	2	40	37	20
Sheffield U	19	8	7	4	43	42	20
Bradford	19	7	7	5	35	31	19
Everton	19	9	9	1	51	46	19
Bath	18	7	7	4	49	46	18
Birmingham	20	8	10	2	32	29	18
Barnsley	17	8	7	3	34	37	18
Nottingham F	18	7	7	4	30	34	18
Crewe	20	7	9	4	44	57	18
Bradford C	16	7	7	2	29	29	16
Wrexham	17	7	7	3	36	37	17
Gateshead	13	6	7	0	29	36	12
Stockport	19	4	11	4	37	76	12
Southport	14	5	4	5	38	58	11
Leeds	16	5	10	1	32	50	11
OLDHAM	15	4	11	0	35	60	8
Middlesbrough	18	5	13	0	31	69	10
Lincoln	10	4	5	1	23	18	9
Burnley	14	3	8	3	17	31	9
Walsall	16	3	11	2	22	35	8
Cardiff	17	2	13	2	22	47	7
Mansfield	10	1	8	1	12	41	3

NORTH
Ending 25 December 1942

	P	W	L	D	F	A	Pts
Blackpool	18	16	1	1	93	28	33
Liverpool	18	14	3	1	70	34	29
Sheffield W	18	12	3	3	61	26	27
Manchester U	18	12	4	2	58	26	26
Huddersfield	18	10	2	6	52	32	26
Stoke	18	11	4	3	46	25	25
Coventry	18	10	3	5	28	16	25
Southport	18	11	4	3	64	42	25
Derby	18	11	5	2	51	37	24
Bradford PA	18	8	3	7	46	21	23
Lincoln	18	9	4	5	58	36	23
Halifax	18	10	5	3	39	27	23
Gateshead	18	10	3	5	52	45	23
Aston Villa	18	10	6	2	47	33	22
Everton	18	10	6	2	52	41	22
Grimsby	17	8	4	5	42	31	21
York	18	9	6	3	47	36	21
Blackburn	18	9	6	3	56	43	21
Barnsley	18	8	5	5	39	30	21
Sheffield U	18	7	5	6	45	35	20
Birmingham	18	9	7	2	37	30	20
Sunderland	18	8	7	3	46	40	19
Chester	18	7	7	4	43	40	18
Walsall	18	6	7	5	33	31	17
Northampton	18	8	9	1	38	44	17
Newcastle	18	6	8	4	51	52	16
Chesterfield	18	5	7	6	30	34	16
WBA	18	6	8	4	35	43	16
Notts Co	18	7	9	2	34	57	16
Manchester C	18	7	10	1	46	47	15
Nottingham F	18	6	9	3	39	54	15
Burnley	18	5	8	5	35	45	15
Leicester	18	5	9	4	32	37	14
Bury	18	6	10	2	53	81	14
Stockport	18	5	10	3	34	51	13
Rotherham	18	4	9	5	28	48	13
Wolves	18	5	11	2	48	61	12
Crewe	18	5	11	2	43	64	12
Middlesbrough	18	4	10	4	30	50	12
Rochdale	18	5	11	2	34	57	12
Wrexham	18	5	12	1	43	67	11
Leeds	18	3	11	4	28	45	10
OLDHAM	18	4	12	2	29	54	10
Bradford C	18	4	12	2	30	55	10
Bolton	18	3	12	3	31	52	9
Doncaster	17	3	11	3	23	41	9
Mansfield	18	2	12	4	25	65	8

1943-44

A run of late season defeats could not obscure the fact that the 1943-44 season was Athletic's best to date in wartime competitions. The form of the side was often exasperating, and yet in the crucial stages of the season, Athletic rose to the occasion and gave the campaign a solid core of achievement. Faced with a stiff series of qualifying competitions and with no extra help from star players to call upon, Athletic surprised even their most ardent supporters by an inspired spell which took them through the qualifying competition of the League War Cup into the first round proper, when they met Liverpool over two matches. After taking an 8-1 hiding at Anfield, Athletic bounced back seven days later to record an impressive 1-0 victory over the Merseyside aristocrats, but lose the tie on aggregate.

This season's record was a matter for congratulation to all concerned, directors, officials, players and supporters, but only those behind the scenes knew what was entailed in keeping a Third Division club going in a competition in which there were First and Second Division clubs, some with apparently unlimited player resources. Athletic had relied, in the main, on the same players week after week, and the team picked against Manchester United in the last match of the season was composed entirely of the club's own players. Few clubs had fielded fewer guest players in the course of this season. Of the 36 matches contested, two players, Tom Shipman and Harold Tilling played in every one. Inside-forward, Arthur Bailey, was Athletic's leading scorer with 9 goals, followed by Edwin Chapman with 8.

AIR RAID PRECAUTIONS ON FOOTBALL GROUND.

If an Air Raid Warning is received whilst a Match is in progress, an immediate announcement will be made over the Loud Speakers, and all play will be stopped. Patrons will be asked to proceed at once to the Exit Gates and to disperse quickly and orderly. **Do not Rush** to any one Exit as **all Exits will be Opened immediately a Warning is received. Do not run** as in this way accidents will be avoided.

Air Raid Stewards will be at every Exit to assist in an orderly dispersal out of the Ground.

The **Loud Speakers will continue to operate until the Ground has been cleared,** and by this means Patrons will be directed to the nearest Exits and Air Raid Shelters. **Under no circumstances may anyone cross the Football Ground,**

Patrons will appreciate that no money can be refunded, or re-admission Tickets issued, if a Game is delayed or abandoned on account of an Air Raid or Air Raid Warning. If it is possible for the game to be commenced or resumed, those who have left the Ground, Stands and Enclosures will be re-admitted and play will again be continued provided of course that the Local Authorities do not object and light permits.

It is requested that at all times Patrons will distribute themselves about the Ground as far as they are able, and so avoid undue crowding at any one spot.

If these instructions are rigidly adhered to, it will not only add to the safety of the individual, but the safety of others.

AIR RAID DISPERSAL.

Wing Stands, Centre Pavilion and Enclosures by the Exits under the Stands.

SEASON 1943-44

1	Aug 28	(a)	Bury	L	1-3
2	Sep 4	(h)	Bury	W	3-2
3	11	(h)	Chester	L	0-3
4	18	(a)	Chester	L	1-6
5	25	(h)	Rochdale	W	2-0
6	Oct 2	(a)	Rochdale	L	1-2
7	9	(h)	Burnley	W	4-2
8	16	(a)	Burnley	L	0-1
9	23	(a)	Halifax T	W	5-1
10	30	(h)	Halifax T	L	0-5
11	Nov 6	(a)	Southport	W	1-0
12	13	(h)	Southport	W	2-1
13	20	(a)	Bolton W	L	0-3
14	27	(h)	Bolton W	W	4-2
15	Dec 4	(h)	Blackpool	D	1-1
16	11	(a)	Blackpool	L	1-3
17	18	(h)	Blackburn R	L	2-4
18	25	(a)	Blackburn R	L	2-5
19	Dec 27	(h)	Stockport	L	1-2
20	Jan 1	(a)	Stockport C	W	5-1
28	8	(a)	Manchester C	D	0-0
22	15	(h)	Manchester C	D	1-1
23	22	(a)	Bury	W	7-3
24	29	(h)	Bury	W	3-0
25	Feb 5	(h)	Halifax T	L	1-3
26	12	(a)	Halifax T	W	3-0
27	19	(a)	Manchester U	L	2-3
28	26	(h)	Manchester U	D	1-1
29	Mar 4	(a)	Liverpool	W	1-0
30	11	(h)	Liverpool	W	1-0
31	Apr 1	(a)	Rochdale	L	0-4
32	8	(h)	Rochdale	L	0-2
33	10	(h)	Tranmere R	L	0-3
34	15	(a)	Tranmere R	L	1-2
35	29	(a)	Manchester U	D	0-0
36	May 6	(h)	Manchester U	L	1-3

Danger from Flying Bombs

Spotters shall be stationed to give warning of imminent danger and a flag will be displayed on the scoreboard.

FINAL LEAGUE POSITION: 36th in Football League North First Championship

FINAL LEAGUE POSITION: 44th in Football League North Second Championship

Matches 19-28 inclusive were also in the League War Cup Qualifying competition. Matches 29-30 were also in the League War Cup Knock-out competitions.

LEAGUE NORTH CUP QUALIFYING COMPETITION
27 December 1943 to 26 February 1944

	P	W	L	D	F	A	Pts
Wrexham	10	9	1	0	26	12	18
Bath	10	8	1	1	30	11	17
Stoke	10	8	1	1	43	19	17
Leicester	10	6	1	3	22	9	15
Sheffield U	10	7	2	1	33	16	15
Bradford	10	6	1	3	23	14	15
Manchester U	10	6	1	3	28	18	15
Everton	10	7	3	0	42	16	14
Birmingham	9	6	1	2	22	10	14
Rotherham	10	6	2	2	32	17	14
Liverpool	10	7	3	0	36	21	14
Newcastle	10	7	3	0	25	20	14
Lovell's	10	6	3	1	33	16	13
Blackpool	10	6	3	1	23	13	13
Barnsley	10	5	2	3	22	16	13
Coventry	10	5	2	3	19	17	13
Blackburn	10	6	3	1	21	18	13
Cardiff	10	6	4	0	23	13	12
Sheffield W	9	5	2	2	17	11	12
Manchester U	10	5	3	2	27	19	12
Bristol C	10	4	2	4	17	16	12
Darlington	10	5	4	1	28	14	11
OLDHAM	10	4	3	3	24	14	11
Rochdale	10	4	3	3	24	14	11
Derby	10	5	4	1	20	16	11
Aston Villa	10	5	4	1	20	16	11
Hartlepool	10	4	3	3	25	25	11
Gateshead	10	5	4	1	27	28	11
Grimsby	10	5	4	1	18	19	11

LEAGUE NORTH CUP
Continued

	P	W	L	D	F	A	Pts
Leeds	10	5	4	1	19	22	11
York	10	5	5	0	22	16	10
Burnley	10	4	4	2	22	19	10
All above qualified							
Stockport	10	5	5	0	23	28	10
Nottingham F	9	3	3	3	8	7	9
Chester	10	4	5	1	31	31	9
Mansfield	10	4	5	1	12	19	9
Huddersfield	10	3	5	2	16	19	8
WBA	10	2	4	4	24	29	8
Doncaster	9	3	4	2	14	24	8
Middlesbrough	10	2	5	3	14	20	7
Bolton	10	3	6	1	15	27	7
Walsall	10	2	5	3	11	22	7
Sunderland	10	3	7	0	25	37	6
Bury	10	2	6	2	18	30	6
Halifax	10	2	6	2	14	25	6
Southport	10	2	6	2	14	25	6
Chesterfield	10	2	7	1	17	25	5
Swansea	10	2	7	1	19	38	5
Crewe	10	2	7	1	21	46	5
Notts Co	10	2	8	0	14	25	4
Northampton	9	2	7	0	9	19	4
Wolves	10	0	6	4	11	27	4
Lincoln	9	1	7	1	14	31	3
Bradford C	10	1	8	1	11	26	3
Aberaman	10	0	9	1	11	39	1
Tranmere	10	0	10	0	11	41	0

NORTH
Ending 25 December 1943

	P	W	L	D	F	A	Pts
Blackpool	18	12	2	4	56	20	28
Manchester U	18	13	3	2	56	30	28
Liverpool	18	13	4	1	72	26	27
Doncaster	18	11	2	5	45	25	27
Bradford	18	11	3	4	65	28	26
Huddersfield	18	12	4	2	48	25	26
Northampton	18	10	3	5	43	25	25
Aston Villa	18	11	4	3	43	27	25
Sunderland	18	10	5	3	46	30	23
Hartlepool	18	10	5	3	44	31	23
Everton	18	9	5	4	60	34	22
Blackburn	18	10	6	2	47	32	22
Rochdale	18	10	6	2	43	41	22
Sheffield U	18	8	5	5	30	26	21
Lincoln	18	8	6	4	51	40	20
Birmingham	18	8	6	4	38	31	20
Manchester U	18	9	7	2	38	35	20
Mansfield	18	9	7	2	32	33	20
Derby	18	8	6	4	43	45	20
Chester	18	9	7	2	40	43	20
Grimsby	18	8	7	3	32	36	19
WBA	18	8	7	3	42	44	19
Gateshead	18	8	8	2	40	51	18
Burnley	18	5	6	7	24	22	17
Walsall	18	5	6	7	27	31	17
Nottingham F	18	6	7	5	33	39	17
Leeds	18	6	7	5	38	50	17
Leicester	18	6	8	4	33	30	16
Darlington	18	6	8	4	49	48	16
Rotherham	18	7	9	2	38	42	16
York	18	7	9	2	35	40	16
Halifax	18	6	8	4	37	36	16
Southport	18	7	9	2	33	51	16
Stoke	18	6	9	3	40	35	15
Chesterfield	18	7	10	1	29	31	15
OLDHAM	18	7	10	1	30	44	15
Stockport	18	5	8	5	24	43	15
Coventry	18	4	8	6	25	23	14
Newcastle	18	5	9	4	32	37	14
Sheffield W	18	5	9	4	34	37	14
Middlesbrough	18	4	8	6	35	52	14
Wolves	18	5	10	3	30	42	13
Bury	18	6	11	1	31	44	13
Barnsley	18	5	11	2	32	42	12
Bradford C	18	4	11	3	27	47	11
Wrexham	18	5	12	1	43	63	11
Notts Co	18	4	11	3	26	53	11
Bolton	18	5	13	0	24	46	10
Tranmere	18	4	13	1	39	71	9
Crewe	18	4	13	1	29	62	9

NORTH SECOND CHAMPIONSHIP
27 December 1943 to 6 May 1944

	P	W	L	D	F	A	Pts
Bath	21	16	3	2	78	26	34
Wrexham	21	15	2	4	62	29	34
Liverpool	21	14	5	2	71	38	30
Birmingham	20	12	3	5	47	19	29
Rotherham	21	12	4	5	54	30	29
Aston Villa	21	13	5	3	50	34	29
Blackpool	20	12	5	3	53	27	27
Cardiff	21	13	7	1	53	28	27
Manchester U	21	10	4	7	55	38	27
Bradford PA	21	11	5	4	50	30	26
Newcastle	20	13	7	0	47	36	26
Everton	21	12	8	1	73	39	25
Stoke	21	10	6	5	66	45	25
Leicester	21	10	6	5	40	32	25
Darlington	21	10	7	4	50	30	24
Nottingham F	20	9	5	6	32	20	24
Sheffield U	21	11	8	2	53	35	24
Coventry	21	10	7	4	48	37	24
Manchester C	21	9	6	6	42	35	24
Lovell's	20	10	8	2	48	30	22
Gateshead	21	9	8	4	45	53	22
Doncaster	17	9	5	3	42	33	21
Derby	21	8	5	3	53	28	21
Rochdale	20	8	7	5	40	36	21
Barnsley	17	9	10	0	44	34	20
Halifax	20	8	8	4	44	42	20
Chester	20	9	9	2	65	65	20
Hartlepool	20	8	8	4	49	50	20
Stockport	19	10	9	0	44	49	20
Sheffield W	20	8	8	4	32	36	20
Blackburn	18	8	8	2	43	40	18
Huddersfield	21	8	10	3	41	40	19
WBA	21	5	7	9	46	48	19
Bolton	21	8	10	3	42	49	19
Leeds	18	8	7	3	34	40	19
Northampton	19	9	10	0	37	39	18
Burnley	18	6	6	6	39	42	18
Bristol C	20	6	9	5	38	42	17
York	20	7	11	2	37	40	16
Middlesbrough	21	6	11	4	41	51	16
Swansea	20	7	11	2	42	67	16
Grimsby	15	6	6	3	23	28	15
Bury	20	6	11	3	38	55	15
OLDHAM	18	5	9	4	28	36	14
Sunderland	19	6	11	2	44	58	14
Chesterfield	19	5	10	4	31	41	14
Mansfield	14	6	7	1	23	25	13
Wolves	20	3	11	6	28	56	12
Walsall	17	3	8	6	17	35	12
Tranmere	20	6	14	0	29	62	12
Bradford C	18	4	12	2	27	47	10
Southport	20	3	14	3	35	67	9
Lincoln	18	3	13	2	25	56	8
Notts Co	20	3	17	0	23	68	6
Crewe	18	2	15	1	31	83	5
Aberaman	18	1	16	1	20	87	3

APPEARANCES:
(In all competitions)

AINSWORTH A.............3	GRAY M.............33	RADCLIFFE M.............27
* BRATLEY G.W.............11	HILTON W.A.............5	* ROXBURGH A.W.............9
BOWDEN J.............6	HURST T.............28	SHIPMAN T.E.R.............36
* BUTLER T.............3	* HAMILTON W.............1	SAMUELS G.............17
BOHAN T.W.............1	HORTON L.............7	STOKES J.............2
BAILEY R.............23	HOOD T.............2	* STEVENS G.L.............2
* CURRAN F.............2	JACKSON J.............1	* TOPPING H.............1
CHAPMAN E.............15	JERRAM G.............1	TAYLOR J.T.............28
* CRAWSHAW H.............5	KEATING R.............5	TILLING H.............36
CROSSLEY J.............1	MARTIN R.O.............11	WILLIAMSON T.............33
COTTRILL W.H.............10	* MILLIGAN G.H.............1	WILKINSON H.............1
DUNNING H.............2		* WORRALL F.............24
FERRIER R.J.............1		

*Guest Player

GOAL SCORERS: (In all competitions)
BAILEY 9, CHAPMAN 8, COTTRILL 7, TILLING 6, WORRALL 5, CRAWSHAW 4, TAYLOR J.T. 3, BOWDEN 2, MARTIN 2, KEATING 2, STROKES 2, HILTON, HURST C., HURST G., AINSWORTH, HORTON, STEVENS, CURRAN ALL ONE EACH. 1 OWN GOAL.
TOTAL 58

Following an indifferent time in the Northern League First Championship, in which Athletic, still desperately short of players, won only seven times in 18 outings, the directors considered it time to give secretary Bob Mellor a well-earned break from carrying the club on his shoulders, a job he'd done without complaint, since May 1934, and advertise the job for a team manager. Athletic received over sixty applications from all walks of life, which were short-listed to include former Latics goalkeeper Jack Hacking, Tom Parker (Arsenal), Warney Cresswell (Everton), T.Wilson (Huddersfield), Jimmy Marshall, a former Latics inside-forward, who cost the club its record fee of £2,250 back in 1920, and Mr.Frank Womack from Birmingham. Mr.Womack had a remarkable record as a 'doctor' to soccer clubs, and he took over at Boundary Park on the 23rd February 1945, after managerial experience at Torquay, Grimsby, Leicester and Notts County.

A new team every week was the Womack way of keeping interest in the end of season games at Boundary Park, as he wanted to see what his younger players could do in League football. The fans responded by producing gate receipts of £40 for a visit from Tranmere Rovers in mid-April. Supporters had cried out for local talent to be given a chance, and when the juniors were selected, they stayed away. Team building at the best of times was a difficult task for Athletic, and the club were tackling the problem before normal football resumed. Womack selected a boy of 17, J.B.Smith from Houghton United, to play centre-half against Liverpool at Boundary Park on V.E.Day 1945. As the crowd lounged in 90° heat, the Liverpool forwards gave Smith a torrid time as they rattled up a 7-0 scoreline. This same day saw street parties, flags, bunting, bonfires and dancing as Oldham people celebrated an end to war, certainly a day young Mr.Smith would never forget.

There was an emotional ceremony before the kick-off with Tranmere Rovers at Boundary Park on April 14th 1945, the sparse crowd of 857 standing bare-headed in the pouring rain, paying tribute to President Roosevelt, who had died the previous day. The only sounds to break the silence were the strains of the Last Post and the roar of a lone Spitfire which dipped in salute overhead. Seconds later, Boundary Park was cheering as centre-forward Cottrill put Athletic in front. Latics 2-1 win gained revenge for a 7-1 hammering only seven days earlier.

Every Football League club supplied most of its professional and amateur players on a manpower conveyor belt throughout the wartime seasons, replacements in the field taking their turn on the assembly line for the armed services. Oldham Athletic had 60 players and staff actively involved with the forces. They served, and not all of them came back.

SEASON 1944-45

1	Aug	26	(a)	Accrington S	L 1-5
2	Sep	2	(h)	Accrington S	W 2-1
3		9	(h)	Preston NE	L 0-1
4		16	(a)	Preston NE	L 1-4
5		23	(a)	Southport	W 5-1
6		30	(h)	Southport	W 2-0
7	Oct	7	(h)	Burnley	W 3-1
8		14	(a)	Burnley	L 0-1
9		21	(h)	Halifax T	L 0-1
10		28	(a)	Halifax T	L 1-5
11	Nov	4	(a)	Blackpool	W 3-1
12		11	(h)	Blackpool	L 2-3
13		18	(h)	Blackburn R	W 3-0
14		25	(a)	Blackburn R	D 1-1
15	Dec	2	(a)	Rochdale	W 3-2
16		9	(h)	Rochdale	L 0-2
17		16	(h)	Bolton W	L 0-5
18		23	(a)	Bolton W	L 1-2
19	Dec	26	(h)	Bury	D 2-2
20		30	(h)	Manchester U	L 3-4
21	Jan	6	(a)	Bury	L 1-3
22		13	(h)	Bury	W 2-0
23		27	(h)	Manchester C	L 3-4
24	Feb	3	(h)	Huddersfield T	L 2-3
25		10	(a)	Huddersfield T	L 1-6
26		17	(a)	Halifax T	W 2-0
27		24	(h)	Halifax T	L 1-2
28	Mar	3	(a)	Manchester U	L 2-3
29		10	(a)	Manchester C	L 2-3
30		17	(h)	Burnley	L 1-2
31		24	(a)	Southport	W 5-2
32		31	(h)	Southport	W 2-0
33	Apr	2	(a)	Burnley	L 1-3
34		7	(a)	Tranmere R	L 1-7
35		14	(h)	Tranmere R	W 2-1
36		21	(a)	Rochdale	W 2-1
37		28	(h)	Rochdale	W 2-0
38	May	5	(a)	Liverpool	L 2-3
39		12	(h)	Liverpool	L 0-7

FINAL LEAGUE POSITION: 38th in Football League North, First Championship

Matches 20-29 inclusive were also played in the League War Cup Qualifying competition.

FINAL LEAGUE POSITION: 49th in Football League North, Second Championship

LEAGUE NORTH CUP QUALIFYING COMPETITION
25 December 1944 to 17 March 1945

	P	W	L	D	F	A	Pts
Derby	10	7	0	3	38	9	17
Aston Villa	10	8	1	1	31	13	17
Bristol C	10	8	2	0	27	10	16
Everton	10	8	2	0	39	15	16
Burnley	10	7	2	1	25	10	15
Cardiff	10	7	2	1	26	11	15
Doncaster	10	7	2	1	30	13	15
Liverpool	10	7	2	1	34	15	15
Stoke	10	6	2	2	35	14	14
Lovell's	10	7	3	0	24	15	14
Barnsley	10	7	3	0	18	14	14
Wrexham	10	5	1	4	30	17	14
Bolton	10	6	3	1	27	15	13
Bradford PA	10	6	3	1	23	19	13
Manchester C	10	6	3	1	23	19	13
Rotherham	10	5	2	3	18	15	13
Newcastle	10	6	4	0	30	21	12
Darlington	10	5	3	2	22	18	12
Bradford C	10	5	3	2	23	21	12
Northampton	10	5	3	2	19	20	12
Wolves	10	5	4	1	23	16	11
Leicester	10	3	2	5	23	16	11
Chesterfield	10	4	3	3	18	13	11
Birmingham	10	5	4	1	19	14	11
Sheffield U	10	5	4	1	24	18	11
Blackpool	10	5	4	1	27	22	11
Bury	10	5	4	1	22	22	11
Crewe	10	4	3	3	23	23	11
Halifax	10	4	3	3	14	14	11
Manchester U	10	5	4	1	16	18	11
Accrington	10	5	4	1	15	18	11

LEAGUE NORTH CUP
Continued

	P	W	L	D	F	A	Pts
WBA	10	3	3	4	20	15	10
All above qualified							
Blackburn	10	5	5	0	31	25	10
Huddersfield	10	4	4	2	21	18	10
Gateshead	10	4	4	2	15	18	10
Hartlepool	10	4	4	2	19	24	10
Nottingham F	10	3	3	4	9	13	10
Leeds	10	4	5	1	29	25	9
Sunderland	10	4	5	1	24	22	9
Grimsby	10	3	4	3	20	19	9
Mansfield	10	4	5	1	18	34	9
Preston	10	2	4	4	14	16	8
Lincoln	10	3	5	2	21	28	8
York	10	3	6	1	25	29	7
Middlesbrough	10	3	6	1	23	30	7
Walsall	10	3	6	1	13	21	7
Southport	10	3	6	1	19	40	7
Port Vale	10	3	6	1	13	30	7
Bath	10	3	7	0	28	34	6
Swansea	10	3	7	0	27	33	6
Hull	10	2	7	1	16	35	5
Tranmere	10	2	7	1	15	28	5
Rochdale	10	1	6	3	9	28	4
OLDHAM	10	2	8	0	19	28	4
Sheffield W	10	1	7	2	14	24	4
Stockport	10	2	8	0	16	35	4
Coventry	10	1	8	1	16	35	3
Aberaman	10	1	8	1	17	46	3
Chester	10	1	8	1	14	39	3
Notts Co	10	1	9	0	12	33	2

APPEARANCES: (In all competitions)

BOHAN T.W.	28	GOODMAN L.	34	OGDEN F.	4
* BUTLER T.	5	HORTON L.	2	* PORTER W.	14
BOWDEN J.	8	HILTON W.A.	1	PHIPPS J.	2
BAILEY A.	6	HURST C.	2	RADCLIFFE M.	34
* BIRCH J.W.	6	HERRICK R.	1	SAMUELS G.	2
BRIERLEY K.	3	IBBOTSON R.	2	SHIPMAN T.E.R.	20
CHAPMAN E.	21	KEATING R.	6	STANDRING N.	16
COTTRILL W.H.	4	LAWTON W.	2	* SMITH J.B.	1
EAVES T.A.	1	LOVELASS W.	1	TAYLOR J.T.	26
EATON C.	1	MARRS B.	1	TIERS J.	3
* EASTWOOD R.	6	MARTIN R.O.	3	TILLING H.K.	1
FARRINGTON J.	1	McMILLAN J.	1	WILLIAMSON T.	29
GRAY M.	7	MELLOR J.	3	* WORRALL F.	24

*Guest Player

GOAL SCORERS: (In all competitions)
BAILEY 9, CHAPMAN 8, COTTRILL 7, TILLING 6, WORRALL 5, CRAWSHAW 4, TAYLOR J.T. 3, BOWDEN 2, MARTIN 2, KEATING 2, STROKES 2, HILTON, HURST C., HURST G., AINSWORTH, HORTON, STEVENS, CURRAN ALL ONE EACH. 1 OWN GOAL. TOTAL 58

NORTH SECOND CHAMPIONSHIP
25 December 1944 to 26 May 1945

	P	W	L	D	F	A	Pts
Derby	26	19	4	3	78	28	41
Everton	27	17	3	7	79	43	37
Liverpool	24	16	5	3	67	26	35
Burnley	26	15	8	3	56	36	33
Newcastle	23	15	7	1	71	38	31
Aston Villa	25	14	9	2	70	45	30
Chesterfield	24	10	5	9	40	24	29
Wolves	24	11	6	7	45	31	29
Manchester U	22	13	6	3	47	33	29
Darlington	24	13	8	3	61	45	29
Bristol C	22	13	7	2	55	33	28
Blackburn	24	13	9	2	62	51	28
Huddersfield	27	12	11	4	52	49	28
Wrexham	22	10	5	7	55	36	27
Bolton	23	11	7	5	45	43	27
Blackpool	24	12	9	3	58	42	27
Stoke	23	12	9	2	67	42	26
Lovell's	19	12	5	4	44	27	26
Cardiff	20	12	6	2	41	27	26
Grimsby	21	10	5	6	51	37	26
Birmingham	24	9	8	7	38	34	25
Crewe	23	11	9	3	50	50	25
Doncaster	20	11	7	2	44	26	24
Bradford PA	22	10	8	4	39	34	24
Accrington	24	9	9	6	39	41	24
Barnsley	24	11	11	2	39	42	24
Rotherham	20	10	7	3	41	37	23
Gateshead	21	9	7	5	46	42	23
Preston	25	9	12	4	41	56	22
Sheffield U	24	9	13	2	56	48	21
Sunderland	25	9	13	3	53	54	21
Leeds	22	9	10	3	53	55	21
Sheffield W	22	8	12	5	53	56	21
Bath	20	10	10	0	50	48	20
Bury	20	8	8	4	38	43	20
York	22	8	10	4	48	56	20
Chester	22	9	11	2	49	61	20
Bradford C	20	8	9	3	43	46	19
WBA	22	6	9	7	39	44	19
Hartlepool	21	8	10	3	34	54	19
Coventry	21	6	9	6	36	53	18
Nottingham F	18	5	8	5	23	25	21
Lincoln	18	4	12	2	32	55	16
Manchester C	19	7	10	2	32	43	16
Northampton	18	5	8	5	33	50	15
OLDHAM	18	7	13	1	39	56	15
Stockport	19	7	12	0	31	50	14
Middlesbrough	24	6	16	2	40	73	14
Walsall	18	5	12	1	24	52	11
Swansea	20	6	13	1	42	63	13
Port Vale	20	5	14	2	27	60	12
Mansfield	20	6	13	1	30	65	11
Hull	18	5	12	1	30	54	11
Rochdale	20	5	13	2	33	82	9
Southport	22	3	16	3	33	82	9
Notts Co	24	4	17	0	29	62	8
Aberaman	17	2	13	2	36	69	6

NORTH
Ending 23 December 1944

	P	W	L	D	F	A	Pts
Huddersfield	18	14	1	3	50	22	31
Derby	18	14	3	1	54	19	29
Sunderland	18	12	2	4	52	25	28
Aston Villa	18	12	3	3	54	19	27
Everton	18	12	2	4	58	25	26
Wrexham	18	11	4	3	40	18	25
Doncaster	18	12	6	0	48	27	24
Bradford PA	18	10	4	4	45	31	24
Bolton	18	9	3	6	34	22	24
Manchester C	18	9	5	4	53	31	22
Stoke	18	9	5	4	37	25	22
Birmingham	18	8	4	6	30	21	22
Barnsley	18	10	6	2	42	32	22
Rotherham	18	9	5	4	31	25	22
WBA	18	9	5	4	36	30	22
Liverpool	18	9	6	3	41	30	21
Grimsby	18	9	6	3	37	29	21
Halifax	18	8	5	5	30	29	21
Chester	18	9	6	3	45	45	21
Blackpool	18	9	7	2	53	38	20
Burnley	18	8	6	4	39	27	20
Leeds	18	9	7	2	53	42	20
Sheffield W	18	9	7	2	34	30	20
Chesterfield	18	8	7	3	30	19	19
Darlington	18	9	8	1	52	45	19
Wolves	18	7	6	5	31	27	19
Rochdale	18	7	6	5	35	33	19
Crewe	18	9	8	1	43	41	19
Blackburn	18	7	7	4	38	34	18
Manchester U	18	8	8	2	40	40	18
Preston	18	7	7	4	26	28	18
Walsall	18	5	7	6	27	31	16
Gateshead	18	7	9	2	45	53	16
Northampton	18	5	7	6	30	38	16
Newcastle	18	5	9	4	30	36	14?
Sheffield U	18	6	9	3	27	25	15
Hartlepool	18	7	10	1	41	47	15
Nottingham F	18	5	8	5	31	40	15
Coventry	18	6	10	2	23	42	14
York	18	6	11	1	49	52	13
Northampton	18	5	7	6	30	36	13?
OLDHAM	18	7	13	1	39	56	15
Mansfield	18	6	9	3	31	40	15
Middlesbrough	18	3	4	5	45	51	15
Bradford C	18	6	11	1	34	57	13
Accrington	18	5	1	29	46	14
Port Vale	18	5	11	2	35	52	12
Bury	18	5	11	2	28	50	12
Swansea	18	5	12	1	30	54	11
Stockport	18	5	12	1	30	54	11
Hull	18	4	12	2	32	56	10
Lincoln	18	4	12	2	32	55	10
Leicester	18	3	11	4	23	63	10
Tranmere	18	2	15	1	20	53	5
Notts Co	18	2	15	1	19	62	5

OLDHAM ATHLETIC · 1944/45
Back: HARGREAVES (Trainer) · BRIERLEY · MARLOR · TURNER · BOOTHMAN · CHAPMAN · KEETING
Front: GOODWIN · BUTLER (T) · WILLIAMSON · HORTON · LAWTON

The Boundary Park enclosure, cleared of all the wartime debris and other paraphernalia, had been painted and whitewashed for the opening of peace-time football in Oldham which saw Athletic defeat Crewe Alexandra 4-2, before 5,000 optimistic supporters. Athletic entered upon this new venture, the Third Division, North West First Championship, with high hopes and a team which bore little resemblance to any in 44-45,—Sawbridge, Marior, Eaves, Horton, Williamson, Goodwin (R), Chapman, Butler, Standring, Brierly and Goodwin (L). Only five victories out of 18 matches saw Athletic finish a disappointing 8th in the First Championship, and fare even worse in the Second, recording only one victory in eight matches.

Athletic's fall from grace had been gathering momentum since the turn of '45, and took its last plunge on the final day of the season with a resounding 1-5 crash at Doncaster Rovers—this ensuring bottom place in the Third North West table. In cold figures, it meant Athletic had proved the worst of the twenty clubs with whom they would have to compete in the coming season, when football would to return to a normal format.

They managed to qualify for the preliminary rounds of the F.A. Cup, defeating Southport over two legs, before losing to Accrington Stanley in similar circumstances. Les Horton and Tommy Williamson led the appearances with a maximum 40 League and Cup. Top scorers were Edwin Chapman on 16 League and Cup goals, closely followed by Tom West on 15, League and Cup.

Athletic's first major attempt to secure financial stability came with the decision to offer club shares to the public in May 1946. Athletic were trying to raise £6,000 to help pay off their liabilities, and mortgage some of the amount in signing well-known players for vital positions. Manager Frank Womack made an urgent, personal appeal to the sporting public of Oldham, pointing out the great importance of the £6,000 worth of shares being taken up in the shortest possible time; they were going slowly to this point. ''The close season is very short, and the money is to be used to put Athletic on the road to success immediately the new season opens,'' said Womack. ''A number of players of experience and proven talent would help us out of our difficulties. I have to get Athletic back in first class football, I made that pledge on my appointment. I must have your help because I am only human, but I am prepared to do the super human to redeem that pledge.''

OLDHAM RIFLES PRIZE BAND
Musical Programme, Saturday, April 8th.

1—MARCH	'' The Rover's Return ''	... ...	*Greenwood*
2—FOX-TROT	'' Lambeth Walk ''	... ...	*G. Mackenzie*
3—MARCH	'' Black Knight '' ...	... ...	*Rimner*
4—FOX-TROT	'' To Mother With Love ''	...	*G. Mackenzie*
5—MARCH	'' Quarter Deck ''	... ...	*Alford*
6—FOX-TROT	''A Penny Serenade ''	... ...	*G. Mackenzie*

SEASON 1945-46

1	Aug	25	(h)	Crewe A	W 4-2
2	Sep	1	(a)	Crewe A	D 0-0
3		8	(a)	Rochdale	L 2-4
4		15	(h)	Rochdale	W 2-1
5		22	(h)	Accrington S	L 0-3
6		29	(a)	Accrington S	D 1-1
7	Oct	6	(a)	Wrexham	D 1-1
8		13	(h)	Wrexham	D 0-0
9		20	(a)	Tranmere R	L 1-2
10		27	(h)	Tranmere R	L 1-2
11	Nov	3	(h)	Stockport C	W 4-1
12		10	(a)	Stockport C	L 1-3
13	Dec	1	(a)	Southport	L 0-3
14		22	(a)	Chester	D 2-2
15		25	(a)	Barrow	L 2-3
16		26	(h)	Barrow	W 3-1
17		29	(h)	Chester	L 2-3
18	Jan	1	(h)	Southport	W 3-0

FINAL LEAGUE POSITION: 8th in Third Division North West, First Championship

19	Jan	5	(h)	Crewe A	D 1-1
20		12	(a)	Crewe A	L 1-3
21		19	(h)	Wrexham	W 2-1
22		26	(a)	Wrexham	W 2-1
23	Feb	2	(a)	Accrington S	D 3-3
24		9	(h)	Accrington S	W 2-1
25		16	(a)	Barrow	W 3-0
26		28	(h)	Barrow	D 0-0
27	Mar	2	(a)	Tranmere R	D 3-3
28		9	(h)	Tranmere R	L 1-2

FINAL LEAGUE POSITION: 4th in Third Division North West, Cup Qualifying competition

29	Mar	23	(h)	Gateshead	D 2-2
30		30	(a)	Gateshead	L 0-3
31	Apr	6	(a)	Halifax T	L 0-1
32		13	(h)	Halifax T	D 1-1
33		20	(a)	Rochdale	L 1-3
34		22	(a)	Rochdale	L 0-4
35		27	(h)	Doncaster R	W 2-1
36	May	4	(a)	Doncaster R	L 1-5

FINAL LEAGUE POSITION: 20th in Third Division North West, Second Championship
Matches 29 & 30 were also in the Third Division North Cup

FA Cup

1	Nov	17	(a)	Southport	W 2-1
		24	(h)	Southport	W 3-1
2	Dec	8	(h)	Accrington S	W 2-1
		15	(a)	Accrington S	L 1-3

THIRD DIVISION NORTH
First half season

West Region

	P	W	L	D	F	A	Pts
Accrington	18	10	4	4	37	19	24
Rochdale	18	10	6	2	43	35	22
Crewe	18	9	6	3	43	31	21
Chester	18	8	5	5	44	38	21
Wrexham	18	8	6	4	30	25	20
Tranmere	18	9	7	2	33	31	20
Stockport	18	6	9	3	38	38	15
OLDHAM	18	5	8	5	29	32	15
Barrow	18	4	10	4	21	44	12
Southport	18	3	11	4	22	47	10

East Region

	P	W	L	D	F	A	Pts
Rotherham	18	12	4	2	56	28	26
Darlington	18	12	4	2	61	36	26
Gateshead	18	11	5	2	51	34	24
Doncaster	18	8	6	4	34	35	20
York	18	6	6	6	34	34	18
Halifax	18	7	7	4	39	46	18
Bradford C	18	6	8	4	45	40	16
Carlisle	18	5	10	3	34	58	13
Lincoln	18	4	12	2	34	54	10
Hartlepool	18	3	12	3	22	45	9

LEAGUE THIRD DIVISION NORTH CUP
Second half season

East Region

	P	W	L	D	F	A	Pts
Doncaster	10	6	1	3	24	15	15
Carlisle	10	7	3	0	30	17	14
Bradford C	10	4	3	3	27	22	11
Hartlepool	10	4	3	3	25	21	11
Gateshead	10	4	4	2	21	23	10
Darlington	10	5	5	0	26	31	10
Rotherham	10	3	5	2	24	26	8
York	10	2	4	4	16	18	8

All above qualified

Halifax	10	2	4	4	15	18	8
Lincoln	10	2	7	1	21	38	5

West Region

	P	W	L	D	F	A	Pts
Stockport	10	7	2	1	26	15	15
Southport	10	6	2	2	20	13	14
Accrington	10	6	3	1	24	17	13
OLDHAM	10	4	2	4	18	15	12
Crewe	10	3	3	4	23	27	10
Wrexham	10	4	5	1	21	20	9
Chester	10	4	5	1	26	25	9
Tranmere	10	4	5	1	17	25	9

All above qualified

Rochdale	10	2	6	2	18	20	6
Barrow	10	1	8	1	13	29	3

APPEARANCES: (In all competitions)

BOOTHMAN J...............14
BOHAN T.W...................5
* BUTLER T...................23
BLACKSHAW H.K..........6
BOWDEN J....................6
* BARCLAY R..................4
BRIERLEY K.................19
* BUCKLEY A..................5
CHAPMAN E................31
CROOKES A...................2
* COLLINDRIDGE C..........2
DIXON M.......................1
DOCHERTY J.................1
EAVES T.A.....................12
FERRIER R.J.................12
GOODWIN L..................23
HORTON L....................40
HAYES W......................3
HOBSON J.....................2
HURST G........................1
HURST C.......................1
HERRICK R....................3
KEATING R.....................2
LAWTON W...................36
MARLOR A.....................34
RADCLIFFE B.................7
* ROOKES P.W..................1
SAWBRIDGE J................14
SCOFIELD M...................6
SHIPMAN T.E.R.............19
STANDRING N...............13
* TURNER H....................13
TAYLOR J.T....................2
TILLING H.K...................4
WILLIAMSON T.............40
WAGSTAFFE E................4
WEST T..........................24
WAITE W.J......................3

* Guest Player

GOAL SCORERS (In all competitions)
CHAPMAN 16, WEST 15, STANDRING 5, FERRIER 4, BRIERLEY 4, BUTLER 3,
COLLINDRIDGE 3, KEATING 2, GOODWIN 2, LAWTON, BOHAN, WAGSTAFFE, BLACKSHAW,
WAITE, CROOKES, BARCLAY, HORTON ALL ONE EACH.
TOTAL 62

BEAUMONT RATCLIFFE

87

INTERNATIONAL XI

THE TOMMY WILLIAM

Back row: WITHINGTON (Blackpool) · LEUTY (Derby) · SWIFT (Man. City)
WESTWOOD (Man. City) · JOHNSTON (Blackpool) · HALTON (Bury)
Front: MATTHEWS & MORTENSON (Blackpool) · HARDWICK (Middlesbrough)
HOWE (Bolton) · GOODWIN (Athletic)

"Keeping the Dream Alive"

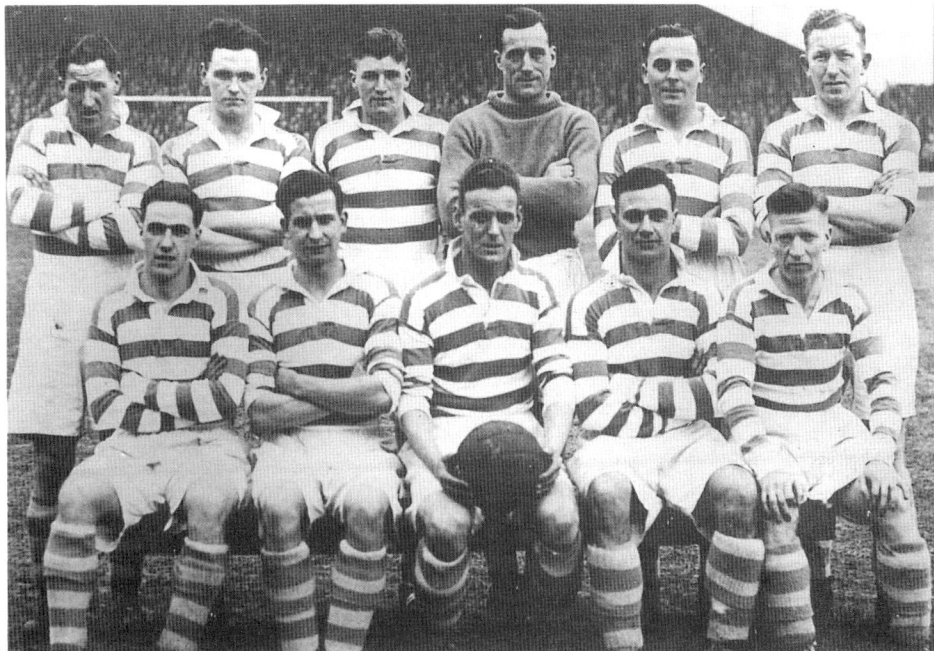

FIT MATCH · APRIL 1947   **ATHLETIC TEAM, WITH GUESTS**
Back: CLARKE (Man. City) · BRIERLEY · BELL · SWINDIN (Arsenal)
BLACKSHAW · WHALLEY (Man. United)
Front: TOMLINSON · BUTLER · WILLIAMSON · HORTON · ORMANDY

THE BOUNDARY PARK ENCLOSURE, CLEARED OF ALL WARTIME DEBRIS

FRED HOWE'S SECOND GOAL FOR ATHLETIC IN THE 3-1 WIN OVER LINCOLN. SEPT. 46

1946-47

The Oldham Athletic Promotion Drive Committee arranged a pre-season cricket match between Athletic and Wood Cup finalists Werneth C.C.,who were represented by their first eleven. Athletic wing-half and Ashton C.C. professional, Billy Lawton, captained the Latics team, which included manager Womack's new signings, Richard Witham, Bill Blackshaw, John Ormandy and Fred Howe. Every penny donated in this, and other pre-season ventures went towards the purchase of new players, winger Tommy Butler re-signing for the club for £500 of the money raised. 3,500 spectators watched the first public trial game at Boundary Park and witnessed the first bit of bad luck before the season had started proper, when inside-forward Bill Waite broke his collarbone, restricting him to only 5 appearances all season.

When normal football was resumed, it was certain that many of the older favourites would no longer grace the arenas of their former triumphs. Six years of war, besides having taken its toll of casualties, had spanned a period in which many players would naturally have retired from the game. Athletic, for their part, provided the answer by giving the youngsters a chance to stake their claim in the re-formed Third Division North. The post-war football campaign promised much, as the young men in the forces returned to civilian life as ardent soccer fans, after having their sporting interests developed whilst serving away. 'Absence makes the heart grow fonder' seemed to be true, as over 7,000 spectators turned up at Boundary Park to watch Athletic's opening match with Carlisle United. They went home disappointed by a 2-0 defeat.

By October '46 Athletic seemed to be battling against the odds, but 'Hope springs eternal', and the New Year it was hoped, would bring a change of fortune. It certainly did, but it was a change nobody expected, as instead of making a swift climb up the Third Division North table, they took a sudden nosedive and found themselves in 19th position out of 22 clubs, perilously close to having to apply for re-election, finishing on a disappointing 32 points. Athletic's brief flirtation with the F.A.Cup came to an end in round 2, losing at Doncaster Rovers 2-1, round 1 had seen a 1-0 victory over old rivals Tranmere Rovers at Boundary Park.

Athletic's slump since the turn of the year brought management matters to a head, and in early April Frank Womack resigned. He left lamenting the scarcity of full time professionals on Athletic's books, saying,"you can't work out your plan of campaign with part-timers, because they either train in the evenings, or on the grounds of other clubs. I have tried to do my best, I am sorry to be leaving". Tommy Williamson's benefit match received the all-clear to be played at Boundary Park on Tuesday, April 15th 1947, after a long struggle against the Government's ban on mid-week soccer. Utility player Les Horton made most League and Cup appearances this season with 44, and ex-Liverpool star Fred Howe top scored with 20 League goals, including two hat-tricks.

Athletic's directors appointed Billy Wootton, the little-known manager of Northwich Victoria, as the new manager of Athletic in June '47. Wootton's appointment was unexpected and surprising, as speculation was rife that either Stan Cullis or Sam Barkas were hot favourites."The board had a very difficult job in making their final choice", said secretary Bob Mellor, "it was a near thing between all three".

RAY HADDINGTON — 1947

1947-48

Nesw manager, Billy Wootton, was confident about his club's prospects this season. "A spirit now prevails among the directors, staff and players that has been absent for a long time, and everyone is anxious to do his job in his particular sphere, for achieving promotion," he said, "to the followers of Athletic, I say thank-you for the support you accorded us last season. Do the same for us this time, and I feel sure you will be rewarded by a greatly improved playing performance." Among Mr. Wootton's new signings, were John Wilson, an inside-forward from Chesterfield, Brendon McManus, a goalkeeper from Huddersfield Town, and a week before the season started, Scottish International forward, John Divers, from Greenock Morton. Divers was appointed team captain and great things were expected, but he injured his knee on his debut against Mansfield Town, and never played for Athletic again, returning to Scotland only a few weeks after signing.

Athletic's difficult start to the programme, resulted in failure to win one of their first eight fixtures, losing six and drawing two, before winning 6-0 away to Darlington at the end of September, Ray Haddington announcing his arrival from Bradford City with a hat-trick. This sparked a slight recovery in fortunes, Athletic winning five of the next ten matches, including an F.A. Cup tie with non-Leaguers Lancaster City at Boundary Park 6-0. The next round saw 21,067 people packed into Boundary Park to witness another disappointing Cup performance, Athletic losing 1-0 to Mansfield Town.

In March '48, Latics signed Lewis Brook from Huddersfield Town and he scored seven times in eleven appearances as Athletic concluded the season with a flourish, winning five of the last seven matches to finish eleventh in the table with 41 points from 42 games. Only two clubs in the Division scored fewer home goals than Atheletic's 25, yet the side's away total of 38 was exceeded only by the fine Rotherham team who scored 39. The League goals were divided among twelve players and one opponent, and only Bill Blackshaw and Ray Haddington reached double figures, with Blackshaw top scoring on 17. Bill Hayes was the most consistent member of the team, turning out 40 times in League and Cup.

ROBERTS, THE ROCHDALE GOALKEEPER IS BEATEN BY THIS SHOT FROM JACK BOWDEN
AS ATHLETIC DREW THIS 1947 DERBY CLASH 1-1

THE MEN FROM BOUNDARY PARK · 1948

STANDING L-R: W. THOMAS (Ass. Trainer) · BROCKLEHURST · LUDLAM (2nd Team Trainer) · CORDWELL · TOMLINSON McMANUS · WATSON · STOKE · N. JONES · OGDEN · BIRKETT (Junior Schoolboy International) · SPURDLE · BIRKETT N. SMITH · BUNTING · JENYANS · BELL · IVILL · ASTON · FRANK HARGREAVES (Trainer)

SECOND ROW: NAYLOR · HADDINGTON · BLACKSHAW · BROOK · IVILL · ASTON · FRANK HARGREAVES (Trainer) · BOWDEN · WILSON · HAYES\AND HURST.
SITTING L-R: PICKERING AND WOOLLEY.

1948-49

The amazing success of the Olympic Games at Wembley Stadium, and attendance records smashed at most sporting events, had given Athletic's officials cause to believe that Boundary Park crowds would rocket this season, especially if the team gave a good showing. The club had 22 professionals on their books, seventeen of them on a full-time basis, a high percentage for a Third Division North club. Among the new players were goalkeeper John Thomas Jones from Northampton, and Ron Birkett, a winger signed from New Brighton.

The team had on paper, the stiffest opening period in recent memory, and that's just how it turned out, losing seven of their first eight matches, scoring only four goals in the process. No club in the Football League had made as bad a start as this, but probably no club suffered such a plague of injuries as there was at Boundary Park during the first two months. The most striking feature of Athletic's revival was the fact that it came about without any excursion into the transfer market. The introduction of centre-forward, Eric Gemmell, in early October coincided with a change in the team's fortunes, his 23 goals in League and Cup helping Athletic to a goalscoring total in excess of the Division's average. Gemmell's partnership with Ray Haddington totalled 45 goals and turned Athletic's season around.

From the turn of the year, Athletic won half of the 22 League matches played, and lost only four times, scoring 52 goals, and finished the season in 6th place in the Third Division North on 45 points, just ten behind champions, Hull City. The F.A. Cup brought wins over Wrexham and non-League Walthamstowe Avenue, before bowing out 3-2 to Cardiff City in round three, before an amazing 28,991 fans. Few Third Division North clubs could boast better support than Athletic. An average of 14,500 had watched the League side this season, the biggest gate being 35,267 for the 1-1 draw with Hull City. Twenty-four players had been called upon for first team duties, and only Bill Pickering, the left-back, had appeared in all 46 League and Cup games.

So pleased were the club's directors, at the change around in fortunes after such a bad start, that they offered manager Wootten a two year contract, which he gladly signed.

HENDERSON, THE SOUTHPORT KEEPER WAS EQUAL TO THIS EFFORT FROM ATHLETIC'S ERIC GEMMELL IN A 1-1 DRAW. OCTOBER '47

PRE-SEASON TRAINING — JULY 1949

ENGLAND SCHOOLBOYS · BOUNDARY PARK · MAY 1950
WITH DUNCAN EDWARDS (Second from the right, front row)

1949-50

There was a steady demand for season tickets at Boundary Park, and last year's sales had been exceeded. All the players who helped raise the club from bottom of the League were still available, and there were few Third Division clubs who had not parted with at least one of their better players to balance their budgets. Athletic turned down bids for three players after substantial fees were offered, deciding instead to stick to their assets. The opinion that there was no outstanding promotion contenders this year fuelled optimism about Athletic's chances. "Our playing strength leaves room for additions, and the management have this in mind, and will not shirk their responsibility should the occasion arise," said manager Wootten, "the dressing room spirit and friendship between the management and players cannot be bettered, and all are eager to be fighting fit." Ernie Woodcock returned to Athletic early season, boosting the clubs playing staff to 24 professionals.

A moderate run of results to Christmas, brought only seven League victories from 22 games, and with only slight improvement afterwards, Athletic finished a disappointing 11th position in the table. They enjoyed a little success in the F.A. Cup, beating non-League Stockton 4-0 in the first round, before emarking on a marathon tie with Crewe, drawing the first two games 1-1 and 0-0 before finally disposing of the 'Railwaymen' 3-0 at Maine Road, Manchester. This gave Athletic a plumb 3rd round tie with a Jackie Milburn inspired Newcastle United. 31,706 people packed Boundary Park to see seven goals enter Oldham's net, with only 2 in reply. Athletic's dreams of Wembley glory ended yet again.

Not one of Athletic's team was able to complete an unbroken run of appearances this season. Ray Haddington and Bill Jessop went close, making 41 League appearances out of a possible 42. Ray Haddington, playing at inside-left and centre-forward, scored 25 goals, 19 in the League, five in F.A. Cup ties and one in the Lancashire Cup, Eric Gemmell notched 12 in League and Cup. Twenty-eight players represented the first team, including all Cup ties, and nine players had joined the professional staff since last year's retained list, notably Les Smith from Huddersfield; Frank McCormack, Clyde; Bill Ormond, Blackpool; Jimmy Munro, Manchester City; Ted Clamp, Derby County; Albert Wadsworth, Stalybridge Celtic; Charlie Campbell, Rutherglen F.C.; Bobby McIlvenny, Merthyr Tydfil; and amateur player Kevin Walsh. Only one player was transferred to another club, Billy Spurdle to Manchester City for £10,000.

Athletic won a cup for only the third time in their history, beating a strong Manchester City side 2-1 in the Manchester Senior Cup final at Boundary Park before 8,321 spectators. Attendances averaged 13,000 for League matches, and the Cup ties against Stockton, Crewe (first replay) and Newcastle attracted 63,266 people to Boundary Park for a Cup average of over 21,000 per match.

The end of season witnessed a Shareholders Association 'ginger group' rapidly obtain control of sufficient shares to help them force a voting decision at the A.G.M. Their objective being the Oldham Athletic board's removal. They had provisionally formed a 'shadow' board to take over in the event of the present board being forced out. At a rowdy meeting of 600 shareholders on the night of the A.G.M., the retiring directors were all re-elected, and despite all the off-field disagreements, things seemed to be taking a turn for the better.

CREWE 0 v ATHLETIC 3, F.A. CUP 2ND ROUND, SECOND REPLAY AT MAINE ROAD

RAY HADDINGTON SLAMS HOME A PENALTY FOR ATHLETIC

A SPURDLE PASS PUTS HADDINGTON THROUGH TO SCORE ATHLETIC'S THIRD GOAL

ROBLEDO BEATS McCORMACK TO THE BALL. WHILE HAYES DUCKS OUT OF THE WAY

THE CUP TIE

"DADDY, BUY ME A ROSETTE
IN SHIMMERING WHITE AND BLUE,
THE BIGGEST RATTLE YOU CAN GET,
A BELL AND BANNER TOO".

"OH LADDIE, FOR WHAT REASON
THIS STRANGE WISH SHOULD I GRANT?
WERE IT THE SILLY SEASON,
I'D UNDERSTAND YOUR WANT".

"DAD, BE SYMPATHETIC,
MY REASONS' VERY SOUND,
NEWCASTLE PLAY ATHLETIC
IN THE F.A. CUP THIRD ROUND".

"I MUST ENCOURAGE GEMMELL,
HADDINGTON AND SPURDLE TOO,
FOR THEY'LL NEED EVERY LUSTY YELL,
IF THEY ARE TO WIN THROUGH".

"IF THEY COULD BEAT THE GEORDIES
IMAGINE OLDHAM'S JOY,
TO SAY NOTHING, DEAREST DADDY,
OF THE SHOCK 'TWOULD GIVE YOUR BOY".

J.M.

THE INCIDENT LEADING TO BILLY SPURDLE'S OPPORTUNIST GOAL FOR OLDHAM

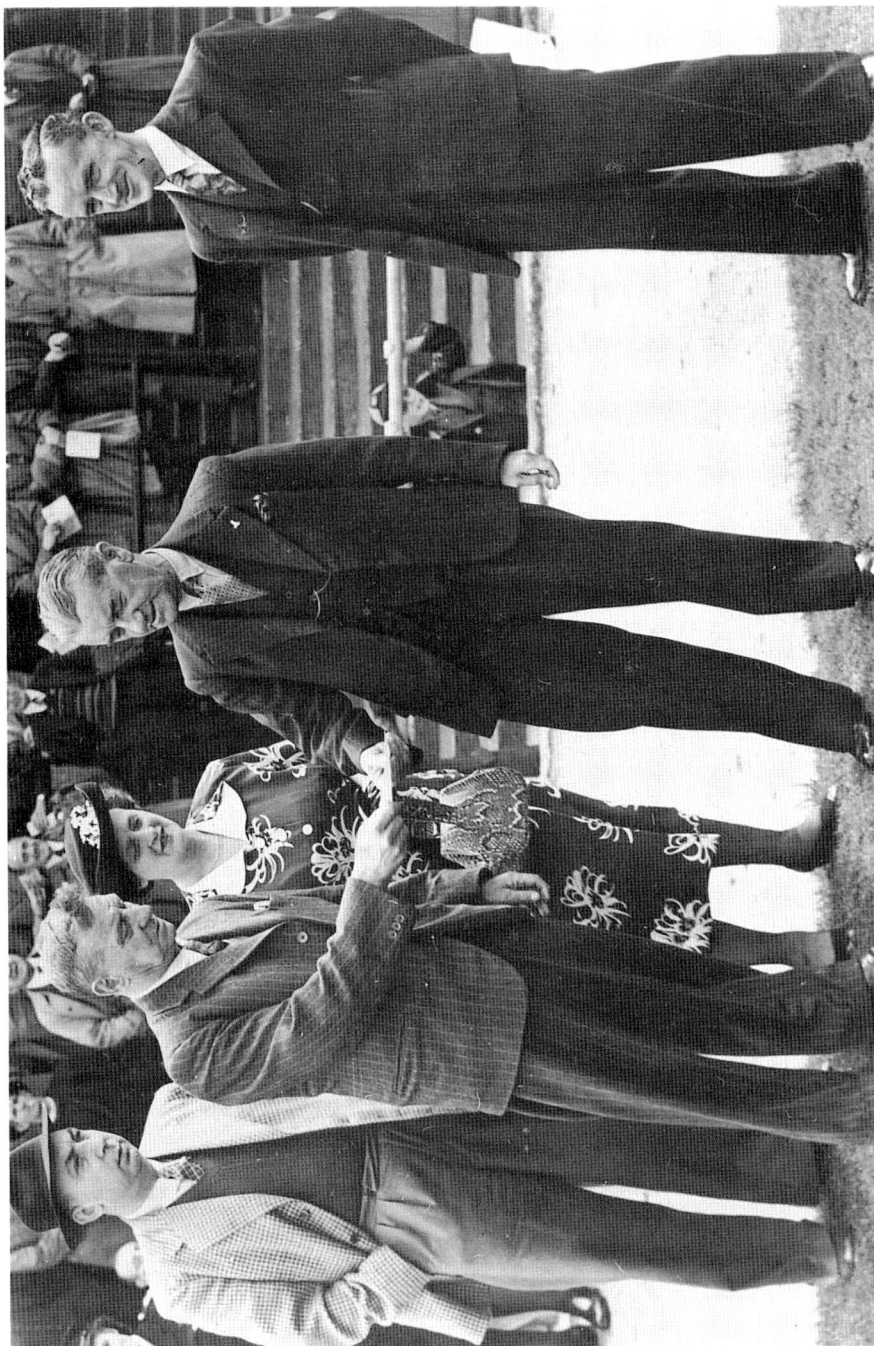

MR. FRED BREEZE (Second from left), CHAIRMAN OF ATHLETIC SUPPORTERS' CLUB HANDING A CHEQUE FOR £500 TO MR. PERCY SKIPWORTH, CHAIRMAN OF ATHLETIC BEFORE THE 5-4 HOME DEFEAT BY ROTHERHAM AT BOUNDARY PARK, AUGUST '50.

The thousands of supporters who tramped the weary 200 yards from the bus to Boundary Park down the rough stretch of Sheepfoot Lane, found it had been transformed into a presentable paved road. From this season, visiting teams and supporters would not have to suffer the bumps and jolts of the dirt track when they came to Boundary Park. Athletic's chances of success appeared brighter than at any time since the war. There was a solid core of support these days, yearning for something better than Third Division football, and given a successful team, crowd potential was at its highest for many years.

The great interest in Athletic was emphasised before the opening League match, when Mr. Fred Breeze, chairman of the Supporters Club, handed over to the club Chairman a cheque for £500, the proceeds of various events organised during the close season. The money was to pay for the cost of new concrete terracing at the Sheepfoot Lane end of the ground, completed during the summer. Despite the well organised, but failed effort by the Shareholders' Association to defeat the three retiring directors, everyone concerned was urged to bury the hatchet, and concentrate on giving the management and players every support at the opening of this season.

Manager Wootton signed several new players, including Ernest Swallow and Archie Whyte from Barnsley, Alan Ball from Southport, Alf Lee from Bolton Wanderers and Ronnie Fawley from Ashton Utd. The air of despondency which hung around Boundary Park towards the end of the last season was disappearing, and a

GEORGE HARDWICK

new belief in the team's ability to gain promotion was evident. Several players had stated last season, that 'lady luck' was against them. A certain player was quoted, "every time I went on the field last season, something seemed to hold me back." He was now convinced that confidence had returned, and it was Athletic's turn to have the ball running for them, but only one win and six defeats in the opening eight matched set the alarm bells ringing again down Sheepfoot Lane. During those eight games, Athletic called upon twenty players, and only once had a change been forced through injury. There had been many positional changes, all to no avail, and many supporters considered the players were unfit, as poor starts had been a feature of the seasons since the war.

Manager Billy Wootton did not survive yet another awful start, resigning on September 28th 1960. His resignation coincided with a change of club chairman, Mr. Herbert Gartside J.P. replacing Mr. Percy Skipworth on the same day. Mr. Gartside made the announcement to the press followed by, "I have nothing to add," nor had Mr. Wootton, beyond, "not a word."

In November Athletic caught the headlines in no uncertain manner by transferring the crowd's favourite, Ray Haddington, to Manchester City for £8,000, then appointing the dapper ex-England captain, George Hardwick, as player/manager, paying Middlesbrough £15,000 for his services. The directors' bold decision to sign Hardwick was vindicated as the team made a fine recovery under his leadership.

In the League, Athletic scored 73 goals, and conceeded the same number, winning only 40 points out of a possible 92, which saw them finish in the obscurity of 15th position in the Third Division North table. In the F.A. Cup, Athletic gained victories over Bradford City and Hartlepools United, before going down fighting 4-1 to Manchester United at Old Trafford in the 3rd round. Tommy Bell was the only player with a 100 per cent appearance record, he played 50 League and Cup matches, but was run close by goalkeeper, Fred Ogden, who made 49 in League and Cup. Leading goalscorer was Eric Gemmell with 22 in League and Cup, including a spendid hat-trick at Stockport County in March.

ATHLETIC'S ARCHIE WHYTE, TRYING TO CLEAR, DEFLECTS THE BALL INTO HIS OWN GOAL DURING THE 1951 F.A. CUP 3RD ROUND AT MANCHESTER UNITED.

UNITED'S ASTON EVADES ATHLETIC'S CENTRE-HALF WHYTE IN THE OLD TRAFFORD
CUP-TIE WHICH ATHLETIC LOST 4-1.

STAN PEARSON SCORES FOR UNITED DURING THE SAME MATCH

ELEVEN ATHLETIC PLAYERS, INCLUDING PLAYER-MANAGER GEORGE HARDWICK (th
BEFORE THEY BOARDED THE MOTOR COACH THAT '

...nt), MR. ARTHUR BARLOW (Director), AND TRAINER BILLY THOMAS (on the left), JUST
...TO HARROGATE FOR A FOUR DAY BREAK, JAN. 1953

ERIC GEMMELL

1951-52

Player/manager, George Hardwick, opened this season with a large bank overdraft at the club, but a fund of enthusiasm and optimism for his job. He had signed several young amateurs and four experienced players, Pat Broadley from Sligo; Jack Warner, Manchester United; Peter McKennan, Middlesborough; and Dennis Grainger from Wrexham in exchange for Bill Jessop. Athletic were now running five teams in the Third Division North, Lancashire Combination, the revived Lancashire League, Mid-Week League, and the Colts in the Levenshulme League. All the home fixtures in the Lancashire League were played on Mossley F.C.'s ground.

Pre-season training and coaching by Manager Hardwick, Jack Warner and Billy Thomas had been very strenuous, to answer any criticism levelled during previous seasons, and they were rewarded with six victories and three draws from the first nine fixtures, giving Athletic the flying start they were praying for. When difficulties arrived in the shape of injuries to key players Burnett, Gemmell, McKennan, Warner, Goodfellow, Smith, McIlvenny, and even Hardwick himself, hopes of overtaking Lincoln City at the top of the Division faded. The team had hovered near the top of the League all season, but finished 12 points behind top spot in fourth place on 57 points. During this season, 27 players had been called on for first team duties, though in the first, highly successful part of the season, only twelve were required.

Athletic visited Nelson in the first round of the F.A. Cup, where a splendid hat-trick by Peter McKennan gave Athletic a resounding 4-0 victory, round two saw Athletic on the receiving end of a 5-0 thrashing at Southend United. The highlight of a good season came in mid-January on a snow-bound Boundary Park, when Eric Gemmell set an Oldham goalscoring record for an individual player, scoring seven times as Athletic beat Chester 11-2 in the Third Division North. Gemmell's feat was even more remarkable as his first six goals came in succession.

In the League and F.A. Cup, Athletic scored an impressive 94 goals, leading scorers being Eric Gemmell on 29, and Peter McKennan on 18. Full-back Tommy Bell made most appearances with 44 in League and Cup. The average home attendance of 16,033 had only been bettered twice before, in the 1920-21 and 1921-22 seasons. Athletic topped the averages for the Third Division North both home and away.

OLDHAM ATHLETIC · 1951/52

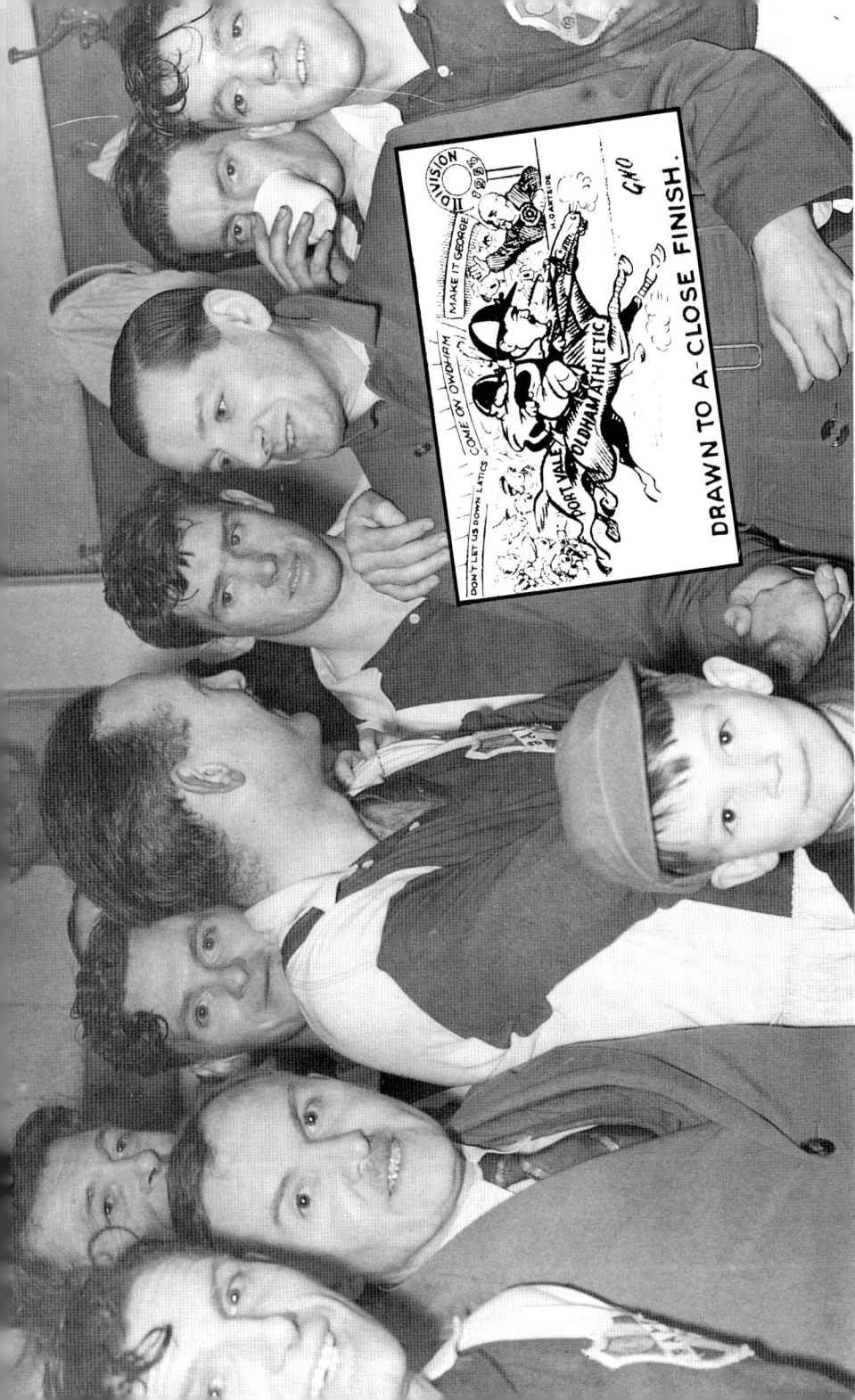

IN THE DRESSING ROOM AT BRADFORD CITY. GEORGE HARDWICK IS CONGRATULATED BY MR. H. THOMPSON (Director). ALSO IN THE PICTURE ARE SMITH, WHYTE, Dr. MacNAMARA, BRIERLY, HARRIS, CLARKE AND LOWRIE.

1952-53

A thletic had built up quite a large following for their cricket team which played friendly games on summer Sundays. The team was usually selected from, Tommy Bell, Eric Gemmell, George Hardwick, Harry Jackson, Eddie Hopkinson, Frank Tomlinson, John Crawford, Bobby McIlvenny, Jimmy Munro, Bill Naylor, Fred Ogden, Archie Whyte and Billy Thomas. The approach to this Coronation season had been remarkably quiet, and it seemed evident that the first class game was returning to normality after the post-war boom.

Player/manager Hardwick was confident this would be Athletic's season, but with so many other fancied clubs knocking on the Second Division door, good luck, particularly on the injury front was needed. The last minute signing of Tommy Lowrie from Aberdeen was quite a capture. A small but dour tackler with clever anticipation and good ball distribution, his signing was seen as the final piece in the manager's promotion jigsaw.

Athletic started this campaign in determined mood, losing only one of the first 18 matches and winning eleven, scoring a healthy 35 times in the process. After a slight hiccup in November, they won six games on the trot, and by mid-January were well entrenched as the Division leaders. Then the cracks began to show, as loss of form and the usual injuries saw only one win from the next eleven games, losing six times and giving the closing pack a glimmer of hope. Athletic never recovered their early-season form, but did enough in the remaining nine matches to clinch their place as Champions.

ATHLETIC'S PROMOTION WINNERS
Back: CRAWFORD · JACKSON (R) · McGLEN · BROOK · MUNRO
Centre: THOMAS (Trainer) · McKENNAN · BURNETT · NAYLOR · GEMMELL · OGDEN · WHYTE
Centre (Sitting): CLARKE · LOWRIE · HARDWICK · ORMOND · SMITH
Front: HARRIS · HOULAHAN · McLIVENNY · BRIERLEY

After 46 years of League football, Athletic had won their first Championship, becoming the first ever Lancashire club to gain promotion from the Third Division North to Division Two. The news that Athletic had achieved promotion was greeted with cheers at the Gaumont cinema in Oldham, where the result from Bradford was flashed on the screen. The cinema manager said that after the half-time score had been shown, the audience were reluctant to leave until they had seen the final score. At the Repertory Theatre, the news was given in a final curtain speech.

As befitting a club which had won promotion, Athletic were given a Civic Reception by the mayor, Councillor H.B. Whittaker, in the mayor's parlour on April 30th 1953. He told the team and officials that they had done a good job of work for Oldham, and once again put the town on the map. Manager Hardwick replied, ''We as players, feel our efforts are appreciated not only by the 'bob-enders', but by all the town. I am grateful to the lads of both first and second teams, and I am also grateful to the directors for tolerating me in the boardroom. We do not always see eye to eye, but I usually get my own way.'' The Championship Shield and medals were presented to Athletic's representatives at the Football League A.G.M. in London on June 13th 1953.

The F.A. Cup saw Athletic win at Boston United in the first round, then travel to close League rivals Port Vale in round two and turn in a memorable team performance in winning 3-0 before a 25,398 crowd. A plumb 3rd round tie at Boundary Park with Birmingham City saw Athletic lose a fog-bound encounter 3-1. 26,580 people struggled to see what little action Athletic could offer.

Attendances this year for League matches totalled 411,103, with an average attendance of 17,835. Athletic won 22 games, drew 15, and lost nine, finishing top on 59 points. Leading scorers in League and Cup games were Eric Gemmell with 25, followed by Bill Ormond and Peter McKennan on 12 each. Finally, the Athletic promotion party, with manager Hardwick in charge, visited Wembley for the 1953 Bolton v Blackpool 'Matthews' Cup Final, as reward for their great efforts.

BILL ORMOND SCORES ATHLETIC'S GOAL IN A 1-1 DRAW WITH STOCKPORT COUNTY AT BOUNDARY PARK BEFORE 27,681 SPECTATORS — APRIL 1953

THE MAYOR OF OLDHAM, COUNCILLOR H.B. WHITTAKER AND ATHLETIC'S CHAMPIONSHIP WINNERS AND OFFICIALS ON THE TOWN HALL STEPS — APRIL 1953.

ORMOND'S SHOT HITS THE POST IN ATHLETIC'S 4-1 VICTORY OVER WORKINGTON AT BOUNDARY PARK — JANUARY 1953

1953-54

"I am making no attempt to go for promotion this season," were the surprising words spoken by George Hardwick, adding, "we shall finish this season nicely in the top half of the Second Divison table. I came to Oldham to manage a First Division club, not a Third, and at the moment we must consolidate our strength and position before making further advancement." Athletic set out this season with the same team which had won them promotion, thinking it only fair the players should get their chance.

For the first time in the history of the Football League, the season opened with practically a full list of League matches on a Wednesday evening in August. Athletic kicked-off with an amazing 4-4 draw at Luton Town, but little else went right as the team struggled to come to terms with their new status, a home win over Lincoln City being the first victory after nine matches. They were lodged firmly at the bottom of the Second Divison from late November and never recovered, winning only eight matches all season, losing 25 times and finishing with a meagre 25 points.

Patients in Oldham and Liverpool hospitals heard one of the first match commentaries relayed to the wards for the last game at Boundary Park against Everton which Athletic lost 4-0. 30,072 people, many from Merseyside, saw Everton promoted to Division One; Athletic had already gone in the opposite direction.

A story which drew attention to the international flavour of the Oldham team, which included five Englishmen, three Scots, two Irishmen and a Welshman, was revealed by manager Hardwick. The Athletic team were staying in a Bristol hotel the night before playing the Rovers at Eastville. Going up to their rooms in the lift were Tommy Walker and Billy McGlen, both Geordies, Joe Harris from Belfast, and Harry McShane, a Scot. They were chatting among themselves when the West Country lift attendant turned to them and said, "I can tell you lads are from Oldham alright." One of the Latics players said afterwards, "He was the only one of us with an Oldham accent."

Fred Ogden, Louis Brook and Les Smith chose the wrong time to hold their joint benefit game. Only 3,500 people paying receipts of £180 turned up, indicating the great disappointment felt by the majority of Athletic supporters. Following a thrilling 3-3 draw at Ipswich Town in the F.A. Cup 3rd round, Athletic lost the replay 1-0 before a good Boundary Park crowd of over 16,000. Wing-half Les Smith made most appearances this season, with 41 in League and Cup. Following Eric Gemmell's unpopular transfer to Crewe in February '54, the team's goals supply dried up, Bobby McIlvenny top scoring with a disappointing 8.

Athletic Player:— "I ought to be a lift-man. I have so many ups and downs in life."
Lift man:— "It's better than being a cellar-man, anyway."

Mr. Stanley Cheetham, Chairman of Athletic, invited the players to a 'reunion' lunch at a local restaurant to deliver a pep-talk on the first day of training. "The football season has started now as far as we are concerned, and the team must get into the pink of condition right away," he told the players, "I want to see Oldham Athletic back in the First Division, where it belongs, and the sooner the better... I would like to think that everyone—especially the team—will, right from the start, forget about last season. It must have been the worst season any club could have had. Everything went wrong for us, and now I would like to think that we are starting this season with a clean sheet... forget what people have said and what they might say again, and get on with the job." He described the club's financial position as far from strong and stressed the continual drain in entertainment tax which last season was £9,834.18s.2d!

Pre-season, Athletic transferred Bobby McIlvenny to Bury for £2,000 after he was refused a guaranteed maximum benefit (£750). Manager Hardwick signed several local boys pre-season, saying the signings were another step forward in his plan to build up a young team at Boundary Park. Joe Brunskill, a close season signing from Sunderland took over at centre-forward for the first two months of the season, before Don Travis returned to his old club, after spending three years at Chester.

An average attendance that showed a decrease of 10,000 a match, a club goal-scoring record that was almost broken by Don Travis, and unpredictable see-saw form that had supporters despairing one week and hopeful the next—were the features of Athletic's first season back in the Northern section. It has been a season of three distinct phases, first came a bad patch in which Athletic failed to score a single goal in no less than seven out of fifteen matches, sinking to 18th in the table. There followed an excellent run of success in the winter months and Athletic moved to seventh—the highest they ever reached. Finally came a period of somersaulting fortunes in which they alternatively lost and won successive games, often by big margins, finally finishing the season in 10th position with 48 points.

During the whole season, not one penny was spent, or was available to spend, in the transfer market. The introduction and development of young players took place with a minimum of outlay. 'Durham wonderkid' Kenny Chaytor, at 16 years and 11 months, one of the younger players to represent Athletic, made his debut in a 2-2 draw at Gateshead late October '54. The same weekend Oldham had a Royal visit, the new Queen Elizabeth and Duke of Edinburgh passing close to Boundary Park on a visit to Shaw, during one of the worst downpours the local weather could muster.

Despite the falling attendances, Athletic's performances at home during the whole season had been good. They lost only four times at Boundary Park in 25 League and Cup matches, all by the odd goal, but only five games were won on opponents' grounds. No player had a 100 per cent appearance record this time, Tommy Walker coming closest with 44 League and Cup, and Don Travis on his return to the club, netted 32 League goals out of a total of 74 scored. He failed by one goal to equal the club's individual record for League goals set by Irishman Tommy Davis in 1936-37. Davies in fact, scored 35 goals that season, but 2 were in the F.A. Cup.

GEORGE HARDWICK'S LAST GAME FOR ATHLETIC, A 1-1 DRAW WITH WREXHAM AT BOUNDARY PARK — APRIL 1956

Down at Boundary Park these days, no one even whispered the word 'promotion'. There was hardly a supporter who believed that such success was even remotely possible, the attitude was a stoical one of hope for the best, but be prepared for the worst. Chairman Mr. Stanley Cheetham's battle cry this year sounded, "Supporters will hear no more from Oldham Athletic about financial distress, bad luck and unfair criticism. The new attitude at Boundary Park is that sleeves must be rolled up and the old moans about lack of financial support forgotton. The club will turn its back on the events of the past year, and start the season optimistically, standing or falling by its record during the year. By that attitude Athletic will stand a better chance of regaining the goodwill of the sporting public." One step in the right direction was taken when the directors decided to cut the price of admission for boys at the Chaddy End from one shilling to 9d. The boys could now stand behind either goal for the same price.

Manager Hardwick said that the team was now training in the continential style, and he hoped they would play like it, but only one win in the first eleven games shattered any illusions about that. Between then and mid-December Athletic won only five more times and the team became rooted in the lower reaches of the table. Between Christmas Eve and March 3rd, Athletic played twelve successive League matches without a win, until things suddenly clicked into place as they slammed Barrow 6-1 at Boundary Park and finished the season with a slight flourish, winning three and drawing five of their final ten games.

They recorded the highest number of draws in the Football League, eighteen, and a similar number of matches ended in defeat. Only one double was achieved, over Tranmere Rovers, hardly surprising as they won only 3 times away from home all season. Athletic's final League position of 20th in the Third Division North was the last straw as far as Manager Hardwick was concerned, and he resigned in April 1956, playing his last game in Athletic colours in late April, against Wrexham at Boundary Park. Mr. Hardwick commented that he felt a move might do both the club and himself a lot of good, "There is no ill-feeling, I have enjoyed my spell with Athletic, and have made a lot of good friends in Oldham."

Once again, Don Travis finished top scorer on 15 goals, and only one player, Tommy Walker, had a 100 per cent record of 47 appearances in League and Cup, with Peter Neale running close on 46. Athletic's average home gate was 6,469, away from Boundary Park, 7,666. The away figure included the 3-1 F.A. Cup defeat at Valley Parade, Bradford in round one. The numbers showed a decrease of a little under 1,500 spectators a match compared with the previous season. George Hardwick's leaving coincided with a change of Chairman. New Chairman, Mr. Frank Swift, made a public appeal for all concerned with Oldham Athletic to sink their differences so that everyone could pull the same way in an effort to put the club back where it belonged.

PRICE

3d.

OFFICIAL PROGRAMME

OLDHAM ATHLETIC FOOTBALL CLUB

PRICE

3d.

ATHLETIC
v. WORKINGTON

Saturday,
October 6th, 1956

1956-57

George Hardwick was replaced in May '56 by Mr. Ted Goodier, former manager of Rochdale and Wigan Athletic, who had played six seasons at Boundary Park during their Second Division days in the 1920's and early 30's. Mr. Goodier came with the reputation of a man who liked a fight, and he felt the work needed to put Athletic back on the rails offered him just that challenge. Mr. Goodier disclosed during a shareholders' meeting, that pre-season he had spent only £1,125 on new players since taking over at Boundary Park. ''That was all there was available'' he said. But the feeling had steadily grown, amid rising enthusiasm, that Athletic were poised to win back much of the support that a persistent succession of failures and disappointments had gradually whittled away. With each subsequent signing by Athletic, the number of season ticket sales rose. Considering that Athletic had been limited to the field of free transfer players, or those with reasonably small fees on their heads, they seemed to have collected a band of useful new men, among them George Torrance from Leicester City and Dave Teece, Hull City, both goalkeepers, Norman Jackson former Bristol City full-back, centre-half Eddie Murphy from Clyde, Laurie Cassidy, a part-timer from Manchester United, Jackie Campbell, former Blackburn wing-half, Eddie Hartley, outside-right from Rossendale United, Dave Pearson former Darwen and Ipswich Town centre-forward, and finally Trevor Hitchen from Southport.

Oldham Transport restored the 'Football Special' buses for a trial

DON TRAVIS — 1956

period only, anticipating the possibility of increased attendances at Boundary Park. This exercise lasted only three months, as Athletic made a poor start to the season, with only one win in the first six matches. The situation improved as thirteen points out of fourteen were picked up during the months of September and early October, and although Athletic had often been lucky, they were getting results. In October came stories about players being placed on the transfer list. High on that list was wing-half, Jimmy Thompson, and Scottish sources reported that Glasgow Rangers were interested. Eddie Hartley, the young right-winger, who played only once, returned to the Lancashire Combination, then came the first serious rift when Jack Campbell announced he was on offer, followed by the crowd's favourite, Don Travis. It became clear that team spirit was not as it should be. At the time Athletic had reached their highest League position, 7th. In November, Trevor Lawless became the third to ask to leave, then Tommy Walker lost his place in the side and became the fourth on the list at his own request.

Athletic's problems showed on the field, and they started to slide down the table. Gates shrunk with the side's fortunes as the crowd's hopes of seeing something better at Boundary Park where shattered again. Athletic slipped into a vicious circle of team changes that caused continuous criticism. In January, Jimmy O'Donnell whom Athletic had given away to Stalybridge Celtic, was signed by Leeds United for £1,400, then goalkeeper Alan Rose had his contract cancelled at his own request. Tommy Walker was transferred to Chesterfield, and the slide

Standing 1-r: HOBSON · MURPHY · THOMF

ND OLD FACES AT BOUNDARY PARK · 1956
.IAMS · BROOK · NAYLOR Front row: TRAVIS · BETTS · CAMPBELL · CROOK · PEARSON

continued. Manager Goodier started travelling on the lookout for new players, but his team was already in serious trouble. He managed to sign former Scottish International, Tommy Wright, from East Fife, to try and stem the tide, but his Boundary Park career lasted only two months before he packed his bags and returned to Scotland. When goalscorer Dave Pearson went to Rochdale, and carried on netting goals, the slide became a slump which saw anxiety and an inferiority complex take hold.

Athletic did not win one of their final twelve matches, and only two of the last 20 ended in victory. Probably the most astonishing record was that between mid-November and mid-March, a run of 18 matches, no one scored from the centre-forward

position. Athletic faced two away ties in the F.A. Cup, winning the first at Halifax 3-2, before losing the second at Accrington 2-1.The total points gained from the 46 League games was 39, and they finished in 19th position. For the third year running, Don Travis finished top scorer, although he played in only 33 of the 48 matches, with 14 goals. No player had a 100 per cent record of appearances. Wilf Hobson had until April, then he missed two games, leaving a total of 46.

The Football Pool run by the Athletic Supporters Club had helped Boundary Park to the tune of £5,000 this season. The pool started in August '56 under the new Small Lotteries and Gaming Act, and was the supporters club's best effort so far.

VOLUNTEERS SMARTEN-UP BOUNDARY PARK

1957-58

A s this season got under way, the promise of promotion was countered by the threat of descending into the depth's of Fourth Division football, which would become a reality the following year. At Boundary Park they were facing the future with the usual determination. In the words of manager, Ted Goodier, ''It will be a do or die battle'', and it was with that thought in mind that he set about building his team during the close season break. Old favourite, Bill Spurdle, returned to Boundary Park after spells at Manchester City and Port Vale, Len Gaynor, ex-captain of Aldershot came in exchange for Arthur Lawless, defender Ted West arrived from Gillingham, and Eddie Shimwell, the distinguished full-back, came from Blackpool. For the first match of the season, Athletic fielded virtually a new team to the one that completed last season's fixtures. Add to that the fact that the team turned out in a new-style continental light-weight strip, and the average supporter might have wondered if he was in the right ground.

Valuable points dropped early in the season would be remembered as the stepping-stones to relegation. After defeating Carlisle Utd. in the first game, Athletic lost the next five, and won only 7 more games to Christmas. January and February were disastrous months for the club; of the seven games played, one four draws were achieved. Although things improved slightly during late March and April, the die had been cast, and Athletic finished in 15th position in the Division Three North, one point and two positions from safety. The bottom twelve clubs of Division Three (N) and Division Three (S) formed the new Division Four as founder members. At Darlington, in the last game, Athletic had the chance to redeem their earlier failings and avoid the trapdoor to Division Four, but they let it slip by losing 3-1. For the handful of faithful supporters, it was a shameful evening, made worse by the team's inability to put up a fight.

Athletic finished the season on a winning note when they won the Manchester Senior Cup for the sixth time, defeating Manchester City 1-0 in the final at Boundary Park. ''If only they had played like that at Darlington,'' was the supporters lament.Athletic crashed ingloriously out of the F.A.Cup competition, losing 5-1 in the second round to a moderate Workington team. Athletic's average attendance for the season's 23 home games was 7,464, with a total of 171,671 spectators paying £17,477. David Teece and Ted West led the appearances with 43 League and Cup outings. Joint top scorers were Gerald Duffy and Peter Neale on 16 League and Cup goals.

Oldham Athletic Association Football Club
Limited

OFFICES: Boundary Park, Sheepfoot Lane, Oldham. Tel. No.: MAIn 4972
CLUB COLOURS: Blue and White Shirts; White Knickers

Directors:

F. Swift, Esq.	W. Bloor, Esq.	F. Mellor, Esq., J.P.
G. Howarth, Esq.	G. Clayton, Esq.	H. Shepherd, Esq., J.P.
S. Cheetham, Esq.	J. Clayton, Esq.	P. Skipworth, Esq.
G. Bloor, Esq.	H. Gartside, Esq., J.P.	H. B. S. Thompson, Esq.
		T. Whittaker, Esq., J.P.

Manager: E. Goodier   **Hon. Treasurer:** R. Mellor
Secretary: F. Buckley   **Trainer:** J. Kelly

JIMMY KELLY (Trainer), INTRODUCES JOHN BAZLEY AND GERRY DUFFY TO
MR. NORMAN DODGIN, ATHLETIC'S NEW MANAGER, WITH THE CLUB SECRETARY
FRANK BUCKLEY LOOKING ON.

JOHN BAZLEY LEAPS OVER THE DENABY KEEPER SMETHURST DURING THE 1ST ROUND
F.A. CUP TIE WHICH ATHLETIC WON 2-0 — NOVEMBER 1958

1958-59

Ted Goodier, Athletic's manager for the previous two years, handed his resignation to the club Chairman, Mr. George Howarth, in June 1958. Mr. Goodier stated he was leaving Boundary Park on the friendliest of terms, adding "I still have the club's welfare at heart. I think a lot about Oldham Athletic, and my decision has come after careful consideration." He continued, "there is the nucleus of a good young team at Boundary Park, which must stand a good chance of getting back into Divison Three." Mr. Goodier's resignation was the 39th managerial change in League football during the previous 18 months. On July 17th 1958, Athletic appointed Mr. Norman Dodgin as team manager, at 37 years of age, one of the youngest in football. A former manager of Exeter and Barrow, he said he would not make any rash promises about Athletic's future, adding, "Football is such an up and down game that one can only give it everything you've got, and I will certainly do that."

The Football League's experiment of a four-up four-down system gave Athletic hope of a quick return to Division Three. There seemed to be a good atmosphere in the dressing room, and a keen sense of competition, basic ingredients for a good season. Since arriving at the club, Mr. Dogin had been out at every training session, assessing the potential of the players and providing that important individual coaching. New players included defender Wally Taylor from Southport who was appointed captain; Ronnie Clark, a left-winger from Gillingham and Albert Bourne from Manchester City.

The first nine games produced only two victories, over Coventry City and Exeter City, both at Boundary Park, and seven defeats, mostly by the odd goal. Athletic continued to lose matches at an alarming rate, and during one period from mid-January to mid-March, lost nine times in ten outings. When the situation was too far gone to retrieve, the team asserted itself, and the final ten matches brought six wins and just two defeats. For the first time in their history, Athletic would have to apply for re-election to the Football League. Season 1958-59 went down as the worst in the history of the club, as they concluded the season in 21st place in Division Four with 36 points.

After being promised money to spend on new players, manager Dodgin was not given a single penny to spend, but in spite of that he had brought promising youngsters onto the staff, Robinson, Stringfellow, Mallon and Elder, to mention a quartet who looked likely to make the first team.

Two non-League outfits, Denaby United and South Shields were defeated in the preliminary rounds of the F.A. Cup, before Stoke City put paid to Cup hopes, winning 5-1 at the Victoria Ground before 22,144 people, the largest crowd Athletic played before all season. Wally Taylor made most appearances with 45 in League and Cup, followed by Peter Phoenix with 43 League and Cup; Phoenix also finished leading goalscorer on 14 in all competitions.

Athletic's officials breathed a sigh of relief when the club was re-elected to Division Four in May '59.

ATHLETIC'S KEEPER DAVE TEECE GOES DOWN IN THE SNOW, AS FORMER ENGLAND INTERNATIONAL, DENIS WILSHAW, WHO SCORED A HAT-TRICK FOR STOKE, RUSHES IN DURING THE 3RD ROUND F.A. CUP TIE AT THE VICTORIA GROUND — JANUARY '59

A thletic made several close-season signings, among them Jimmy McGill from Partick Thistle; Jimmy Ferguson, Falkirk; Peter Corbett, Workington; Charles Ferguson, Rochdale; Stuart Richardson, Q.P.R.; 'Percy' Player, Grimsby Town; and Brian Jarvis from Wrexham. Manager Dodgin was non-committal about the ability of his new signings. "Only time will tell", he said, but the fact that Reserve Team trainer, Archie Whyte, was wearing a broader and more optimistic smile these days, suggested he could see a more promising side under his control, and this, it was hoped, would mean a stronger senior side.

Boundary Park had been smartened up, and although to outward appearances, it was only a coat of paint, there was more to it than that. It was a sign that the club was determined to regain its status as a proud member of the Football League, a task which began immediately the new Board of Directors, under Chairman Mr. Gordon Bloor, took the reins. The directors were under no illusions about the enormity of the job that faced them. Mr. Bloor said, "If we fail, I fancy it will be the end for Oldham Athletic."

This season turned out to be highly controversial, on and off the field. It would be depressing to dwell too long on Athletic's performances, but after winning the first two games without conceding a goal, came a run of 16 games without a win, suffering twelve defeats in the process. Only six more victories from 28 League matches, plus an F.A. Cup 2nd round exit to local rivals Bury, sealed Athletic's fate as the second worst team in the entire Football League. They scored fewer goals than any other team in Division Four with 41, and conceded 83. Athletic had to apply for re-election for the second consecutive year after finishing a disastrous 23rd in Division Four on 28 points, narrowly avoiding the 'wooden spoon' which was taken by Hartlepool United on 27 points.

Amidst all the turmoil of this 1959-60 season, Jimmy McGill and Billy Spurdle managed to represent Athletic 40 times each in League and Cup. Top scorer was Peter Stringfellow with eleven, all in the League.

Headlines in the local press in early May 1960, spoke of allegations of attempted match fixing in games involving Athletic players. A statement was issued by Oldham Police concerning these stories: "Following police interviews with five members of the playing staff of Oldham Athletic F.C., respecting alleged conversations between them, and which have been reported to the management of the club by some of the players concerned, a file was prepared and sent to the Director of Public Prosecutions. Consequent upon correspondence which has passed between the Chief Constable and the Director of Public Prosecutions, the Chief Constable has decided there will be no further police action in relation to the alleged conversations."

Manager Norman Dodgin's contract was cancelled by mutal agreement, soon after the announcement and he departed amicably. It was continually depressing for the soccer-loving public of Oldham to read of trouble and yet more trouble. Club Chairman, Mr. Gordon Bloor said, "I am very glad that this matter has now been cleared up. While it has been hanging over the club my hands have been tied. I shall still make an investigation of my own of course, and out of courtesy, I shall be making a report to the Football League to put them in the picture." Mr. Bloor also insisted that financial help at Boundary Park was desperately needed for the summer months. "Being blunt, the days of life saving appeals by Athletic are finished. The general public cannot, and will not come to Athletic's aid with donations. I am not being pessimistic therefore, when I say that unless some responsible help can be found, then Athletic are on the brink of closing their doors." He went on to suggest that the Athletic Directors would resign 'en bloc' if suitable people could be found to take over and help the club better than them.

Some rare good news came Athletic's way on May 28th, when they were re-elected to the Fourth Division at the annual meeting of the Football League in London. Gateshead, who finished one place above Athletic, were voted out, and replaced by Peterborough. Athletic topped the voting with 36 clubs favouring their re-election.

ATHLETIC'S NEW MANAGER DANNY McLENNAN TAKES A LOOK AT BOUNDARY PARK, WITH JIMMY KELLY (Trainer), AND FRANK BUCKLEY (Secretary) — MAY 1960

PETER PHOENIX DRIVES OFF FROM THE 2ND TEE, WATCHED BY (left to right), TED WEST, KENNY CHAYTOR, MANAGER DODGIN, GEORGE WALTERS AND KEITH ROBINSON — SEPT '59

A KISS FROM MAN. CITY'S DENIS LAW FOR OLDHAM'S SOCCER QUEEN MISS DELIA BLOOR. ALSO IN THE PICTURE ARE LATICS' GOALKEEPER JIMMY ROLLO, T.V. ANNOUNCER GERRY LOFTUS, AND ACTOR ALAN ROTHWELL

JACK ROWLEY AND HIS PLAYERS DISCUSS TACTICS IN THE RAIN — JULY 1960

1960-61

Oldham's new mayor, Alderman G.F. Holden, pledged his support for 'one of the best-known features of the town's recreational life—Oldham Athletic,' saying, ''we must, as a town, find some way to keep Athletic in being. The town of Oldham is big enough to keep the club going, and as an ardent rugby fan, I can see many advantages in having a first class soccer team in the town.'' He continued, ''there is opportunity here for some public-spirited person to come along and help Athletic in its playing and financial difficulties.''

Just two days before the club sought re-election to Division Four, Athletic had appointed a new manager, Mr. Danny McLennan, former Berwick Rangers boss. Mr. McLennan, who had cleared a five-figure debt at the Scottish club, and lifted the team into the top six of the Scottish Second Division was making no prophecies for Athletic, ''I shall simply be concentrating on the first team to begin with.'' He said, ''there is obviously a great potential here, but everyone wants to see an improvement in the first team. The club cannot afford to build and wait for the future.'' Mr. McLennan added, without any direct reference to the club's recent troubles, ''it does seem clear that any improvements can only come with everyone pulling together, both inside and outside the club.'' He went on to say that he was very pleased Athletic had signed Jimmy Frizzell the previous week, ''I have seen him play often, and I think he will fit quite well in Fourth Division football. I know that other English clubs were keen on signing him.'' Athletic had paid out their biggest fee for some time for Frizzell's services, £1,500 securing him from Greenock Morton. Seven new Directors were voted onto Athletic's board amid some confusion, claiming the proxy poll was invalid. They were elected by 300 shareholders who packed the King Street Baptist School on July 19th 1960, for one of the stormiest meetings in the club's history.

One month after appointing Danny McLennan, Athletic were again without a manager when he accepted a better offer from Scottish club, Stirling Albion and packed his bags, leaving the club in the week which saw the deadline for players re-signing and a time when Athletic should have been jumping into the transfer market. Director Frank Buckley was forced into duties of acting manager. Athletic's fortunes were due an upturn, and on August 2nd, Mr. Jack Rowley was appointed manager. Under normal circumstances it was a position any football manager would approach with apprehension, but after the happenings at Boundary Park during the past year circumstances were anything but normal. ''It is too early for me to make any predictions for the future, but it will be my aim to put a team on the field which tries to play football. I have no time for kick and rush tactics,'' said Mr. Rowley. As a player with Manchester United, Jack Rowley had won six England Caps and F.A. Cup and Football League Championship medals, scoring over 200 League and Cup goals. He was therefore a manager who would command the total respect of his players.

New players were signed, but the manager would have to strengthen the staff even more if he was to achieve his aim of putting Athletic in the top half of the table. Along with Frizzell, the new players were Johnny McCue from Stoke City, Bob Rackley from Bristol Rovers and George Greenall from Southampton. The minimum admission charge this season was increased from two shillings to two shillings and six pence, and the faithful who paid out their extra 'tanner' were rewarded with one of the most adventurous seasons in Athletic's recent history. It began on an ambitious note, and ended in similar fashion.

Season 1960-61 could have witnessed the end of professional football in Oldham, instead it signalled the re-birth of the town's soccer hopes. The team finished the campaign in a mid-table position (12th), but behind that fact was one of the most thrilling chapters in the club's existence. After a disastrous start with only one win and nine defeats from the first twelve matches, manager Rowley signed Bert Lister and Ken Branagan from Manchester City for a combined fee of £10,000 and fortunes changed. Then came the master stroke as Bobby Johnstone, the former Scottish International inside-forward, was signed from Hibs in October '60. Suddenly Athletic were a soccer power again. The team blended together, and with a brilliant run of ten successive victories, lifted itself right from the bottom

of the table to within striking distance of the top. Oldham's 'soccer boom' was in full swing when along came plans for the floodlights on the ground. On the playing front the run couldn't last, but manager Rowley and his team had achieved their object, they were back in business.

This season saw the birth of the League Cup competition and a 6-2 defeat at Norwich City in round two. The first round brought a 2-1 win over Hartlepool United at Boundary Park. The F.A. Cup provided three matches. A first round away win at non-league Rhyl, followed by a 3-0 home replay defeat by Chesterfield, who had been held 4-4 on their own ground. Bert Lister finished with most League and Cup goals, scoring 21; Peter Phoenix making most appearances with 49 in all competitions.

TO CUT DOWN TRAVEL FATIGUE, ATHLETIC'S TEAM, SUPPORTERS AND CLUB OFFICIALS FLEW SOUTH FOR A FIXTURE AGAINST EXETER CITY, THE CLUBS' FIRST EVER FLIGHT TO A FIXTURE — MARCH 1961

WORKMEN BUSY ERECTING THE STEEL STRUCTURE FOR BOUNDARY PARKS' NEW
NORTH STAND — FEBRUARY 1961

THE PARTLY-COMPLETED NEW STAND AT BOUNDARY PARK IS THE BACKGROUND TO THIS
GOAL FROM JIMMY FRIZZELL IN THE 5-2 VICTORY OVER ACCRINGTON STANLEY— FEB 1961

SHORTLY BEFORE CHRISTMAS 1960, ATHLETIC'S DIRECTORS, OFFICIALS AND PLAYERS RECEIVED THEIR NEW CLUB BLAZERS, BADGES AND TIES

HAVE A SWEET! DONCASTER'S GOALKEEPER WILLIE NIMMO FOUND A YOUNG FRIEND BEHIND HIS GOAL IN THIS FIXTURE WITH ATHLETIC, PROVING THAT NOT EVERYONE THROWS APPLE CORES AND ORANGE PEEL AT THE VISITING GOALKEEPER.

1961-62

The leakage of confidential information to the press, had Athletic's directors worried and suspicious during the weeks leading up to the 1961-62 season's commencement. In mid-August, the matter came to a head when the club attempted to sign the Stirling Albion winger, Johnny Colquhoun. Althetic definitely didn't want it known they were after the player, because of the danger of other clubs stepping in, but before manager Rowley, and club director, Mr. Fred Williamson, had even set foot in Scotland, the news was out. Colquhoun did eventually sign for a reported £6,000, and the mole at Boundary Park went to ground.

Would this year bring glory or disappointment? Jack Rowley invested in nine new faces to try and make the promotion dream a reality. Besides Colquhoun, Alan Williams arrived from Bristol City; Ian Greaves from Lincoln; John Horsbrough from Dundee; Jimmy Scott from Burnley; Stan Ackerley, Manchester United; Alan Shackleton, Everton; John Robinson, Bury; Len Dickenson, and Ken Ford, both Sheffield Wednesday. Bobby Johnstone re-signed for the club, after originally rejecting new terms. Manager Rowley said, "It will be harder than last time, but I feel sure we will finish higher up the table. I don't want to make any promises, but we have strengthened our staff, and it can be a very good season for Athletic."

In many ways it turned out to be Athletic's finest season in years. There was a fine F.A. Cup run, and a never-to-be forgotton 4th round clash with Liverpool as the climax. The crowd of 41,733 who packed Boundary Park on that thrill-charged January day, saw a glimpse of Oldham Athletic back as soccer power.

Athletic's brilliant Cup run killed the club's promotion hopes. From that peak of achievement, the team slipped steadily downhill, finishing the season in 11th place on 46 points. A crowd of over 8,000 turned up for the season's last match at Boundary Park, and showed that the public's enthusiasm was still strong. Floodlights were switched on at Boundary Park for the first time on Tuesday, October 3rd 1961, League Champions Burnley being the visitors for a friendly fixture. Jimmy Scott topped the appearances with 51 League and Cup, and Jimmy Frizzell headed the scoring list with 25 in all competitions. Alan Williams was voted 'Player of the Year.'

ALL SMILES DOWN SHEEPFOOT LANE, AS LATICS PLAYERS PREPARE FOR THE 1961-62 SEASON

WORKMEN BUSY SINKING BORE-HOLES TO TAKE THE FLOODLIGHT PYLON FOUNDATIONS
AT BOUNDARY PARK — JUNE 1961

AS A REWARD FOR THEIR SUCCESSFUL RUN IN THE F.A. CUP, OLDHAM INDUSTRIAL CO-OPERATIVE PRESENTED ATHLETIC PLAYERS WITH NEW BOOTS — JANUARY 1962

ATHLETIC 1962-63
Back row: WILLIAMS · MARSHALL · McCALL · BOLLANDS · SCOTT · COLQUHOUN
Front: LEDGER · JOHNSTONE · LISTER · BRANAGAN · FRIZZELL

'**P**romotion or Bust' was the motto around Boundary Park, but manager Jack Rowley was more cautious, "No predictions, that's a fool's game, but I certainly think we have a better chance this season than last. One thing is essential, we must get a good start. It's remarkable to think how well we did last year after winning only eight points from the first ten games". Althetic played three pre-season friendly games, all against other League clubs, winning two of them. In the old days, a couple of public trial games between Blues and Reds would be as much as was expected at Boundary Park. Last season, an annual 'Rose Bowl' charity match between Athletic and Rochdale was inaugurated. "Those old practice matches between first and second team players often gave false impressions", said manager Rowley. "First teamers normally don't pull everything out, and second teamers are usually trying that little bit extra, with these competitive games, I've been able to draw a truer picture of the club's strength. It has also given the new players a chance to fit into our style of play." Bill Marshall, a full-back from Burnley; Peter McCall, an industrious wing-half from Bristol City; Bob Ledger, a utility player signed for £5,750 from Huddersfield Town, and Jim Bowie, a 6'2" Scot from Arthurlie. New faces, same old hopes.

The Boundary Park club achieved its cherished aim of promotion, but the words of Chairman Frank Armitage, 'Promotion or Bust' became almost too prophetic. For Athletic, season 1962-63 came close to bringing both promotion and financial ruin. For almost the entire

BERT LISTER PUTS MORE PRESSURE ON THE SOUTHPORT GOALKEEPER — DEC. '62

season, Athletic had been at the head of the Fourth Division table. Every team they played treated the fixture as a Cup tie, and were determined to knock them off their perch. The strain of holding that top place told on Athletic in the months of March and April, and almost brought disaster, but the side had the character to recover from its bad spell just in time, finishing 2nd place in the table on 59 points.

As the season reached its conclusion, the club dropped a bombshell by dismissing manager Jack Rowley, and leaving the Athletic Board effectively split into two camps. Rarely can a soccer manager have been sacked after leading a team to promotion. Mr. Jack Clayton, club President was quoted, when pinpointing the troubles: "The problem started as far back as 1962, but recently a section of the board have wanted to pick the Oldham Athletic team. This was manager Rowley's job, and he stuck to his guns." Chairman Frank Armitage, said in a T.V. interview, "The next manager must have few brains, the skin of a rhinoceros, and the heart of a lion."

On the playing front, the 5-2 defeat by Bradford City in the opening round of the F.A. Cup, was seen as a blessing-in-disguise, enabling the team to concentrate on the job at hand. This season, the Cup competition straddled month after month of weather-ruined soccer, and would have been a distraction. Athletic's promotion team cost in the region of £45,000, making this season probably the most expensive in the club's history, but when Athletic could point to promotion, the outlay was justified in the end.

DLY DAMAGED DURING THE GALES OF JANUARY 1963, THE CHADDERTON-END STAND
BOUNDARY PARK WOULD SOON BE THE SCENE OF INTENSE ACTIVITY AS WORKMEN
MOVED IN TO CARRY OUT REPAIRS

Player of the Year was Bert Lister, whose wonderful six goal display in the fantastic 11-0 win over Southport on Boxing Day had supporters reaching for the record books. Lister scored six right-footed goals, a unique performance in itself. Athletic's win was also a record for the Fourth Division, the club's biggest ever win, beating the 11-2 demolition of Chester ten years earlier, and was Southport's heaviest defeat.

Three players made maximum appearances, Ken Branagan, Johnny Colquhoun and Alan Williams with 49 League and Cup. Bert Lister topped the goalscoring charts with an impressive total of 33 in all competitions. Many supporters believed if Lister had not been dropped for a spell in March, he would surely have established a new goalscoring record for Athletic.

WITH THE AID OF A BULLDOZER OWNED BY CLUB DIRECTOR MR. HARRY MASSEY, ATHLETIC TRY TO BEAT THE ELEMENTS — FEBRUARY 1963

'IT'S A DOG'S LIFE'; YOU JUST CAN'T GET A GAME ANYWHERE THESE DAYS. I JUST NIPPED ON TO TRY HELP BERT LISTER NOTCH ANOTHER GOAL IN THAT RECORD BID AND I'M COLLARED — v. CHESTERFIELD, BOUNDARY PARK, APRIL 1963

OLDHAM ATHLETIC 1963-64
Back: SIEVEWRIGHT · FRIZZELL · BOLLANDS · BRANAGAN · LEDGER · TAYLOR
Front: JOHNSTONE · WILLIAMS · LISTER · WHITTAKER

1963-64

A thletic's new manager was Les McDowall, who began his duties at Boundary Park on Monday 17th June '63. The former Manchester City boss, who resigned from Maine Road in a storm of controversy was hoping a change of job would bring another success story to a career which had reached the heights and the depths. "It's perfectly true that things have not been going too well for me recently, but I'm sure that position will change now," he said. There were over 30 applicants for the position, including former Athletic boss, George Hardwick, but experience swung the vote in McDowall's favour. As he settled into his new managerial chair, he spoke of his plans for Athletic. "It's a great club, and it's riding on the crest of a wave. Consequently, as far as I'm concerned, it will be status quo to start with. You don't start making rash changes when things are going well."

Athletic kicked-off with high hopes and the priority job of consolidating the position they so richly earned last season. Manager McDowall made no wild promises or bold forecasts, but one thing seemed certain, if Athletic reproduced their attractive soccer and enthusiasm, it should sweep the team to further heights. The club had made only the minimum of buys during the close season, goalkeeper Alan Halsall; full-back Barry Taylor; half-back George Sievewright, and ex-Manchester City inside-forward Colin Barlow. Alan Williams, Athletic's defensive kingpin was the last of the club's 18 professionals to re-sign. Last season, Latics crowds increased to an average of 14,000, even without a Cup run, and with the prospect of many attractive fixtures this season it was hoped this would increase the average even further. "Give the fans a winning team and they'll turn up", said manager McDowall, "Divisions don't mean a thing to them."

A GROUP OF LATICS PLAYERS TAKE A BREAK FROM ROUTINE TRAINING AT THE OLDHAM CONSERVATIVE CLUB — AUGUST '63

147

Early season, Athletic were the promotion pacemakers with eight victories from the first eleven fixtures, and were on top of the table in early October with 17 points. Coventry City took over when Athletic lost to Shrewsbury a week later, but with a win over Crystal Palace, became joint leaders with the Sky Blues on 19th October. By January 11th, Athletic had dropped to fourth spot, but following a great win over Coventry on January 22nd, got back into second place, just .01 of a goal behind the leaders. Then came the fall from grace, losing at Crewe on January 25th, and between that date and March 30th picking up only two points from six home games and dropping down the table. Bobby Craig's arrival from St. Johnstone for £2,000 in March helped to stop the slide, but Athletic could only finish 9th in Division Three on 48 points.

Athletic had the third worst home record in the Division, losing seven games at Boundary Park, and drawing three. They reached the third round of the F.A. Cup, losing 6-3 at Ipswich after home victories in rounds 1 and 2 over Mansfield and Bradford. Both home Cup ties attracted over 17,000 spectators. Out of a maximum of 50 possible appearances, Bob Ledger led the averages with 49. Bert Lister finished top scorer on 17 goals in League and Cup, despite missing many games through injury. The average home League attendance at Boundary Park was 11,745.

BERT LISTER MAKES A SPECTACULAR LEAP TO FLASH A GREAT HEADER INTO THE PORT VALE NET TO GIVE ATHLETIC A 1-0 WIN — SEPT '63

ATHLETIC'S CAPTAIN ALAN WILLIAMS HANDS OVER HIS ROLE AS COIN-SPINNER TO THE OLDHAM SOCCER QUEEN YVONNE WOOD, BEFORE ATHLETIC'S 2-1 VICTORY OVER Q.P.R. — AUGUST 1963

ALBERT QUIXALL IS WELCOMED TO BOUNDARY PARK BY MANAGER LES McDOWALL AND
TRAINER JIMMY KELLY — SEPTEMBER 1964

1964-65

"**A**ll at Boundary Park are quietly confident of their chances to keep in the running in the Third Division race following what, after all, was a pretty good effort last term. With the solid nucleus of last season's team, our new signings, and the promising band of youngsters who were blooded towards the end of last season, our supporters can rest assured that there will be no lack of effort from the boys" promised Les McDowall.

The close season signings, centre-forward, Jimmy Harris, and two Scots, full-back, Alex Cameron and wing-half, Alan Lawson, all made their League debuts in the first home game, a 5-1 defeat by Grimsby Town. After two more consecutive heavy defeats, 5-0 at Peterborough and 4-1 at Mansfield, manager McDowall bolstered his defence by signing Barrie Martin for £10,000 from Blackpool, the second highest transfer fee paid in the club's history. Athletic continued to struggle with only two wins in the first seventeen matches, losing ten, form which rooted them at the foot of the table. A bold effort was made to overcome the disability of such a bad start as Athletic plunged into the transfer market in September, signing former Manchester United 'golden boy', Albert Quixall for £8,500, and winger Tony Bartley from Bury for £7,500. Even that double transfer brought disappointment in the limited appearances of Quixall who was dogged by injury right from the start. The same period saw the highly popular Bert Lister sever his ties with Athletic and join Rochdale.

ROCHDALE OBSERVERS' MR. SCOTT PRESENTS THE ROSE BOWL TO ATHLETIC'S CAPTAIN JIMMY FRIZZELL — AUG '64

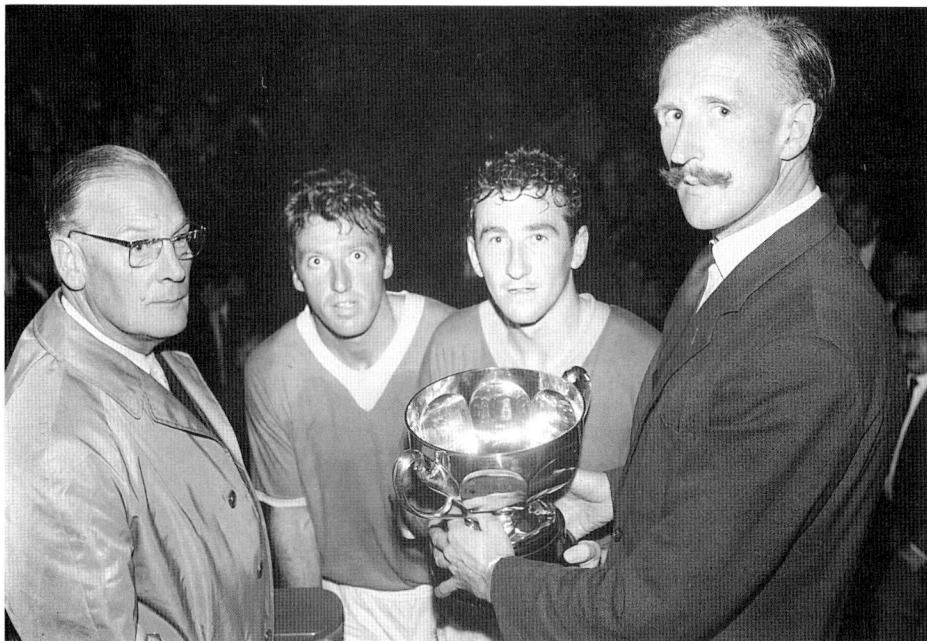

Even the Life Members were unable to remember a season that started so disastrously, progressively worsened, and ended up by the club being saved from relegation by a freak goal with one game to go. The events in the Boardroom, with directors resigning over club policy, and poor form on the field were closely interwoven into an overall picture of disappointment and depression, and one which the soccer fans of Oldham wanted no part of, judging by the increased number of stay-aways, an equation that was proving the undoing of many famous old clubs at this time.

Prior to the home fixture with Walsall on March 20th, Athletic dismissed manager Les McDowall. ''That's the way it goes in football, but the parting was an amicable one,'' was McDowall's only comment. Chairman Harry Massey said, ''In my opinion I don't think any further managerial appointment will be made before the end of the season.'' A further development saw former Chairman, Frank Armitage, resign from the board, followed by director Fred Williamson. The sorry tale of failure and lack of recent success brough a cash crisis to Boundary Park, with gates down to an average of 8,000, a figure about half that on which the club could subsist.

From the turn of the year to the end of the campaign, Athletic won only four matches, and lost eleven from 19 outings, finishing down in 20th place with 36 points. The clubs below them were all relegated. The F.A. Cup saw ties with non-League Hereford and Crook Town, won 4-0 and 1-0 respectively, before a third round defeat at Middlesbrough by 6-2. The record for most appearances this disappointing season went to Alan Williams who played 48 consecutive games out of a possible 50 in all competitions. Club captain Jimmy Frizzell top scored, along with Tony Bartley, with 10 goals apiece in League and Cup.

SUPPORTERS CLEAN-UP BOUNDARY PARK — 1964

ATHLETIC 1964-65
Back: FRIZZELL·JACKSON·BRANAGAN·BOLLANDS·LAWSON·CAMERON
Front: LEDGER·CRAIG·HARRIS·BOWIE·COLQUHOUN

A GOAL BY TONY BARTLEY (OR WAS IT LISTER?) AGAINST MANSFIELD TOWN — DEC '64·

ATHLETIC 1965-66

BOUNDARY PARK LOOKED MORE LIKE AN ICE HOCKEY STADIUM THAN A FOOTBALL
GROUND, VERSUS SHREWSBURY DECEMBER '64
(inset) JIMMY FRIZZELL AND BARRIE MARTIN CLEARING SNOW FROM THE PENALTY SPOT.

1965-66

Memories of the sorry tale of failure last season, which plunged the club into a cash crisis that made survival touch and go, were still vivid in the minds of the majority of fans, and only a spectacular revival would erase them. A surprise choice for the Boundary Park hot-seat was the former Oldham Athletic wartime amateur player, Gordon Hurst. With a colourful and distinguished playing career spent with Charlton Athletic, where togetherness meant more than star players, he was banking on the staff he already had to show the effort and determination needed to revive the club's fortunes. He began under the handicap of having lost key players of the calibre of Johnny Colquhoun, Alan Williams, Peter McCall and Barrie Martin, and consequently the side struggled from the first match, recorded only three wins in 22 games, before the New Year brought Ken Bates as chairman, who rolled into Oldham to breath life into an ailing Athletic, and make his name a household word in the town.

A wealthy young Cheshire businessman and well-known in City circles, Mr. Bates had come to the financial rescue of Athletic after five weeks of secret negotiations. It all started with a chance phone call to Chairman Mr. Harry Massey. "He rang up and told me that he had picked out Oldham Athletic as the club he wished to join because the potential was there and just needed re-organising," said Mr. Massey. The two met over dinner in a Manchester hotel and discussed plans to rescue and re-build Athletic. Eventually, negotiations were officially opened between Mr. Bates and the club, and at a Board meeting on 21st December 1965, Mr. Massey stepped down to vice-Chairman so that Mr. Bates could assume full control. "It is a happy mutual arrangement between him and I," said Mr. Massey.

KEN BATES AT THE WHEEL OF HIS SILVER CLOUD ROLLS-ROYCE ON HIS WAY TO TAKE
OVER AS CHAIRMAN AT BOUNDARY PARK — DEC. '65

MANAGER GORDON HURST TALKS WITH
GROUNDSMAN MIKE CASSIDY — JUNE '65

JIMMY McILROY SIGNS THE CONTRACT THAT
MADE HIM ATHLETIC'S NEW MANAGER — JAN '66

Mr. Bates modestly claimed to know little about football, but was good enough in his youth to command a place as centre-half in Arsenal's famous nursery team. "Soccer nowadays," he said, "is business, big business, and I do know something about business." The first thing he did when he took over, was to confirm that manager Gordon Hurst would be given a chance to prove himself. "Gordon has asked for a free hand and backing. He'll get both from me," he said, "Europe is our goal, and it can be done." Athletic swept into the New Year with a fanfare and a flourish, and the future looked brighter than even their most loyal fans could have dreamed of only a matter of weeks before.

Mr. Bates put money where his mouth was and financed the signings of Frank Large, a £7,500 capture from Carlisle United, Reg Blore from Blackburn for £8,000, Dennis Stevens from Everton, Ian Towers from Burnley for £20,000, and Bill Asprey from Stoke City, all in January 1966. The new players were still settling in at Boundary Park when Athletic pulled a plumb third round F.A. Cup tie with West Ham United out of the hat, over 25,000 people packing Boundary Park to witness an epic 2-2 draw, Albert Quixall missing a penalty for Athletic, who lost the replay 2-1.

A surprise in late January saw Jimmy McIlroy join Athletic from Stoke City as Team Manager on a five year contract. A somewhat perplexed Gordon Hurst said, "I will give Jimmy McIlroy all the backing I can until the Chairman returns from South Africa and my position is sorted out. But that does not mean to say I am accepting the job as assistant manager. I want to know under what conditions I am to be assistant manager and, apparently, until the chairman returns in five weeks' time, no one can tell me." When Chairman Bates did return, he persuaded Jimmy McIlroy to become player/manager, and help the side in another relegation fight. McIlroy's first game brought an instant dividend, a 2-0 win at Southend United.

NEW SIGNING BILLY JOHNSTON AND HIS WIFE CHAT TO (left to right)
DIRECTOR ARTHUR HUDSON, JIMMY McILROY AND GORDON HURST — JULY '66

Before Chairman Bates appeared on the scene, and delved into the transfer market, Athletic had played 11 home matches, with a total attendance of 67,597. The biggest gate was 7,986, for the first home match against Reading, but by October it had dropped to 3,746 for the visit of Bristol Rovers, the lowest gate since the last match of the season in May 1960. The 11 home games of 1965 averaged 6,145. But on New Years day, when four new players made their League debuts in the same Athletic team—Dennis Stevens, Reg Blore, Ian Towers and Frank Large, it shot up to 14,099, the season's best League attendance. In the months of January and February, the eight home matches, including the F.A. Cup tie against West Ham, had totalled 111,504 for an average of 13,938, more than double those of last year.

Unfortunately, despite an outlay of nearly £50,000 in the transfer market to bring fresh talent and new hope to Boundary Park, fans had seen the new-look Athletic win only nine times in 27 outings, and finish a disappointing 20th in the table—just above the relegation positions—for the second season running. The dependable Jimmy Frizzell made most appearances this year with 50 out of a possible 56 in all competitions. Fewest appearances went to Ian Wood, who completed his first match in a career which would see him break the club's all-time appearance record. Ian Towers top scored with nine goals, all in the Third Division.

JIMMY PENNINGTON'S FREE KICK BEATS JIM STANDEN TO PUT ATHLETIC ONE UP IN THE 3RD ROUND CUP REPLAY DEFEAT AT WEST HAM — JAN. '66

REG BLORE SLAMS IN ATHLETIC'S FIRST GOAL IN THE CUP-TIE WITH WEST HAM UNITED

THE WEST HAM KEEPER STRETCHES ACROSS HIS GOAL TO SAVE ALBERT QUIXALL'S
SPOT KICK IN THE 2-2 F.A. CUP 3RD ROUND DRAW WITH WEST HAM UNITED AT
BOUNDARY PARK — JANUARY '66

ATHLETIC RETAIN THE ROSE-BOWL WITH A 1-1 DRAW WITH ROCHDALE IN AUGUST '65.

ALAN LAWSON, JIMMY FRIZZELL AND JOHNNY COLQUHOUN ADMIRE THE MANCHESTER SENIOR CUP WHICH ATHLETIC WON BY DEFEATING BURY 2-0 — APRIL '65

" "The past is forgotten, we are starting absolutely afresh from today. The poor state of the pitch, the poor facilities for fans, the free transfers are all in the past. The only thing that matters now is where we are going from here," said Manager, Jimmy McIlroy, "Oldham Athletic is going to be run like a professional club should be run. The players are all going to be pro's, and I shall expect from them, professional performances. This is a new job to me, and I realise that I have a lot to learn, but I reckon that experience is the best teacher, and since I joined Athletic it's been quite an experience. I am excited at the prospect of working with the youngsters who are joining us. No doubt there will be criticism, but I feel that I have the patience and confidence to wait for things to develop. I have been at Stoke City, and quite a long time at Burnley, and if the Athletic fans are given a fraction of the success that these two clubs have had, I feel that their response to the players would be overwhelming."

Chairman Bates made a bold decision to give Boundary Park a much needed facelift which he thought would have a psychological effect on the players. It was a tough job persuading First Division players to drop a couple of Divisions without having to combat the drawback of an out-of-date ground with old-fashioned facilities. The critics who said improve the team and never mind the ground had their answer when Athletic invested another £40,000 in signing Keith Bebbington and George Kinnell from Stoke City, and goalkeeper David Best from Bournemouth.

ATHLETIC'S CAPTAIN BILL ASPREY ACCEPTS THE ROSE BOWL FROM THE ROCHDALE OBSERVER DIRECTOR MR. J. LANDLESS AFTER ATHLETIC HAD BEATEN ROCHDALE AT SPOTLAND 2-1 — AUG. '66

Despite increased prices, the support was there at the start of the season, which opened with a flourish, Athletic winning five of the first seven fixtures, new signing George Kinnell prominent, scoring eight times and becoming the crowd's favourite, but after only three months in Athletic's colours, he was transferred to Sunderland for £20,000. This unpopular move was countered to some extent in November with the signing of Ken Knighton from Wolves for £12,000, but by this time the team was slipping, yet still in contention. December saw only one win in six outings setting the pattern for the remainder of the season, Athletic winning only seven times from January 1st to the end of the season, finishing in 10th position on 48 points.

After F.A. Cup victories over Notts County and Grantham, Athletic played Wolves at Boundary Park, in the 3rd round, drawing 2-2 after leading 2-0 with 90 minutes completed. They lost the replay 4-1. It seemed a bold decision by manager McIlroy to give youth its fling in a struggling team, but teenagers, Ronnie Blair, Ian Wood and Les Chapman came into the side with impressive contributions, and proved that Athletic now had a youth policy which would be a great boon to the club. In the League, with youngsters being blooded, Athletic gained 19 points from nineteen matches, in comparison with 24 points from nineteen games early season when Athletic still had George Kinnell,Frank Large (transferred to Northampton for £14,000), and Billy Johnston, who was forced to retire due to injury. Out of a possible 51 League and Cup games, Ian Towers completed a maximum, followed by Reg Bloor on 48. Towers completed an impressive double, also being top goalscorer with 27 League strikes. The average home crowd in League and Cups was 10,626, a slight increase on the previous season.

After the last match, Athletic's players started a three week holiday before reporting back for several day's training in preparation for a tour of Rhodesia and Malawi. The club party flew from London on June 16th to Salisbury, Rhodesia, where they played nine matches against local teams. Meanwhile in Malwi, the National Football Association was staging a series of trial games to select players for a national team to represent them against Athletic. The game was included among the celebrations on the first anniversary of the establishment of Malawi, formerly the Central African British Colony of Nyasaland.

LATICS CENTRE-FORWARD IAN WOOD'S EFFORT IS SAVED BY THE Q.P.R. GOALKEEPER SPRINGETT, IN A 1-0 DEFEAT — APRIL '67

KEITH BEBBINGTON SLAMS A LEFT FOOT SHOT OVER THE UPRAISED RIGHT ARM OF THE WOLVES'S KEEPER DAVIES TO PUT ATHLETIC ONE UP IN THE F.A. CUP 3RD ROUND 2-2 DRAW AT BOUNDARY PARK — JAN. '67

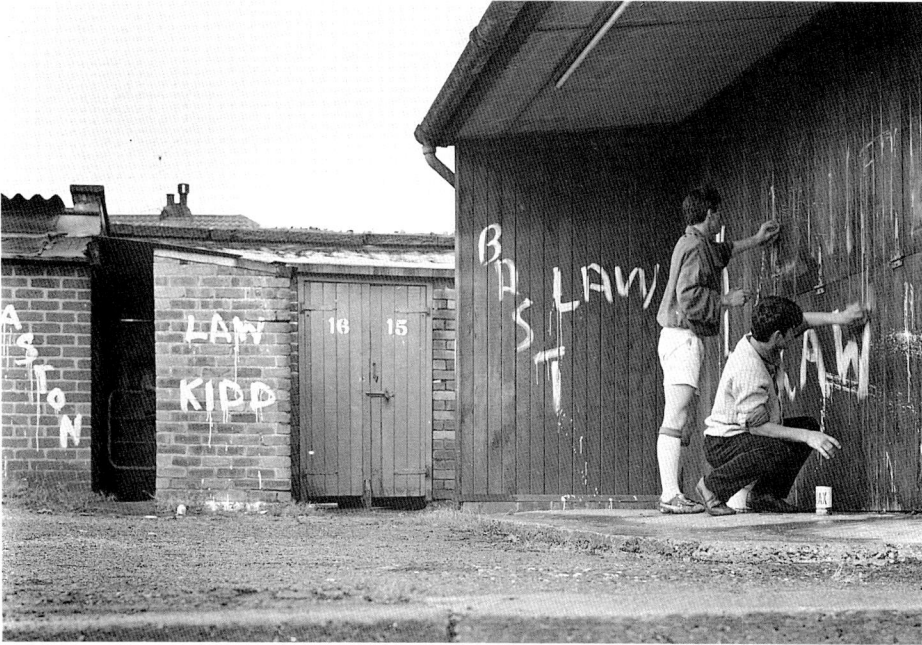

VANDELS SMEAR BOUNDARY PARK — AUG. '67

ATHLETIC EXPERIMENT WITH A TAPED FILM OF THE FRIENDLY FIXTURE WITH STOKE,
WHICH WAS RE-LAYED ON T.V. BY CLOSED CIRCUIT — AUG. '66

IAN WOOD (left) WATCHES HIS SHOT IN THE FINAL MINUTE BEAT THE GRANTHAM KEEPER SMALL FOR GOAL NUMBER FOUR IN THE 4-0 F.A. CUP 2ND ROUND WIN — JAN. '67

OLDHAM ATHLETIC · 1967/68 Front: CHAPMAN · WOOD · FRIZZELL · TOWERS · DOYLE
Back: MAGEE · SHEFFIELD · BOWIE · BEST · BLAIR · BLORE

—— 1967-68 ——

Despite criticism of Athletic's visit to Rhodesia in the House of Commons by the Minister for Commonwealth Affairs, Mr. George Thomas, the venture had proved an overwhelming success, not only in the shape of match results— they won 10 of the 11 games played—but also in the way they had been received and welcomed. Chairman Ken Bates said, "I now know why the Oldham population is declining, they are all living in Rhodesia. Wherever we went we constantly meet people from Werneth, Greenfield and Failsworth, and every part of the town itself, many of whom watched Athletic play before and after the war."

Assistant-manager, Gordon Hurst, decided to leave the club in mid-July and join Rochdale as trainer-coach. Although close-season signings were restricted to the capture of Irish Inter-League forward, Eric Magee from Glenavon for £4,000, and goalkeeper Bill Molyneux on a free transfer from Liverpool, hopes ran high at Boundary Park that the club could make an all out challenge for promotion. Athletic's success in preserving an impressive record on their tours of Rhodesia and Ulster delighted the party, and no one more so than manager McIlroy who saw it as an optimistic pointer to the club's chances in the Third Division. Events, however proved such optimism misplaced, and Athletic supporters could be excused for looking back in anger on a season that seemed to have brought only frustration and bitter disappointment. An attendance of just over 2,000 for the last match, the lowest for many years, was a positive indictment of the men who made the 1967-68 season such a failure.

"STEADY ON, HE'S ONE OF OURS!"
THE GROUNDSMAN RESTRAINS BOUNDARY PARK'S GUARD DOG 'CAPTAIN NEMO' AS IT
TRIES TO TACKLE ATHLETIC'S BILLY JOHNSTON

In their first 15 matches of the campaign, Athletic picked up four League points, and were ejected from the League Cup in the first round by Workington. By mid-October, Athletic were bottom of the League with just four points from 12 games, no fewer than 14 behind leaders Walsall. They had scored fewer goals than any other side in the Division and there was an air of gloom and despondency about the club that was reflected in the play. Then, without drastic surgery to the team, Athletic suddenly hit upon a winning burst that took them on a seven-match sequence of success. That was where the crunch came, for despite their supreme effort they climbed just five places and were by no means out of danger. Reaction set in, and Athletic lost another three games, including the F.A. Cup first round tie at Barrow.

The season's two signings, Walter Joyce and Alan Philpott, had both helped to strengthen the side, Joyce with a rugged defensive approach, Philpott with some subtle attacking touches. Mid-December saw the popular Ken Knighton sold to Preston North End for £35,000, Bob Ledger move to Mansfield Town for £3,000, and Laurie Sheffield, a £17,000 buy from Rotherham take his place at centre-forward. Without the drive of Knighton at wing-half, and the goal flair of Ledger, Athletic hit another dismal patch, losing five consecutive matches which pushed them back into the relegation zone in early March. Centre-half Allan Hunter went down with injury, allowing Alan Lawson a chance in the centre of defence which he accepted

ATHLETIC'
Back: BOWIE · LAWSON · FRIZZELL · HUNTER · MOLYNEUX ·
Front: MAGEE · TOWERS · BLORE · CH.

with telling impact. Working closely with his ally, Jimmy Frizzell, Lawson zipped tight Athletic's defence with courage and inspiration. In the final twelve matches, Lawson persuaded, pushed and bullied the side into a fighting unit that collected a life-saving 17 points and finished the season in 16th position with 43 points. Athletic's reserve team dominated the Lancs Combination from the word go and completed a notable double when adding the Combination Cup to the League title they won with ease.

Winding up a disastrous season, Athletic hit an all time low in average attendances at Boundary Park for League matches—6,000. The Boundary Bulletin ended its career this season, voted second best programme in the Football League, the Bulletin had suffered under the season's drastic economy cuts. The last Bulletin was the 52nd. Problems at boardroom level resulted in Mr. Eric Beard resigning, bringing to the surface the question of unity and solidarity. This season had been a bad one for chairman Ken Bates, and ill-feeling created by disputes with his board members made it obvious there was some dissatisfaction in the way the club was being run.

Goalkeeper David Best made most appearances with a maximum 50, and Bob Ledger's 11 goals from only seventeen appearances in League and Cup, before his transfer, were enough to make him top scorer.

LL · 1967/68
ST · BLAIR · KNIGHTON · FOSTER · LEDGER · KELLY (Trainer)
OD · JOHNSTON · McILROY (Manager)

ATHLETIC'S SKIPPER ALAN HUNTER HOLDS ALOFT THE ROSE BOWL WITH
ALAN PHILPOTT, FOLLOWING LATICS 2-1 VICTORY OVER ROCHDALE — AUG. '68

NUMBER 10, BILLY JOHNSTON COULD ONLY NUDGE THE BALL AGAINST A POST AS
MANSFIELD BEAT ATHLETIC 4-0 SEPT. '68

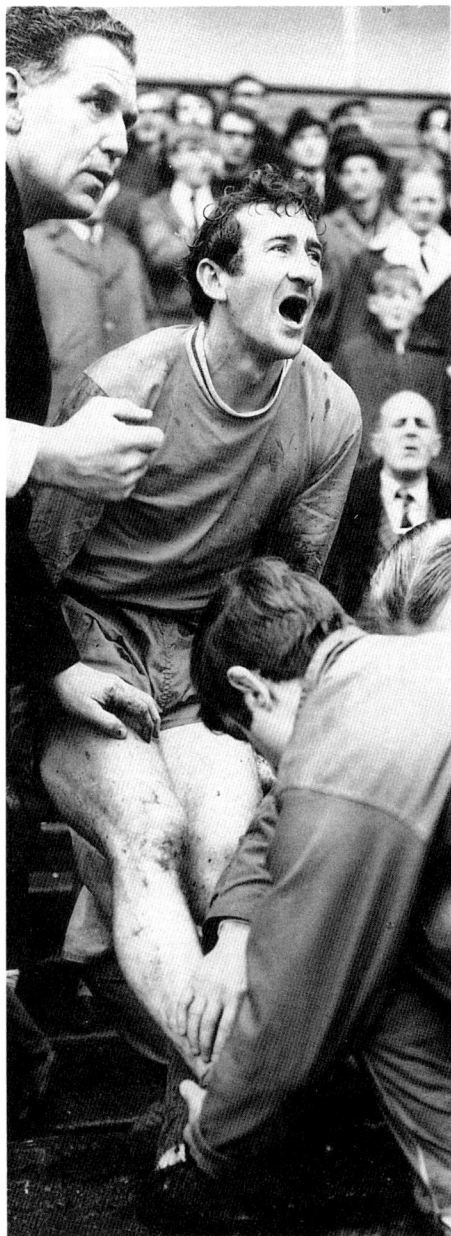

PAIN AND TENSION IN FRIZZELL'S FACE,
v. HARTLEPOOL — NOV. '68

Athletic's failure to capture the imagination of the town's sporting public had hit the club where it hurt most, in the pocket. Season ticket sales where more than £5,000 down on the previous year. A pre-season of rumours, suggested manager McIlroy was resigning due to the pressure of the job, Chairman Bates was also claimed to be leaving for business reasons; not the ideal preparation for a new campaign. Athletic made no major signings, the playing staff being virtually unchanged from the previous May, except for the transfer of Ian Towers to Bury in July. His average of a goal every other game would be badly missed.

Two days after the opening match of the season, a 4-0 defeat at Luton, Chairman Bates returned from holiday, met with Jimmy McIlroy and stated, "I am not leaving Athletic, and neither is the manager", but following an opening in which the team conceded eleven goals and scored only one from the first three matches, and with Bates again away on business in the Virgin Islands, manager McIlroy did resign. The board of directors agreed to cancel his contract which still had over two years to run, and for a short time the club was managed by three directors, Mr. Harry Massey, Mr. Ronnie Clayton and Mr. Arthur Hudson. McIlroy refused to comment at length on his two and a half years at Boundary Park; "All I can say is that it has been an experience," he offered tersely. Mr. Massey stated that he did not know what Mr. Bates' reaction would be to the news, adding that, "he had been informed of the situation in a cablegram, and we intend to go on running the club until he returns.''

The terrible run of defeats continued, and on September 17th 1968 Ken Bates returned to England, and resigned his position as Chairman of Athletic, but retained a seat on the board. He said, ''The time has come when I have to concentrate more on my job than on football. After all, football has always been a hobby to me, an expensive hobby at that, and I have devoted more time and energy to it than a lot of people would have done.'' He continued, ''I have no intention of withdrawing my money now, or doing so in the future.'' Mr. Bates denied he was leaving the Chairmanship at Boundary Park with any feelings of failure. He said that when he looked back on what had been achieved in the two years since he took over at Athletic, he had considerable cause for pride.

Within six months he had also resigned as a director.

In the midst of one of the worst runs in Athletic's history, Jack Rowley returned on September 26th 1968, to manage Athletic after a spell as manager at Bradford. After signing a two-year contract he said, ''I am very pleased indeed to be back with Oldham. I realise, of course, that it will be a struggle, but it cannot be any worse than it has been.'' Performances did improve but Athletic's season of disappointment turned into eventual despair, finishing bottom of Division Three on a poor 35 points. The mid-season signings of Alan Spence from Southport, and the return of old favourite Johnny Colquhoun from Scunthorpe helped Athletic in a tremendous fight to stave off relegation, and with a better start to the season they

NEW MANAGER JACK ROWLEY HAS A QUIET WORD WITH VICE-CHAIRMAN
MR. RON CLAYTON — OCT. '68

CLUB CAPTAIN ALAN LAWSON PRESENTS A CHRISTMAS SAUSAGE TO
JOHNNY COLQUHOUN WITH JIMMY FRIZZELL LOOKING ON — JAN. '69

PLAYER OF THE YEAR KEITH BEBBINGTON RECEIVES THE TROPHY FROM MISS OLDHAM
ATHLETIC LYNN THOMAS, WITH LES CHAPMAN LOOKING ON — MAY '69

would have finished in the top half of the table. Just before Christmas they had only nine points from 21 matches, since then they had averaged more than a point a game, but never looked likely to overcome that nine point handicap. Manager Rowley said, "The lads have done a tremendous job since Christmas, and it is a great pity that we didn't have a better start to the season."

Jimmy Frizzell was appointed first team coach this season, but he still carried on playing, appearing eighteen times. From a possible 49 League and Cup games, Keith Bebbington, Reg Blore, Les Chapman and Allan Hunter all notched 44 appearances. Keith Bebbington led the goalscoring chart with 13 in League and Cup, closely followed by new signing Alan Spence on 12. Athletic's Cup exploits were short-live affairs, beaten 2-1 on aggregate by Preston in the League Cup, and losing 4-2 at Wrexham in round one of the F.A. Cup. The average Boundary Park attendance slumped to 3,889, a further decrease from the previous season. The 1968-69 season was a troublesome voyage indeed!

ATHLETIC TAKE THE FIELD AT OLD TRAFFORD FOR A LANCS. SENIOR CUP TIE — JAN. '69

MANCHESTER UNITED 4, ATHLETIC 2; LANCS. SENIOR CUP — JAN. '69

ATHLETIC'S YOUTH TEAM · 1968/69
Back: SWEENEY · COOK · HOOLICKIN · FITTON · CRUMBLEHULME · SCHOFIELD · ROBINS
Front: GRIMBLEDESTON · MAKIN · HENRY · SMITH · AITKEN

PHOTO-CALL IN NEW BLAZERS — PRE SEASON 1969-70

1969-70

Manager Rowley persuaded full-back Ray Wilson, a member of England's 1966 World Cup winning team, to sign for Athletic, hoping his experience would lead the club straight out of the Fourth Division. It was hoped he would be the key figure in Athletic's efforts to recapture the interest of the Oldham public, and was appointed club captain. Athletic were not in a position to turn down good offers for players, and pre-season Allan Hunter was transferred to Blackburn Rovers for £30,000, followed shortly after by Les Chapman to Huddersfield Town in exchange for David Shaw plus £35,000. Athletic signed defenders Maurice Whittle from Blackburn and Mike Faulkner from Sheffield United, plus forwards John Bingham from Manchester City and Jim Beardall from Blackburn. It was considered that with their new tactical plan for away games, a 4-4-2 formation devised by coach Jimmy Frizzell, Athletic would give very little away on their travels from Boundary Park.

Athletic undertook a pre-season tour of Scotland. Based in Perth, they played three matches, beating East Stirling in the opener, drawing with East Fife, and losing by the odd goal in five to Arbroath. When the League campaign got under way, Athletic did not start too badly, winning two and drawing two of the first six games before the rot set in, and a string of defeats and draws plunged Athletic in deep trouble by December. Manager Rowley's signings had failed to justify his confidence in them, and on December 29th he received an unwanted New Year's gift, the sack for the second time in seven years. The team's dismal League form, coupled with a second round F.A. Cup knock-out by non-Leaguers South Shields forced the board's hand. Jimmy Frizzell took over as caretaker manager on the 30th December with Walter Joyce in charge of the reserves. Under Frizzell's leadership,

JIMMY FRIZZELL AS A PLAYER   ... AND MANAGER

Athletic were picking up points and steadily improving their position, then in early February came the turning point when Jim Fryatt was signed from Blackburn Rovers for £8,000. With Fryatt leading the attack, and Frizzell coaxing the best out of his players, Athletic finally overcame their re-election worries. In appreciation of his efforts, Jimmy Frizzell was given a two year managerial contract. A delighted Frizzell said, "I am very pleased with the appointment and the confidence that the board have shown in me. I will do my best to justify it," adding "as it was before, there was always the thought at the back of my mind that if things went wrong someone else would be brought in. Now that problem had gone, and there is a little more security."

While the situation on the field was improving, events in the boardroom had seen local businessman, John Lowe join the board and save the club from possible extinction by reaching agreement with former club Chairman Ken Bates over re-payment of monies owed. "This had to be done to save the club from being closed up. We all know that Mr. Bates had the power to close the club," said Mr. Lowe, who had been a friend of club Chairman Massey for some time, "I want to stress that I will not be another Ken Bates. I am John Lowe, and I do not intend to go about wielding the big stick."

This had been one of the most traumatic seasons in Athletic's history as they had faced not only the threat of re-election, but the agonising threat of extinction. To finish in 19th position in the Fourth Division on 39 points was, under the circumstances, a triumph in itself. Ian Wood completed a maximum 50 appearances, followed by Jim Bowie on 48. David Shaw, in his first season at Boundary Park, did well to score 12 League goals, as did Jim Fryatt on 11 from only sixteen appearances. The average Boundary Park crowd rose to 4,473 as more supporters realised the club's new-found potential.

IAN WOOD COLLECTS THE PLAYER OF THE SEASON AWARD FROM
VICE CHAIRMAN MR. HARRY MASSEY — APRIL '70

ATHLETIC PLAYERS THOMPSON, WOOD AND HEATH PREPARE FOR FATHERHOOD — 1970

ATHLETIC · 1970/71
Back: McGREGOR (Physio) · McNEILL · HEATH · CRANSTON · DOWD · WHITTLE · WOOD · SWEENEY · FRIZZELL (Manager)
Front: BEBBINGTON · FRYATT · BOWIE · BRYCELAND · SHAW

1970-71

This season, Athletic put the years of disappointments and frustration firmly behind them, as they won both cash and honours. The money came as the product of the Ford Sporting League scheme whereby teams in all four Divisions, earned points for goals scored and had them deducted for players being booked or sent off. Athletic won the cash prize every month, as they did the end-of-season bonus, to pick up £70,000 in total. The effort was commemorated by the construction of the Ford Stand. The honours came in the shape of promotion to Division Three, by finishing third in Division Four with 59 points. It would have taken a brave man to have forecast these events, after the near disaster of the previous campaign.

Jimmy Frizzell and his backroom staff had worked feverishly to plan this season's success, and even they must have been surprised at the way things dropped into place.

Goalkeeper, Maurice Short, was signed from Middlesbrough, Bill Cranston from Preston North End, Don Heath from Swindon, and Barry Hartle from Stockport County. Athletic never found any sort of form in the first game at Grimsby and lost 4-1, causing doubts in the town about the team's potential, but they swept to a shock 3-1 League Cup win over Bury at Gigg Lane, and three days later followed this by a convincing victory over Exeter City at Boundary Park in the first home fixture of the season. Despite a defeat at Cambridge United, the League's newcomers, Athletic now had an appetite for success, and victories over Scunthorpe, Brentford and Newport started the promotion ball rolling. Middlesbrough handed out a League Cup defeat, which could have been a blessing, as over the next weeks Athletic consolidated their position as one of the Division's leading lights.

ONE OF JIM FRYATT'S THREE GOALS IN THE 4-2 WIN OVER LINCOLN CITY AT BOUNDARY PARK — NOV. '70

FRYATT AND SHAW CAN'T BELIEVE IT — A 3-1 HOME DEFEAT BY WORKINGTON, SEPT. '70

A FRYATT HEADER GOES WIDE IN A 5-1 WIN OVER BRENTFORD — SEPT. '70

Throughout October there was a mixed bag of results, but after Crewe were beaten 5-3 at Boundary Park, Athletic won the next three matches, before taking a disappointing F.A. Cup knockout from neighbours Rochdale. Southport caught Athletic on the rebound from their F.A. Cup defeat to win 4-2 at Boundary Park, but Athletic won their next five matches in great style to re-affirm their Third Division aspirations. At this stage Athletic were firmly established in second place. Notts County were top with 39 points from 24 games, Athletic had 37 points from 26 games and Northampton 36 points from 25 games. Early January saw a 5-0 hammering at Bournemouth, but Athletic bounced back with victories over Darlington and Southport. The win at Southport was the last game before the twin pressures of chasing promotion and the Ford Prize caught up with Athletic and threatened their dreams. Despite a win at Crewe, Athletic lost to Notts County, Lincoln and Southend, and dropped points at Northampton, Aldershot, York, Chester, Brentford and Barrow. By this time, with only four games left, the promotion issue was far from settled. Athletic were in fourth place on 53 points, with Chester and Colchester breathing down their necks. It was a cliff-hanging finish, but fears that Athletic might fail were dashed with one dazzling performance before 10,405 people at Boundary Park. Close rivals Colchester were sunk 4-0, with Keith Bebbington scoring twice, David Shaw getting a third and an own goal sealing the rout. A great victory at York City, and draws at Workington, and at home to Southport clinched a promotion place, making manager Frizzell the hero of the hour.

Jim Fryatt finished leading goalscorer with 26 League and Cup, followed by David Shaw on 24. The two most consistent players were Jim Bowie and Maurice Whittle making a maximum 49 appearances. The average attendance figures were a little disappointing considering the nature of Athletic's season 9,575 in League and Cup.

ATHLETIC'S SPANISH TOUR 'SNAP' — 1971

ATHLETIC TEAM GROUP — 1971/72
Back: BOWIE · SHAW · OGDEN · HEATH · DOWD · CRANSTON · MULVANEY
Front: McNEILL · WOOD · WHITTLE · BRYCELAND · BEBBINGTON · CLEMENTS · FRYATT

JIM FRYATT GETS TO THE BALL BEFORE THE WORKINGTON KEEPER BURRIDGE, SEPT. '70

FRYATT'S FLYING HEADER FINDS THE NET IN A 3-1 WIN AT NORTHAMPTON — DEC. '70

1971-72

This season was, in many ways, a time for consolidation and examining the side's strengths and weaknesses in preparation for better things but at the end of it all nothing emerged, other than the fact that Athletic had established themselves as an average Third Division side. Athletic quickly discovered the team that had played so boldly to pull clear of the Fourth Division, was not quite good enough in the higher grade. Players like Jim Fryatt, transferred to Southport in November, and Tommy Bryceland, who joined St. Mirren as player/manager in January '72, heroes last season, could not re-produce the form that was so much a part of Athletic's promotion drive. The men called in to replace them, Colin Garwood and the tireless Paul Clements, did not immediately come off. On the credit side, Athletic did stiffen their defence, a master stroke of opportunism getting centre-half Dick Mulvaney on a free transfer from Blackburn Rovers, after he had been initially listed at £50,000. Mulvaney replaced another pre-season signing at centre-half, John Sleeuwenhoek, who played only twice before leaving the club.

The team could not score enough goals, relying too much on David Shaw, and although he finished the season with a good return of goals, 19 in League and Cup making him leading scorer, he could have had many more with decent support. This weakness was displayed at Boundary Park, where Athletic dropped point after point simply because they couldn't score goals. On opponents' grounds, when the emphasis was on defence, the team did well, their away record as good as anyone's in the League. In the final reckoning it was the points gained away that enabled them to finish in the respectable anonymity of 11th place on 45 points.

Both the F.A. and League Cups were again full of disappointment for Athletic. In the League Cup they had a first round win over Bury at Boundary Park, but then lost unluckily in the 2nd round at Torquay United. The F.A. Cup provided just one game, a 3-0 defeat at Chesterfield to maintain Athletic's dismal recent run in knock-out competitions. The most outstanding feature of the entire season was the emergence of a squad of young players who looked potential first team material, Ian Robins, Keith Hicks, Ian Buckley, Kevin Crumblehulme, Derek Spence and Andy Sweeney. Ian Wood with a maximum 49 points again topped the appearance charts. He had missed just one match in three seasons which was a tribute to his stamina and fitness. The average attendance at Boundary Park totalled 8,027.

ANOTHER HEADED GOAL BY FRYATT IN THE 3-1 WIN OVER DARLINGTON — JAN. '71

TEAM GROUP — 1972/73

MANAGER FRIZZELL RE-SIGNS RONNIE BLAIR — AUG. '72

Problems befell Athletic before the season started with an injury to new signing, Tony Hateley, and seemed a key factor in the dismal start that forced manager Frizzell to rewrite his script for the entire campaign.

Athletic's season had been more disappointing for its level of entertainment than its level of achievement. To finish fourth in the League table was no failure. Climbing from the 12th position they occupied last season was a fair indication of the progress the club had made. They were so well placed for so long, that it needed only a genuine strength of character over the last six weeks to achieve their avowed intention of Second Division football.

Statistically, there were factors that proved how important the final 14 match phase was to Athletic. In that time they collected only 17 points out of a possible 28, and scored just 15 goals. That gave them an average, over the final 14 games, of 1.07 goals per game. Over the initial 32 matches, the average was a much more impressive 1.78.

How much the departure of striker, David Shaw, an £80,000 transfer to West Bromwich Albion, affected the goals per game statistics was debatable, but it must have had some significance. Athletic's best run of the season came in a 20 match spell that stretched from the end of October until late February. During that time they moved up from the foot of the Third Division table, and emerged as promotion contenders.

In mid-January, they capped their tremendous surge, by securing a point at Shrewsbury, and taking over at the top of the Third Division. Sixteen hours later they were down to second place, but at least they had sampled life at the top. In late January, Athletic beat Watford 2-1 to move clear at the top of the table by two points. At that time the future looked bright indeed.

Then came disaster. In early February, Southend United visited Boundary Park and caught Athletic on a bad day, winning 1-0 to start a slide that by March 1st saw Athletic down to seventh place. Over the entire campaign, Athletic dropped a decisive 15 points at Boundary Park.

No team that sacrificed so much to opponents on its own ground had any right to expect promotion, but Athletic were close to that ambition for two reasons. Firstly, the Third Division this season consisted of very ordinary teams, all could be beaten, and all regularly were. Secondly, Athletic had an excellent away record that allowed them to pick up points to compensate for those dropped at home. Normally it is the other way round. These two factors combined to keep Athletic on the shirt-tails of the League leaders for a long time.

The vast improvement in Athletic's position this season was not reflected in the gates. Although there had been an increase in the attendances at Boundary Park, the actual average was up by less than 200 on last year. Just as there had been black spots this season, an amazing crop of injuries and the suspension by the club of Johnny Morrissey for a breach of discipline, to mention just two, there had been highlights. Notably the emergence of two youngsters, Mike Lester and Keith Hicks. The influence defender Paul Edwards had on Athletic was significant, and he was considered to be the player to build around the following season. Edwards was a £15,000 signing from Manchester United.

Once again, the F.A. and Football League Cups failed to provide Athletic with any lucrative diversion from the League campaign. In the League Cup they were dismissed by Bolton and, in the F.A. Cup, took a first round knock-out from Northern Premier League side Scarborough after a replay.

Ian Wood was an ever-present again this season, playing in all 49 League and Cup games. Keith Hicks in his first full season in League football had also been ever-present, as had Maurice Whittle. Despite missing the final 14 League games following his transfer, David Shaw was again leading scorer with 18 League and Cup goals.

A double taste of European soccer awaited Athletic at the season's close. Early May they flew to Portugal to play the Portuguese 2nd Division club 'Cintra.' Nine days after returning to England, the team jetted out to Greece where 40,000 crowds were expected when Athletic met First Division sides Salonika and P.O.A.K., before completing the tour with a game against Kala Maria.

GEORGE BEST HAS BEEN CONTACTED

by JIM WILLIAMS

ATHLETIC have been in contact with Manchester United star George Best. After a round of exhaustive inquiries, I am now firmly convinced that manager Jimmy Frizzell and club secretary Bernard Halford met Best at a Manchester boutique on Wednesday afternoon.

The talks, I understand, were carried out in the presence of Best's business manager, and Athletic went as far as offering to match the player's wages at Old T...

Until he has made some sort of peace with United, however, he is not free to express anything more than "interest" in any offers that are made to him.

The timetable of events that led up to the interview between Frizzell, Halford and Best on Wednesday — a timetable which, incidentally, is in dispute — is very complicated indeed.

ARRANGEMENTS

I gather that it all started over the week-end when the club chairman, Mr. John Lowe, decided that if Swansea City could make an offer to Best, then so could Athletic. Plans to open negotiations then set in motion and, shortly ...esday, the club secretary and ... home of Best's landlady, Mrs. ... Grove, Chorlton-cum-Hardy. ...l, was in bed at the time, but ...ade to see the player later at a ... which he owns. Best drove to ...hite Rolls Royce and there he ...e club secretary. Talks with ...s manager, went on for some ... Frizzell and Bernard Halford

... on Wednesday evening and he ...aving seen or spoken to Best ... all during that day. Frizzell ...1 told me: "Best is tied to ...nchester United and, until he ... made his peace with them, ...r is nothing that anybody can

" We had to rush through the expansion of nursery school places in time to catch George Best "

ATHLETIC'S BOARD OF DIRECTORS · 1973/74
Back: HARRY WILDE · JACK KERSHAW · FRED WHITEHEAD
Front: DICK SCHOFIELD · BILL SHORE (Chairman) · ARTHUR HUDSON (Vice-Chairman)

ATHLETIC'S PHOTO-CALL · 1973/74

1973-74

The lash of criticism that greeted Athletic's failure to clinch promotion last season, drew an immediate response from club Chairman Mr. John Lowe. "We failed by just three points after fighting for it to the last match of the season and I, along with my co-directors, are bitterly disappointed that promotion had not been achieved. We shall continue with the same aim next season and, even if we win promotion, we shall carry on afterwards and will not be satisfied until the Latics are a First Division side." Sadly, Mr. Lowe died in January 1974, and missed the successful promotion push which would have made him so proud.

Between the anxiety of a stuttering start and a nervous finish, Athletic produced a consistent spell of brilliant football to win the Third Division Championship. Athletic deserved the title. By the middle of January, they were in tenth place in the table, and trailed leaders Bristol Rovers by a seemingly irretrievable 13 points. To haul themselves back from such a position was clearly Championship form.

They started their winning run at Wrexham in mid-January, when goalkeeper, Chris Ogden, had probably the game of his life, as Latics won 2-1. They went on to beat Halifax, Bournemouth, Tranmere, Rochdale, Aldershot, Blackburn, Cambridge, Walsall and York City, before losing by the only goal of the game at Chesterfield.

In February, Atheltic signed the fleet-footed Alan Groves from Bournemouth for £10,000. His entertaining style, combined with powerful and aggressive wing play, charmed the Boundary Park faithful, and his arrival coincided with Athletic's great victory charge.

ATHLETIC'S CAPTAIN DICK MULVANEY RECEIVES THE 3RD DIVISION CHAMPIONSHIP CUP FROM SAM BOLTON, VICE-PRESIDENT OF THE FOOTBALL LEAGUE

It was an incredible run that encouraged Athletic to believe in themselves and give them confidence to befell the setbacks which overtook them in the final phase of the previous season. The team's brilliant success over Easter brought six points from three games, one of which was at rivals Bristol Rovers; it was probably that victory which gave Athletic the title.

In a week of speeches, celebration and public acclaim, a handful of words from the Athletic Vice-Chairman, Mr. Arthur Hudson, summed up best the club's achievement this season, ''Four years ago when we were bottom of the Fourth Division, we were a joke and commonly referred to as Oldham pathetic. Now we can meet our public with heads held high. We have won back our pride and self-respect and are Oldham Athletic again.''

Athletic received the Championship cup from Mr. Sam Bolton, Vice-President of the Football League at a civic reception at Oldham Town Hall on Tuesday, May 7th 1974.

The whole senior squad deserved credit for the achievement, because in the final reckoning it was essentially a team triumph. The decision to appoint Andy Lochhead, a £15,000 signing from Aston Villa, as team captain was an inspired move. He had the ability to motivate those around him, even when not playing well

COLIN GARWOOD'S 2ND AND DECISIVE GOAL, v. BRISTOL ROVERS AT EASTVILLE, APRIL '74

himself. Of all the skippers this season—Edwards, Mulvaney and Wood had turns leading the side—Lochhead was the most influential. Colin Garwood emerged as one of the most deadly strikers in the Third Division, and finished top scorer with 17 goals in League and Cup.

Athletic's dismal League Cup run continued, losing to Bury 3-2 after a 0-0 scoreline at Gigg Lane. They fared better in the F.A. Cup with first and second round wins over non-League Formby and Third Division Halifax. The third round witnessed a marathon with Cambridge United. The first game at the Abbey Stadium took place during the power crisis of 1974, and was the first ever Sunday fixture played between first class clubs. This 2-2 draw was contested on January 6th. After a replay scoreline of 3-3, Athletic finally settled the tie 2-1 on the neutral ground of Leicester City's Filbert Street. Burnley put paid to any serious Cup aspirations at Boundary Park, winning 4-1 before a crowd of 22,350.

Proving that success does pay in football, Athletic were watched by 108,000 more fans this season that last, with an average at Boundary Park of 10,356. Ian Wood, normally an ever present, missed the final two games through injury, enabling George McVite and Maurice Whittle to take the appearance honours with a 54 maximum in all competitions.

TRIUMPHANT ATHLETIC AFTER CLINCHING THE 3RD DIVISION CHAMPIONSHIP WITH A 0-0 DRAW AT PLYMOUTH — MAY '74

COLIN GARWOOD SHOOTS FOR GOAL — v. HEREFORD UTD, MARCH '74

GARWOOD SIDE-FOOTS ATHLETIC INTO A 1-0 LEAD AT SOUTHPORT — APRIL '74

ANDY LOCHHEAD SCORES IN THE 3-1 WIN OVER ROCHDALE — FEB. '74

ALAN GROVES
HIS ARRIVAL AT BOUNDARY PARK COINCIDED WITH ATHLETIC'S
GREAT VICTORY CHARGE, FEB. '74

RONNIE BLAIR CELEBRATES A GOAL IN A 4-0 WIN OVER SHEFFIELD UNITED IN THE TEXACO CUP — AUG. '74

1974-75

It was question time at Boundary Park. The bright new paint, the lush, fresh turf, the sharp-edged terracing and the promise of new seats in the main stand, all gave way to the biggest poser Athletic had faced in recent seasons. How would they fare against the elite of the Second Division? Looked at logically, the pre-season Texaco Cup matches proved very little. Athletic did not play well in the tournament, and it was difficult to judge just how seriously the opposition, which included Sheffield United and Manchester City, treated the competition.

A solid start to the season saw four wins, two draws and two defeats over the first two months of the campaign, with crowds hovering around the 13,000 mark at Boundary Park. But Athletic were stalked by disaster from October onwards, turning this season into one long battle for survival. The team finally defied the prophets of doom by clinging on to Second Division status with three points to spare, and because survival was always the ambition behind Athletic's campaign, the season had to be viewed as a success, finishing in 18th position on 35 points.

Survival would probably not have been achieved without an inspired mid-season transfer deal that brought Les Chapman and David Holt to Boundary Park in place of Colin Garwood and Tony Bailey. Chapman's contribution to the final months of the season was crucial. His commitment lifted the team, and gave them the extra competitive edge which finally took them to safety. Holt also played a

LES CHAPMAN

DAVID HOLT

199

ATHLETIC'S IAN ROBINS VOLLEY'S ATHLETIC'S FIRST GOAL PAST THE DESPAIR
OLD TRA

... OF MANCHESTER UNITED'S GREENOFF AND BUCHAN IN LATICS 3-2 DEFEAT AT
...ARCH '75

decisive part, with Paul Edwards flitting in and out of the side, Holt was given a busy time in a defence which proved far better than that of any of their fellow strugglers. Athletic's front line seldom looked the part. The meagre goals return confirmed where the weakness lay. Ian Robins with nine goals, and Alan Young with seven, bore the brunt of the attacking responsibility.

Those early weeks of the season, with Athletic crushing First Division Sheffield United 4-0 in the Texaco Cup, and then beating Sheffield Wednesday and Bristol City in League matches at Boundary Park, gave a promise which was never fulfilled. The team which carried Athletic to the Third Division Championship looked good enough to contest at least a top ten place in Division Two, but the bubble burst in mid-October, when Athletic lost 3-2 to York City at Boundary Park. At that time, Athletic were tenth in the table, but the slide towards the danger zone began with that defeat. There were highlights after that. Athletic shared the points in thrilling games with Norwich and Sunderland, and then, in the highlight of the season, a Maurice Whittle penalty sunk Manchester United 1-0 in a Boxing Day clash at a packed Boundary Park.

Athletic's failure to win a single away fixture eroded any ground gained by a reasonable home record. The best away performance came at Sunderland over Easter. Athletic, two goals down and apparently destined for a heavy defeat, fought back to earn a point. The good work at Roker Park was undone in typical fashion, as they lost 1-0 to a modest Hull City team at Boundary Park on Good Friday. Athletic lost both their Cup matches at the first time of asking. In the League Cup, a 2-0 defeat at Bury, and in the F.A.Cup, a 3-0 reversal at Villa Park.

Said manager Frizzell, ''We have learned so much this year, but our biggest lesson has been that we have to become consistent if we are to avoid a similar struggle next season, but we have once and for all I hope, laid the spectre of George Hardwick's team, which went straight back down to Division Three after just one season. It has haunted us for months, but I think we have seen the last of it now''.

Goalkeeper Chris Ogden was the only player to appear in all senior matches this season. His run of consistency carried him through all 44 League and Cup games, two more than his closest rival, Ian Wood. The average attendance at Boundary Park was 13,248, but with the club's pre-season finances geared to average home crowds of 15,000, meant the club was losing money.

MAURICE WHITTLE

ALAN GROVES SCORES ATHLETIC'S 2ND GOAL IN THE 2-0 WIN OVER NOTTINGHAM FOREST — FEB. '75

IAN WOOD CLEARS A SUNDERLAND ATTACK IN THE 2-0 F.A. CUP 3RD ROUND DEFEAT AT ROKER PARK — JANUARY '76

1975-76

Sixty-six to one outsiders for the Second Division Championship, Athletic were joint favourites with York City for relegation to Division Three, but manager Jimmy Frizzell took no heed of the bookmakers' gloomy prediction, and forecast a comfortable mid-table position for his side at the end of the season. On paper Athletic's squad looked to have the makings of a stumbling block rather than a chopping block for Second Division opposition. Athletic, who had struggled to hold onto Second Division status the previous season, started this new campaign with no new players. The board could not afford to give manager Frizzell the necessary cash backing, although new players were needed. In October, David Shaw re-signed for Athletic from West Brom on a free transfer, and although not fully fit, he scored 13 times in thirty outings to finish top scorer.

From the first 26 League matches, the team collected 30 points and climbed to fifth in the table. From the final 16 games, they mustered only eight points and slumped to sixth from bottom. From talk of promotion in the middle of January, Athletic found themselves, by the start of April, fighting the threat of relegation. The vast majority of the players on Athletic's books had only the Third and Fourth Divisions inscribed on their pedigree. They did well to lift Athletic from Division Four, and even better to hoist them from Division Three, and their early season form this time had been inspired. The bubble burst in mid-January, exhausted by their efforts, they slipped back to their own true level.

George McVitie was sold to Carlisle and not replaced, George Jones left to join Halifax without replacment. Without McVitie and Jones, Frizzell did not have enough scope for team changes. Players out of form were guaranteed a team place because there was no one else to put in. Athletic were further hit by the loss, through injury, of the promising striker Alan Young, and suddenly Athletic were

DAVID SHAW SCORES ATHLETIC'S SECOND GOAL IN A 3-0 WIN AT CHELSEA — JANUARY '76

three forwards short, and they couldn't cope. From then on, the only way the team could go was down, and down they went. After a run of eleven games without a victory, Athletic finally broke the sequence with a 5-2 home win over Portsmouth, which put paid to the fast growing fears of relegation, but Latics ended the campaign by taking only one point from the final four matches to finish 17th in Division Two with 38 points.

Problems over money, which first came to the surface before a ball had been kicked this season, raised its head again. Alan Groves, already on the transfer list at his own request, brought cash problems back into the limelight with a plea for a higher basic wage. There were other rumblings behind the scenes, and Athletic finished the season with a major pay revolt on their hands.

Although Athletic were beaten 2-0 in the second round of the League Cup by Aston Villa, they scored six times over the two legs of the first round against Workington, George Jones netting a hat-trick at Boundary Park. Since the League Cup competition started in 1960, Athletic had never progressed beyond the second round. In fifteen tournaments they had taken ten first round defeats, and gone out five times in the second round; it was one of the worst League Cup records in the country. The one F.A.Cup tie, at Sunderland, ended in a 2-0 win for the home team.

No player appeared in all the club's 56 League and Cup games. Les Chapman came closest with 45, and there were four other players with 40 or more games. Ian Wood broke the club's all time appearance record at Southampton on January 31st. It was his 370th appearance and beat a record set back in 1921 by David Wilson. Large increases in admission charges, coupled with the club's failure to make any significant signings, lopped nearly 55,000 off the Boundary park attendances this season. The average gate for home games was down to 10,191.

GROVES SCORES IN THE 5-2 DEFEAT OF PORTSMOUTH — APRIL '76

PHOTO-CALL · 1976/77

Back: HURST · SHAW · OGDEN · HOLT · PLATT · BLAIR · IRVINE

Middle: FRIZZELL (Manager) · JAY (Physio) · DUNGWORTH · BRANAGAN · EDWARDS · YOUNG · HALOM · HICKS · GROVES · LOCHHEAD

Front: CARROLL · WHITTLE · CHAPMAN · ROBINS · BELL · WOOD · VALENTINE

LIVERPOOL 3, ATHLETIC 1, F.A. CUP 5TH ROUND AT ANFIELD
ATHLETIC'S IAN WOOD CLEARS FROM KEVIN KEEGAN — FEB. '77

LIVERPOOL'S JOEY JONES AND ATHLETIC'S DAVID SHAW IN A HEADING DUAL —
F.A. CUP 5TH ROUND — FEB. '77

It was hoped Athletic's close-season signings would give the side a balance and strength-in-depth they had not possessed since promotion to Division Two. Jimmy Frizzell, now the longest-serving manager in Division Two, after seven years and five months in the chair, was looking for players who would "die for the cause of Oldham Athletic." John Hurst, a free signing from Everton, brought all the qualities of an experienced First Division defender to Boundary Park. Vic Halom, a £25,000 signing from Sunderland, was a well-built and aggressive striker, and David Irving was a free transfer signing from Everton, were he had been the leading scorer in their Central League side. Club Chairman, Mr. Harry Wilde, renewed the declaration of intent to bring First Division football to Boundary Park, "Since moving from the Third Division, we have had our sights set upon Division One. That remains our ambition and our objective."

This turned out to be a campaign of no real progress in Second Division terms. The hope and optimism which shone through to February, was suddenly gone during the final three months of the season. A string of disasters saw Athletic lose 12 times, and plunge into the relegation-zone in late April. It was difficult to understand how an Athletic side, so sharp and positive over the first six months, could lose its way so dramatically.

Frizzell's three signings had been successful. Vic Halom finished leading scorer with 23 goals, Hurst emerged as a marvellous professional, and Irving showed genuine potential, but the manager accepted that he should shoulder a lot of the blame for his team's decline during the final few months. "There is no point in hiding behind the players. The responsibility for the decline is collective, and I have to take my share," said Frizzell.

That decline meant that Athletic made no progress at all in League terms. They finished the campaign with 38 points, exactly the same number as last time. The League position was better, finishing 13th, but the real significance lay in Athletic's failure to pass last season's points total.

CARL VALENTINE SCORES ONE OF ATHLETIC'S THREE GOALS IN A 3-1 F.A. CUP VICTORY OVER NORTHWICH VICTORIA AT MAINE ROAD — JANUARY '77

The F.A. Cup was kinder to Athletic, with wins over Plymouth and non-League Northwich Victoria. The big Cup test was at Liverpool, where Athletic played very well despite finishing on the wrong end of a 3-1 scoreline.

On the credit side, this season saw the emergence of Carl Valentine as a player of great potential, and Gary Hoolickin made his debut in the final match of the season as a sign that he also was on the fringe of the first team squad. Les Chapman was the only player to have appeared in all the club's senior matches. Chapman, who missed only one game last season, was clearly the most consistent competitor at Boundary Park at this moment. Athletic's average Boundary Park attendance was a disappointing 9,998.

PHIL NEALE SCORES LIVERPOOL'S THIRD GOAL FROM THE PENALTY SPOT IN THE
F.A. CUP 5TH ROUND TIE WITH ATHLETIC AT ANFIELD — FEB '77
(INSET) WOOD'S TACKLE ON HEIGHWAY GIVES AWAY THE PENALTY

1977-78

Jimmy Frizzell, starting his seventh full season as manager of Athletic, accepted that this could be his toughest challenge yet at Boundary Park: "There is no doubt in my mind that the Second Division this season is a lot tougher than last. It is probably the most competitive Second Division in which we have played". But Frizzell believed, despite the poor showings in the pre-season Anglo-Scottish Cup ties, that his team would hold their own.

Athletic signed ex-Evertonian Mike Bernard in July for £10,000 and his midfield experience, it was hoped, would bring the best out of Graham Bell and Les Chapman, Bernard's arrival coincided with the transfer of Ian Robins to Bury. In October, Steve Taylor signed from Bolton for £38,000, and his presence certainly pepped up the Latics forward line, being the only player to score a goal in his first seven games. Rebel, Alan Groves, finally had his wish to leave Athletic in November, signing for Blackpool with the promise of First Division football. They were relegated to Division Three!

The season glowed with promise after a faltering start, and finished disappointingly, as Athletic stuttered through the final 16 games to produce only two victories. In statistical terms, Athletic made progress by finishing in 8th place in Division Two. Their total of 42 points was the best since 1933-34 when they finished with 44.

In mid-November, with the team third from bottom of the table with 12 points from 16 games, they won at Mansfield Town, and catapulted through a run of 12 League games without defeat. Significantly, they included in this sequence six away matches of which four were won. The side looked to have finally come to terms with life in the Second Division. By late January, with the weather taking huge bites out of the League programme, Athletic had battled to sixth in the table, and were only four points adrift of the promotion group. A terrible toll of late season injuries decimated the playing staff, already too thin, and so disappointment followed hot on the heels of delight, with Athletic papering over the cracks in the team, with players short of experience playing out time to the season's end.

VIC HALOM'S HEADER DRIFTS WIDE OF THE NOTTS COUNTY GOAL DURING ATHLETIC'S 2-1 VICTORY — OCT '77

The season had its fair share of turning points. There was the arrival, and departure, of Mike Bernard, the transfer of Alan Groves to Blackpool, the arrival of Steve Taylor and Steve Gardner, and major injury blows to Vic Halom, Graham Bell and Ronnie Blair. Athletic manager, Jimmy Frizzell, admitted that he had been under more personal pressure this season, than at any other time in his managerial career. Looking back to the depressing days of November and December, Frizzell said, "The pressure was terrible, largely because there was nothing we could do about it at the time. We were playing some marvellous football but not putting the ball in the net, and all the results were going wrong". Frizzell saw the signing of Steve Taylor as the turning point, his 21 goals in 34 games being the decisive factor in the change of the club's fortunes.

After a marathon 1st round League Cup tie with Brighton, which went to a 2nd replay at Leicester's Filbert Street before Athletic won 2-1 in front of a paltry 1,840

spectators, Oldham lost 2-0 at Hull in round 2. They lost 2-1 in the F.A.Cup to Luton, after a commendable 1-1 draw at Kenilworth Road.

For the second successive year, the energetic Les Chapman topped Athletic's appearance list, playing 44 times out of a possible 48 League and Cup matches. The most encouraging signs this year were the number of young players creeping into the team. Steve Edwards, Mark Hilton and Paul Heaton all making their League debuts. Despite enjoying their best League position for almost 40 years, Athletic suffered a slight drop in League attendances at Boundary Park. The average fell from 9,998 last year to 9,456 this time.

ATHLETIC'S STEVE TAYLOR SCORES AGAINST SPURS IN A 1-1 DRAW — MARCH '78 (INSET) VALENTINE AND TAYLOR INTERVIEWED BY PAUL DOHERTY OF GRANADA T.V.

STEVE TAYLOR FAILS TO REACH A CROSS FROM HALOM IN THE 2-0 WIN OVER BURNLEY, DEC '77.

1978-79

The death of Alan Groves at the age of 29 was a tragic loss to football, and especially to followers of Oldham Athletic, who had grown to appreciate his talents more than anyone else. A crowd of 4,396 saw Athletic meet Blackpool in a benefit match for his dependants on July 29th 1978.

Athletic's manager, Jimmy Frizzell, turned down the chance of an £80,000 five year contract with Walsall to stay with Athletic. The club responded by awarding Frizzell a pay rise, but no increase in the length of his contract which had two years to run. A club spokesman said, "A four year contract is a four year contract, and we can't be changing it or adding to it every year. If we do we are simply playing ducks and drakes with documentation". He continued, "The Board is unanimously agreed that we do not want Jimmy Frizzell to leave. We are impressed with his record here, and we know that he is the best man for the job". Jimmy and his team finished with an end of season dogfight to avoid relegation, when they should have been pushing to beat the previous season's best Second Division points total.

Athletic were on course in November for as good a season as, if not better than, 1977-78. When they beat Cardiff 2-1 at home on November 18th, they had 15 points from 15 games, but had to wait until April 13th, five months, for another home League win when they thrashed Blackburn Rovers 5-0. It had been an away success at Blackburn in mid-March that had put Athletic on the road to recovery after going 12 matches without a League win. From Easter onwards Athletic turned in the sort of form that promotion candidates would have been proud of. From their last nine matches they took 14 points to stay up.

ALAN YOUNG (left), AND SIMON STAINROD A £60,000 SIGNING FROM SHEFFIELD UTD.

On the Cup front, Athletic enjoyed a good Cup run in the Anglo-Scottish Tournament, losing to Burnley in the two legged final, and performed creditably against Nottingham Forest in the League Cup second round. Held 0-0 at home they did well in the replay, although they lost 4-2. There was a brief flirtation with F.A. Cup glory surprisingly at the time when League form was suspect. A fortunate 3rd round win at snow-bound Stoke City, was followed by a tremendous 3-1 result over Leicester at Boundary Park, Alan Young netting a hat-trick. Due to fixture congestion, Athletic were forced to play their 5th round tie with Spurs just 2 days later, tired legs contributing to a 1-0 defeat at Boundary Park. It was a pity Athletic couldn't pull it off to earn a glamorous 6th round date with Manchester United.

Throughout the closing weeks there had been moments of great hope for Athletic. Simon Stainrod, a late season signing from Sheffield United, showed super skills, Steve Edwards produced determined left-back performances, and there emerged Jim Steel, Tim Jordan, Paul Heaton and Mark Hilton as players of tremendous promise, now with greater confidence and experience.

Alan Young dominated Athletic's goal charts, but the fact he scored 14 in forty two games, almost three times more than any one else, indicated where the side toiled. For the third successive season, Les Chapman topped the appearances with a maximum 47 before a free transfer took him to Stockport County. In all, Chapman had played 267 times for Athletic, a great club man. Goalkeeper Peter 'Barabas' McDonnell matched Chapman for appearances this year, playing the majority of games with a cartilage injury. Ronnie Blair was awarded a testimonial, a reward for ten years of loyalty, versatility and dependability. Bolton's manager and ex-Athletic player Ian Greaves said of Blair, "It would be a manager's paradise to have eleven players as totally committed as Ronnie". A major transfer occured in February '79, when Vancouver Whitecaps of the North American Football League, paid Athletic a healthy £86,000 for young winger, Carl Valentine, with a clause allowing him to return to Boundary Park on loan the following year.

ST. MIRREN v. ATHLETIC·ANGLO SCOTTISH CUP SEMI-FINAL, 2ND LEG·OCT '78
ATHLETIC'S PLAYERS CELEBRATE A WIN ON PENALTY KICKS

REFEREE KEITH HACKETT BOOKS ATHLETIC'S YOUNG v. WREXHAM — APRIL '79

ALAN YOUNG SCORES HIS 2ND GOAL IN A 3-1 F.A. CUP 4TH ROUND WIN OVER
LEICESTER CITY — FEB '79

1979-80

Walter Griffiths, the longest serving administrator in the Football League, and general manager/company secretary at Athletic for six years announced his retirement pre-season. Team manager Frizzell admitted to being worried and frustrated at the way pre-season preparations had gone, but he needn't have bothered as Athletic, after a patchy start, played some excellent football, especially after record signing, Kenny Clements, £200,000 from Manchester City, had settled into the heart of the defence in September. In early December, Athletic signed their first overseas player, Ryszard Kowenicki joining the club from Polish side, Widzew Lódź for £12,000, a price that proved to be a bargain.

The vital ingredient Athletic lacked this season was consistency, no matter which eleven players turned out. They lost at Boundary Park to Shrewsbury Town, Fulham, Cardiff City and Wrexham, yet defeated fancied teams like Birmingham City, Chelsea, Sunderland and Newcastle United. Athletic had to learn to treat all opposition alike and not kid themselves there were any easy games. A goalkeeping blunder gave Coventry City a 1-0 win at Boundary Park in the F.A.Cup 3rd round, and Athletic bowed out of the League Cup yet again in round one, losing 4-3 on aggregate to Northampton Town.

Ian Wood was given a free transfer by Athletic ending his 14 years' association with the club, but he once again topped the appearance charts, along with Simon Stainrod, playing 39 out of a possible forty-five League and Cup games. Consistency had been Wood's hallmark over the years, and it was little wonder that he established a club record of 525 League appearances (eight as sub), a total which, in days of freedom-of-contract, will probably never be bettered.

Simon Stainrod finished the season as Athletic's leading goalscorer with 11 from 39 matches. He was run close by young Scotsman, Jim Steel, who hit 10 in 36 games. Athletic's average home League attendance showed a slight increase on last season, but still came nowhere near to making the club self-sufficient on attendances alone. They still relied heavily on lotteries and other fund-raising efforts.

STAINROD SCORES DURING A 3-2 WIN OVER PRESTON — SEPT '79

ATHLETIC'S FIRST OVERSEAS SIGNING, POLISHMAN RYSZARD KOWENICKI — A
£12.000 TRANSFER FROM WIDZEW LÓDŹ.

Manager Jimmy Frizzell sounded a defiant note to the bookmakers who reckoned Athletic were prime candidates, yet again, for relegation. "It annoys me intensely when people outside Lancashire regard Oldham as a dirty little mill town", said Frizzell, "though I am a Scot, I have lived here for 20 years, and I don't like anyone criticising the place, whether it is this club, the Rugby League club, or our local cricket sides. I don't care what the bookmakers say, we can look forward to this season with as much optimism as any other side, and more than some"

Athletic were forced to install crowd control fencing under the Safety of Sports Grounds legislation. The fencing, on all sides of the ground, was part of a £250,000 scheme to upgrade Boundary Park to the required standard. They also became only the second club in Division Two to install undersoil heating with the help of local business sponsorship and lottery money. The 'Meltaway' under-pitch soil-warming system was installed by a Swedish company at an approximate cost of £60,000.

RODGER WYLDE

Athletic's major pre-season signing was Paul Futcher, a £150,000 buy from Luton Town. His vision and aggression, it was hoped, would add a new dimension to the team's midfield which, with the flair and goal-scoring ability of Ryszard Kowenicki and Paul Atkinson, looked capable of holding its own in Division Two.

Hold their own they did, but this season had a surprising new twist. It was Athletic's normally excellent home record which deteriorated, while their away form was perfectly

PAUL FUTCHER

flourish with only one home defeat, which saved the season. The side finished 8th from bottom on 39 points, only 11 points behind promoted Swansea, and dropped 19 points at Boundary Park, the worst home record since promotion. Rodger Wilde did well to finish with twelve goals, and should have been among the Division's leading scorers; instead he lost form and confidence, as did the team, as early season form evaporated.

The £250,000 sale of Simon Stainrod to Queens Park Rangers was an unpopular move at the time, for the entertaining goalscorer was a crowd-puller and potential match winner. From an attendance viewpoint, Stainrod's departure and the run of poor form contrived to send gate figures plunging to a 6,502 average. Manager Frizzell invested £70,000 of the Stainrod transfer cash on Roger Palmer in November 1980.

The turn of the year, and the introduction of fresh young players, was a turning point in putting the team back on the rails, and the appearance of 17-year-old Darren McDonough as a prospect for the future was one of the highlights.

Athletic departed both Cup competitions at the first hurdle. An unlucky defeat by Bournemouth in the League Cup was followed by an F.A.Cup 3rd round defeat by League newcomers Wimbledon.

Scoring goals was the major problem this season, totalling only 42 in 46 League and Cup matches, and failing to register a score on twenty occasions. Rodger Wylde came good at the end of the season, his seven goals in the final nine matches proving vital in Athletic's relegation struggle. Wylde was top scorer with 12, all in the League. Ronnie Blair, surprisingly given a free transfer by the club, topped the appearance charts with 46 League and Cup outings, the only 100 per cent record this season.

A ROGER PALMER GOAL v. SHREWSBURY TOWN — MARCH '81

MARTIN NUTTALL SCORES FOR LATICS IN A 2-0 VICTORY AT CARDIFF CITY — JAN '81.

ROGER PALMER SCORES, SAME FIXTURE

PHOTO CALL · OLDHAM ATHLETIC · 1981/82

1981-82

This season saw one of the youngest first team squads ever to represent the club. Five of the 15 strong squad on duty for the pre-season friendlies was aged 20 or under, and the average age was just 22. With many of the older, established players having left the club over the previous couple of years, goalkeeper Peter McDonnell found himself the veteran at the age of 28. A dash of experience was added by the likes of Kenny Clements, Rodger Wylde, Paul Futcher, and new club captain, Ged Keegan, all in their mid-twenties, but basically it was a youthful and largely unproven panel of players for what promised to be a hard, keenly-contested Second Division.

Club Chairman, Mr. Harry Wilde, insisted the only way forward for Athletic, particularly when money was in such short supply, was through a flourishing youth policy. "If you can't buy players, which doesn't guarantee success anyway, you have to find and mould them yourself", Mr. Wilde stated.

This youthful squad gave Athletic their most successful season in the Second Division for four years, and could so easily have gone down in the record books as the season they made the breakthrough to Division One. Their final position of 11th was bettered only in 1977-78 when they finished 8th with 42 points. In terms of points gained, this season was, in fact, their best. Under the old two points for a win system, Athletic would have had 44.

Athletic's record up to December was excellent. They were the last team in the entire Football League to lose their unbeaten record, which went at Charlton in October in a 3-1 defeat. They were the only team in the Second Division to score in every League match up to November 21st, when Crystal Palace held them 0-0 at Boundary Park. In November they became the first team to keep a clean sheet on Q.P.R.'s new artificial pitch when they earned a 0-0 draw. When they beat Grimsby Town 3-1 at home on December 5th, Athletic reached their highest League position since March 1930, second place in Division Two.

RODGER WYLDE SCORES AGAINST NEWCASTLE IN A 3-1 WIN AT BOUNDARY PARK — OCT '81

Right through until February 27th, when they lost 2-0 at Champions-to-be Luton Town, Athletic were in with a chance of promotion, then injuries to key players began to take their toll as did mounting problems over players being suspended.

Athletic needed strength-in-depth and were found lacking. Their supply of goals dried up, only 11 in 18 matches from Boxing Day, when their unbeaten home record was shattered 3-0 by Blackburn, to April when they slumped 4-0 at Crystal Palace. Only two wins in that period set Athletic on the path down the Division, and as fast as their promotion hopes receded, so did support. It was Athletic's inability to take maximum points at Boundary Park which cost them dear. Although beaten only three times at home, they dropped another 18 points in nine home draws. Had they won five more home matches, Athletic could have been promoted.

Youngsters like Darron McDonough and John Ryan served the club well, and we had a glimpse later on in the campaign of a few more teenagers who would add to the first team squad's strength: John Bowden, Dougie Anderson and Andy Goram. Athletic's excellent youth policy, and the board's decision to push youngsters into senior action early, would reap its rewards.

Athletic progressed beyond round 2 of the League Cup for the first time this season. After wins over Bolton and Newport, they lost 4-1 on aggregate to Fulham.

The F.A.Cup saw a disappointing 3rd round loss at Gillingham. Club captain Ged Keegan, voted Player of the Year by supporters, made more appearances than any other player, featuring in 47 of the possible 49 League and Cup matches. Rodger Wilde was once again top scorer with 17 League and Cup goals. Despite recording their worst attendance since promotion, a 2,904 crowd against Charlton, Athletic managed to increase their average League gate from 6,502 to 7,027.

Manager Jimmy Frizzell, believed he could exploit the free transfer market to give his squad the added strength-in-depth they needed for the coming season. However, on June 14th 1982 the football world was rocked at the news that Mr. Frizzell had been sacked after 22 years as player and manager. A club spokesman said,"The board has decided to terminate the manager's employment. The two years remaining on his contract will be honoured along with his testimonial arrangements. There is no particular reason for our decision, but we do feel that the club needs a new challenge, and people coming through the turnstyles. We are hoping for a new impetus throughout the club". Mr. Frizzell remained tight-lipped, offering a diplomatic, "No comment".

ROGER PALMER'S SHOT IS HANDLED BY LEICESTER CITY'S KELLY (4) ENABLING WYLDE TO EQUALISE FROM THE PENALTY SHOT IN A 1-1 DRAW — DEC '81

ATHLETIC CELEBRATE A GOAL AT ROTHERHAM — OCT '81

ROGER WYLDE (7) SHOOTS WIDE OF THE BARNSLEY GOAL IN A 3-1 DEFEAT

1982-83

Thirty-three-year-old Joe Royle, whose playing career was ended the previous season by injury, was confirmed as the new Boundary Park boss on Wednesday July 14th 1982. Chairman, Mr. Harry Wilde said, "From a list of 30 applicants we got down to three, and Joe was a unanimous choice. From our point of view it is a marvellous signing. We are very impressed with him and we are sure he will do a great job". Royle replied,"I am delighted to be at Boundary Park, because this is a job which offers an excellent chance for success. From what I saw of Oldham last season I am optimistic. If we can put out a winning team and an attractive team, I am sure we can bring back supporters". Royle continued, "Although I am a novice as a manager, I am not too proud to ask for advice from the people in the game who I respect, and I am sure that we can make a good job of things at Oldham".

Royle may have been new to the world of soccer management, but it didn't take him long to spot that Athletic needed strengthening in key positions if they were to sustain a genuine promotion push, but the Athletic board made it clear that they couldn't raise money to add the missing pieces to the promotion jig-saw. In fact Royle found himself under pressure to sell players just to keep the club ticking over.

Boardroom politics induced Mr. Harry Wilde to resign mid-September after eight years as Chairman, and thirteen years as a director. The new Chairman was Mr.Ian Stott, who had been on the board since 1974. Athletic had a much needed cash injection in November when the club's major shareholders and long-time associates, J.W.Lees Brewery, bought the Boundary club and sports hall complex, discharged the club's bank overdraft, loans and other debts, and breathed an air of hope and optimism into the club.

NEW MANAGER JOE ROYLE ARRIVES AT BOUNDARY PARK — JULY '82

Royle's first signing as a manager was goalkeeper, Martin Hodge, on loan from Everton, but after only four games for Athletic, he returned to Goodison Park, allowing teenager Andy Goram to take his first steps to stardom.

Athletic's record of ten home draws, and only eight victories was not good enough to sustain a promotion challenge. They finished only nine points behind promoted Leicester City, but squandered as many, if not more, points at Boundary Park. Only that comparatively poor home record stood between Athletic and the First Division. That criticism apart, Athletic played some of their most attractive football, home and away, since promotion. They recorded their highest Second Division position, seventh. They scored more goals, 64, and achieved their best points total, 61, which translated to the old two-points-for-a-win system still came out on top with 47.

They made their usual early exit from the Cup competitions. Losing to Gillingham in the League Cup, and to Fulham in the F.A.Cup, but manager Joe Royle could still feel rightly proud of his first season's achievements since taking over from Jimmy Frizzell.

Midfield players, Roger Palmer and Paul Atkinson, were the only men to boast a 100 per cent appearance record, playing in all 45 League and Cup matches. Rodger Wylde topped Athletic's scoring charts for the third season in a row, with 19 goals, all in the League, and Roger Palmer made a valuable contribution from midfield, notching 15 goals. Paul Futcher, Steve Edwards and Jim Steel were all transferred during the season.

GED KEEGAN'S FIERCE VOLLEY HITS THE CHELSEA BAR IN A 0-0 DRAW — APRIL '81

WYLDE'S HEADER GOES CLOSE v. SHREWSBURY TOWN — AUG '82

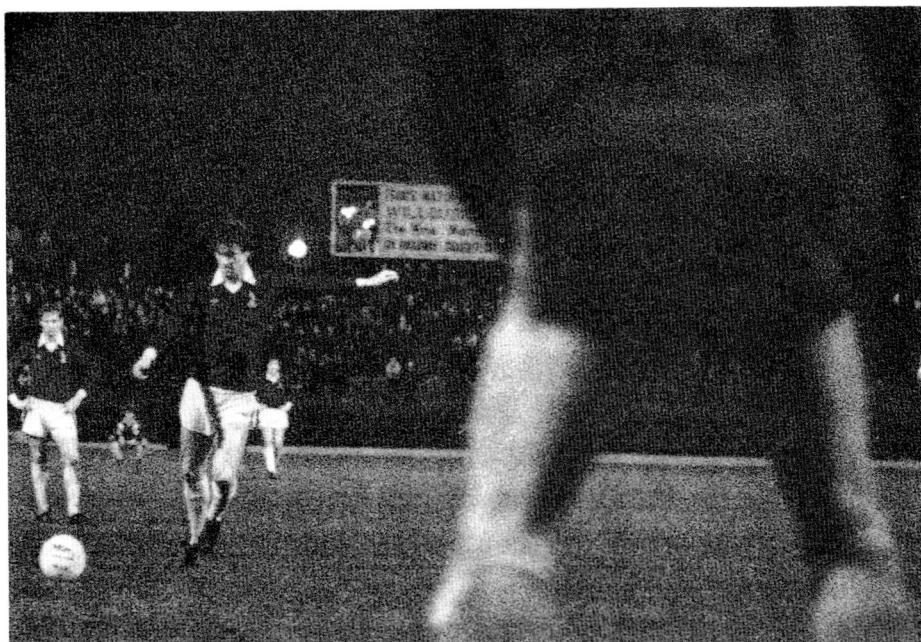

A RODGER WYLDE PENALTY HELPS ATHLETIC TO A 3-1 WIN OVER GRIMSBY — DEC. '81

JOE ROYLE SIGNS ON MARTIN BUCHAN — AUG '83

NICK SINCLAIR SCORES A RARE GOAL v. ROTHERHAM — JAN '83

1983-84

Martin Buchan's free transfer from Manchester United, it was hoped, would add prestige and class to what was still basically a young squad. Buchan's signing had overshadowed Athletic's other team-building activities during the close season. The departure of three popular players in John Ryan, Paul Atkinson and Rodger Wylde left many supporters unhappy, but Athletic's new recruits, it was hoped, would quickly become favourites of the Boundary Park crowd. The fans who insisted on a 'big name' signing got their wish with Buchan, but Derrick Parker and the diminutive Mark Ward looked equally capable of making valuable contributions. However the team struggled this term, and escaped relegation by the skin of their teeth. Athletic scored only 45 League goals, and suffered 21 defeats, finishing with a points total of 47, five more than Derby County who occupied the third relegation place.

Athletic were hampered from the start, as injuries took a devastating toll, Royle struggling to field the same team in successive matches. There were additional problems, with newcomers Derrick Parker and Joe McBride struggling to settle in. It was all reflected in away performances, with Athletic managing only three wins and two draws in 21 attempts.

Having to use four different goalkeepers, Andy Goram, Brian Parkin the on-loan Mark Grew and Jeff Wealands, and twelve players in various defensive combinations, left the team lacking stability at the back, as underlined by a dreadful goals-against total of 73. They improved their home record through collecting 36 points as opposed to 34 the previous campaign. The emergence of promising youngsters like Mark Ward, Bob Colville, Steve Bullock and Andy Hodkinson, now with Second Division experience, would strengthen next season's squad.

NEW SIGNING JOE McBRIDE SCORES HIS FIRST GOAL FOR LATICS AT DERBY COUNTY
IN A 2-2 DRAW — SEPT '83

After a first round victory over Stockport, Athletic again failed to progress beyond the second round of the League Cup, losing 3-1 at Wimbledon. The F.A.Cup was another disappointment, Oldham going down 3-1 at Shrewsbury Town in round 3.

Late season, Athletic snapped up striker Mike Quinn from Stockport County for £52,000, and great things were hoped of him. Mark Ward ended his first season in League football by matching Roger Palmer's 100 per cent appearance record for Athletic in 46 League and Cup games. Roger Palmer kept up his splendid record, scoring 14 League and Cup goals, followed by David Cross, who scored seven times in 21 matches. His goals in November and December were vital in the relegation fight, before his return to the North American Football League. Athletic's average home League attendance dropped from 6,961 to 6,027 this season, despite the bonus of a 20,320 crowd against Manchester City. Without the City attendance, the average would have been only 5,312.

MICK QUINN ARRIVES AT BOUNDARY PARK

JOE ROYLE INTRODUCES JOE McBRIDE TO A SLICE OF OLDHAM WEATHER

GOALKEEPER GORAM LEAVES THE FIELD INJURED, BLACKBURN — OCT '83

MARK WARD IN ACTION AGAINST BRIGHTON — AUG '83

A ROGER PALMER GOAL v. CARLISLE — OCT '83

JOE ROYLE AND HIS PLAYERS (PLUS PICCADILLY RADIO D.J. MIKE SWEENEY) LISTEN TO THE F.A. CUP 4TH ROUND DRAW — JAN '85

The current betting list showed Athletic 100-1 outsiders for the Second Division Championship. Together with Cardiff City on the same odds, they were favourites for relegation, and prompted Manager Joe Royle to insist, "Those odds are an insult and dictated by money. If all our supporters put money on us it still wouldn't have much effect on the betting, but it does make us all even more determined to prove the bookies wrong".

Royle believed that the Second Division title race was as wide open as ever and that, granted a relatively injury-free campaign, Athletic could match any of their rivals. "Last season was very much a transitional phase after losing key players, trying to settle in newcomers and being badly hit by injuries. But we still have a strong squad, on paper at least", said Royle. Athletic's only summer recruit was free transfer man Willie Donachie from Burnley. "Left-back was our biggest weakness last season", said Royle, "Willie has already shown that his experience in that position could be vital to us. There is no substitute for class and experience".

This season Athletic laid the foundations for possible success with a much improved record. Despite the financial problems of dwindling attendances, Athletic had managed to assemble a squad which had held its own after a stuttering start to the season. Athletic took only 17 points from their first 21 League games, and conceded 41 goals in the process, then after switching to a sweeper-style system in March, conceded only 14 goals in 14 games and five of those came in one match, at champions-elect Oxford United.

MIKE QUINN SENT SPRAWLING IN A 2-0 WIN OVER PORTSMOUTH — SEPT '85

Striker Mike Quinn's 21 goal contribution proved his value in the Second Division, and he looked worth considerably more than the sum Athletic paid Stockport for his services. Ever-present Mark Ward found it harder in this, his second professional season, but had still made 93 consecutive senior appearances.

A £250,000 bonus came Athletic's way in January, when little-known teenage striker, Wayne Harrison, joined Liverpool after making only a handful of senior appearances at Boundary Park. Fellow teenager, Andy Barlow's first campaign in professional football summed up Athletic's season. At times they struggled, but when the penny dropped and they found confidence, they were as good as anyone in the Division.

Athletic met Bolton Wanderers in a highly entertaining League Cup tie. After losing the first leg 2-1, Athletic were held 4-4 after extra time at Boundary Park, losing the tie on aggregate 6-5. The F.A.Cup saw a 2-1 Boundary Park victory over Brentford, followed by a 5-1 4th round hammering at Sheffield Wednesday. Athletic's average home League attendance slumped again this season to 4,725, the only five figure gate being for the game against promoted Manchester City.

A WAYNE HARRISON GOAL, v. MANCHESTER UNITED IN A MID-SEASON FRIENDLY — JAN '85

GOALKEEPING PRACTICE ON CLAYTON FIELDS, ANDY GORAM, ANDY GORTON AND COACH ALAN HODGKINSON — 1985

TONY HENRY TUSSLES WITH MAN. UTD'S NORMAN WHITESIDE DURING THE 1985 FRIENDLY FIXTURE AT BOUNDARY PARK

A CRACKING GOAL FROM ROGER PALMER v. CHARLTON AT BOUNDARY PARK — SEPT '85

FUTCHER GOES CLOSE, AGAINST LIVERPOOL, MILK CUP 2ND ROUND — SEPT '85

The introduction of summer signings Ron Futcher, Paul Atkinson and Gary Williams had given the senior squad a stronger look, but team planning took a blow when Mark Ward signed for West Ham United in a £250,000 deal before this season started.

Despite the problems facing football in the aftermath of the Hysel Stadium disaster, Chairman Mr. Ian Stott believed that Athletic were winning the continuing fight to strike a balance between improving the playing squad, boosting commercial activities, and up-grading spectator facilities. He admitted that, for the first time for several years, the club directors had backed the team to clinch promotion, as an air of optimism pervaded at Boundary Park.

A new Full Members Cup competition looked certain to get the go-ahead from the F.A. after backing from the Football League this season. Restricted to interested clubs in the top two Divisions, the Members Cup would be a mid-week knockout competition, regionalised in the early stages, with a final at Wembley. ''We have got to examine all ways of raising extra cash, and this could be an attractive proposition'', said Royle.

Liverpool visited Boundary Park for a pre-season friendly, and left on the wrong end of a 1-0 scoreline. This was the first game Liverpool had played following the ill-fated European Cup Final in Brussels, and also marked the first game in charge for Anfield's new player/manager Kenny Dalglish.

Athletic's season began and ended with promise, but in between came one of the worst spells of form since the club was promoted from Division Three, 12 years earlier. They lost only three of their opening 14 fixtures, occupying second position in the table in early November, but then lost ten of the next eleven games and slumped to fifth from bottom by the turn of the year. They took only one point from a possible 30 during those dismal days of November and December, before finishing the campaign in style by losing only four of the last seventeen.

Considering the disastrous spell of form, it was quite an achievement for manager Joe Royle and his team to finish the season in eighth place in the table, and go close to their best record since promotion. Athletic's results against the seven teams to finish above them were impressive. They lost twice to champions Norwich, and seventh placed Sheffield United, but they won at home against promoted Charlton, Wimbledon, Portsmouth, Crystal Palace and Hull.

FORMER LIVERPOOL 'SUPER-SUB' DAVID FAIRCLOUGH SCORES FOR ATHLETIC AGAINST HIS OLD CLUB DURING THE MILK CUP 2ND ROUND SECOND LEG AT BOUNDARY PARK — OCT '85

Despite the injury and subsequent retirement of Brendan O'Callaghan, and the sales of Mark Ward and Mike Quinn, transferred to Portsmouth in March for £150,000, Athletic had the makings of their strongest squad for many years. The January signing of the towering defender Andy Linighan, a £55,000 capture from Leeds United, was significant in halting Athletic's mid-season slump. Youngsters like Mike Milligan, Gary Williams and Steve Bullock had shown they were not out of place in the first team and would improve.

In the Cups, Athletic received a football lesson from Liverpool, losing 8-2 over two legs in the League Cup. Fourth Division Orient caused Athletic embarrassment in the F.A.Cup by winning 2-1 in a third round tie at Brisbane Road.

Viewed overall the season showed signs of improvement, which if maintained would see the club move closer to its First Division goal. Scotland goalkeeper Andy Goram, who would represent his club and country in the Mexico World Cup Finals during this summer, had the distinction, along with Roger Palmer, of making most appearances for Athletic with 44 League and Cup each. Ron Futcher pipped Roger Palmer in the race to be the club's leading goalscorer. Futcher scored in each of the last two home games to take his total to 17, all in the League, which was one more than Palmer, who hit 15 in the League and one in the F.A.Cup. The home League average attendance slipped again to 4,649.

ATHLETIC'S PLASTIC PARADISE TAKES SHAPE — AUG '86

1986-87

This season Athletic launched their ground re-development scheme and laid a £385,000 plastic pitch which was the largest artifical sports surface in Great Britain. Working together with Oldham Leisure Services, Athletic hoped to convince the public that the 8,415 square metres of fibriliated polypropylene was more than just a plastic football pitch. After removing thousands of tonnes of turf and soil, completely clearing the old grass pitch and undersoil-heating system, the contractors put down 225mm of crushed and graded stone, 65mm of macadam, a rubber shock pad, and 23mm of sand on the final top layer of plastic carpet. Also gone was the famous Boundary Park slope. The pitch had been 6'-4½" higher at the Rochdale Road End of the ground than at the Chadderton End. The gradient had been reduced by more than half. The sand helped the pitch to bed in and, surprisingly for plastic grass, needed plenty of watering until it settled down. Having a true, consistent surface to play on in 21 home games, it was hoped, would be an advantage, suiting Athletic's passing game. When Athletic played their first home game, a 1-0 victory over Barnsley in gale force conditions, the surface resembled a beach instead of a sports arena.

Pre-season, manager Joe Royle was offered a new three year contract which he gladly accepted. ''There was never any doubt I would sign, I have started a job here that I would like to finish. I believe we have made steady progress towards our ambition for First Division football, and now I hope we can go from strength to strength,'' he said. Royle believed that a First Division place was

RON FUTCHER SCORES THE ONLY GOAL OF THE GAME, FOR ATHLETIC
v. DERBY COUNTY — AUG '86

the only way for the club to achieve financial security. He added, "We can soldier on with money from having an artificial pitch, a busy commercial department, and from selling players. But what we really need is to bring in the crowds. The only way to achieve that is by rubbing shoulders with the big clubs".

The bookmakers were offering kinder odds this season, making Athletic just 25-1 for the Second Division Championship, but those at Boundary Park were naturally more confident about their chances of clinching a top five place and qualifying for the new end-of-season promotion play-off's. The top two in the Division would automatically be promoted, with the third, fourth and fifth clubs joining the 19th in the First Division in a play-off for one more place in Division One.

Athletic took a gamble this season by spending £100,000 on Grimsby Town's captain, Kevin Moore, and £80,000 on Tommy Wright from Leeds United. Denis Irwin also joined the club on a free transfer, again from Leeds United.

After an excellent season in which Athletic provided some superb football, memorable goals, and a tremendous improvement in away form, they were plunged into the play-off trauma when, in any other recent season, their third place would have guaranteed automatic promotion.

Lack of concentration at two vital moments in both legs of the play-off against Leeds United, gave the Yorkshiremen two goals and a chance of First Division football. At Elland

HAT-TRICK HERO MIKE CECERE WITH MATCH BALL v. BLACKBURN ROVERS, MAY '87

Road, Athletic held their own until the final minute when substitute Keith Edwards scored his first killer goal. At Boundary Park, Athletic set off with a 1-0 deficit, but soon equalised with a Gary Williams goal. Athletic, with the three ex-Leeds players, Andy Linighan, Tommy Wright and Denis Irwin in their team, had plenty to prove, and when Mike Cecere headed them in front with only minutes remaining, it seemed their point had been made. But Leeds stormed forward, and that man Edwards scored his second last-minute goal in three days, enabling Leeds to qualify for the play-off final on the away goal ruling.

Athletic had proved themselves to be worthy promotion contenders, never out of the top three all season, and eight of the twelve players on duty against Leeds were aged 23 or under, an obvious promise for the future. Although the season ended in disappointment, it went on record as one of significant all-round progress, and a launch-pad to better things.

Roger Palmer topped the goalscoring charts with 17 in League and Cup, and the early season contribution of Ron Futcher, who scored ten goals in the opening ten games of the campaign, finishing with 15 from 31 outings before his £40,000 transfer to Bradford City, couldn't be underestimated. Andy Goram, Denis Irwin and Roger Palmer shared the distinction of making most appearances for Athletic this season. The trio missed only one of the possible 50 matches in League, play-offs, F.A.Cup, Littlewoods (League) Cup and Full Members Cup.

Athletic were knocked out of the F.A.Cup by Bradford City after a replay, lost to Coventry City in the Littlewoods (League) Cup, after beating Leeds United in the first round, and in the new Full Members Cup, lost 1-0 at Derby County in the first round.

Average home League crowds at Boundary Park went up to 6,883, excluding the Leeds play-off match, but the club still recorded the poorest attendance figures of the top ten sides in the Division.

MANAGER ROYLE CONSOLES IRWIN AND LINIGAN FOLLOWING ATHLETIC'S 1-0 DEFEAT IN THE PLAY-OFF SEMI-FINAL, 1ST LEG AT ELLAND ROAD

CHAIRMAN MR. IAN STOTT PRESENTS ROGER PALMER WITH THE SUPPORTERS'
'PLAYER OF THE YEAR' AWARD — MAY '87

PALMER'S GOALBOUND HEADER IS TIPPED OVER BY LEEDS KEEPER DAY IN THE PLAY-OFF
SEMI-FINAL, 2ND LEG — MAY '87

A DEVASTATED TOMMY WRIGHT IS CONSOLED BY LEEDS UNITED'S ANDY RITCHIE
FOLLOWING LATICS PLAY-OFF DEFEAT — MAY '87

ANDY RITCHIE'S £50.000 TRANSFER FEE FROM LEEDS WAS FIXED BY AN INDEPENDENT
TRIBUNAL — AUG '87

1987-88

From the team that finished the last campaign, only one player, other than loan signing, Ian Ormondroyd, had left the club. Kevin Moore's £125,000 departure to Southampton was a great disappointment, but a clause in his contract allowed him to move if Athletic failed to gain promotion. The loss of Moore was compensated for by the signing of the Blackburn Rovers skipper, Glen Keeley, for £15,000, and the versatile Andy Ritchie from Leeds for £50,000. Both transfer fees being set by independent tribunals.

After early-season problems with injuries, confidence and settling in newcomers, Athletic emerged stronger than ever. The signing of Frankie Bunn from Hull City in December transformed Athletic into a formidable attacking unit. Four defeats in the last 25 League games, unbeaten at Boundary Park in ten (nine victories), and some wonderful attacking performances, gave grounds for great optimism for the future. In beating the likes of Aston Villa, Manchester City, Middlesbrough, Blackburn Rovers and Crystal Palace, they proved they needed fear no team.

The senior squad was stronger in depth and versatility than for many years, and the standard of players available for reserve and youth-team duty seemed better than ever. The club's overall financial position looked much brighter, the years of careful management and transfer wheeling and dealing had left Athletic in their healthiest condition for many seasons. The transfer of Andy Linighan to Norwich City for a club record £350,000 in March, bolstered Athletic's coffers even more.

FRANK BUNN PICTURED DURING HIS DEBUT FOR ATHLETIC v. BOURNEMOUTH AT DEAN COURT — DEC '87

For the second successive season, Denis Irwin and Roger Palmer shared the honour of appearing in more of Athletic's matches than any other players, figuring in 49 of the 51 League and Cup games. Andy Ritchie and Roger Palmer dominated Athletic's goalscoring charts with 20 each. Palmer's total was his best ever for a season, including his 100th Football League goal, and three hat-tricks. It was the first time for 17 seasons that the club had two players reaching the twenty mark since Jim Fryatt (24) and David Shaw (23) did so in 1970-71 when Athletic won promotion from the Fourth Division.

Average league attendances rose this season to 6,903, and the club had the bonus of a 16,931 turn out for a 3rd round F.A.Cup tie with Tottenham, which Athletic lost 4-2.

Athletic surprised their supporters by reaching the 4th round of the Littlewoods (League) Cup before losing a close encounter with Everton at Goodison Park 2-1. Earlier rounds had seen entertaining victories over Carlisle and Leeds United.

THOMAS SCORES FOR SPURS AS ATHLETIC CRASH OUT OF THE F.A. CUP 3RD ROUND AT BOUNDARY PARK — JAN '88

TOMMY WRIGHT SCORES FROM AN ACUTE ANGLE v. LEEDS UNITED IN THE LITTLEWOODS
CUP 3RD ROUND REPLAY AT BOUNDARY PARK — NOV '87

ROGER PALMER BREAKS THE CLUB'S ALL-TIME GOAL SCORING RECORD. HIS FIRST GOAL AGAINST IPSWICH TOWN AT BOUNDARY PARK IN APRIL '89 BEING HIS 111TH FOR ATHLETIC IN A 4-1 VICTORY

J oe Royle looked forward to his seventh season as Athletic's manager, quietly confident that it would be the lucky one for the Boundary Park club. No longer was it a question of 'will the Latics survive another Second Division campaign?'' as thoughts were now turned towards the distinct possibility of mounting a serious promotion challenge.

Royle's astute leadership, backed by an enthusiastic Board of Directors, had seen Athletic emerge from the crisis of the mid-80's to a respected force in the Second Division. Manager Royle said, ''We won't start as promotion favourites on most people's lists, but plenty will have us pencilled in as the dark horses''. Athletic believed they had their best panel of players for many years, both in terms of numbers and quality.

The only area in which Athletic needed more competition was goalkeeper. During the previous 12 months they had lost Scotland international, Andy Goram, to Hibs for £325,000, and his talented, if rather unpredictable understudy, Andy Gorton, to Stockport. Athletic had signed Andy Rhodes for £55,000 from Doncaster Rovers towards the end of the previous season, and manager Royle believed his new goalkeeper behind a solid defence held the key to the team's fortunes. ''If we can keep 20 clean sheets this season, and keep up our goalscoring record, then we won't be far away'', said Royle. However, only the bottom two clubs, Walsall and Birmingham conceded more goals than Athletic, throwing Royle's pre-season planning to the wind.

ROGER PALMER SCORES THE 2ND OF HIS THREE GOALS IN ATHLETIC'S 4-1 WIN OVER MAN. CITY AT MAINE ROAD — AUG '88

Athletic had problems with injuries, which had a dramatic effect on the team's fortunes, but the real problem was that poor defensive record. Athletic scored more League goals (75) than all bar the two clubs promoted, Chelsea and Manchester City. Of the twelve League and Cup victories, only three of them came when Athletic scored fewer than three goals, but there were not enough times when Athletic could rely on the defence to earn a share of the points. They figured in only four goalless draws but, on the other eight occasions that they failed to score, they lost every time. The loss of the defensive combination, Goram, Linighan and Moore had taken a time to sort out, but Royle was now pinning his faith in new signings Jon Hallworth, Ian Marshall and Andy Holden to provide a similar service as they settled at the club.

One of the highlights of the 1988-89 season was the sight of Roger Palmer smashing the club's all-time record for League goals. The first of Palmer's two goals in the 4-0 win over Ipswich Town on April 4th took his total for Athletic to 111, and past the record set 35 years before by Eric Gemmell. Palmer extended his total to 113 by the end of the season, and finished with 15 League goals. Top of Athletic's overall scoring charts was Andy Ritchie. His total of 16 League and Cup goals coming in 34 appearances. Roger Palmer topped the appearance lists to maintain his remarkable record for Athletic since his £70,000 signing from Manchester City 9½ years earlier. He had missed only a handful of matches during the last decade and was the only player to appear in all 51 League and Cup fixtures this time. Earl Barrett came closest to matching Palmer's record, missing only two games, in this his first full season in League football.

It said something for the adventurous nature of Athletic's performances, that the average crowd rose this season to 7,202, even allowing for the fact that they had only two Cup ties at Boundary Park, both in the Littlewoods (League) Cup, beating Darlington 4-2 on aggregate in round 2, before losing 2-0 to Everton, after a creditable 1-1 scoreline at Goodison Park. Athletic's F.A.Cup hopes faded at Selhurst Park, the adopted home of Charlton Athletic, who luckily won 2-1.

PALMER'S CLOSE RANGE HEADER GOES WIDE IN LATICS 2-0 LITTLEWOODS 3RD ROUND
REPLAY DEFEAT AGAINST EVERTON — NOV·'88

254

TONY COTTEE BEATS ATHLETIC'S KEEPER ANDY RHODES TO SCORE EVERTON'S FIRST
GOAL IN THE LITTLEWOODS CUP 3RD ROUND REPLAY — NOV '88

ATHLETIC'S MANAGER JOE ROYLE IS INTRODUCED TO HRH THE DUCHESS OF KENT PRIOR
TO THE LITTLEWOODS CUP FINAL AGAINST NOTTINGHAM FOREST — 29TH APRIL '90

1989-90

Sponsorship deals were now part and parcel of most sports, as more companies recognised the benefits of a high public profile through leisure activities. It was therefore appropriate for Athletic, trying to build a promotion team, to complete their biggest ever sponsorship deal with a national building company, Bovis, who would be the team's shirt sponsors for the next three years.

Joe Royle, second only to Nottingham Forest's Brian Clough in length of service as manager with one club, hoped his eighth year in charge at Boundary Park would be the lucky one. Over the previous few seasons, Athletic had been rebuilding the senior squad, strengthening and improving, wheeling and dealing in the transfer market, the outcome being a team that had only six survivors from the play-off squad of '87, Denis Irwin, Willie Donachie, Andy Barlow, Roger Palmer, Mike Milligan and Gary Williams. Although Athletic had lost the services of Tommy Wright, a £300,000 transfer to Leicester, Peter Skipper and John Kelly to Walsall for a combined total of £65,000, Joe Royle remained optimistic that Athletic could carry on in the same entertaining way which was their hallmark. The signings of Neil Adams, £100,000 from Everton, Rick Holden £165,000 from Watford and Scott McGarvey, £25,000 from Bristol City, had given Athletic increased competition and cover for places in the forward line. The emergence of the versatile Paul Warhurst, plus the return to fitness of Gary Williams and Willie Donachie provided the manager with increased options.

CLUB CHAIRMAN MR. IAN STOTT SHAKES HANDS WITH BOBBY COLLINS AT THE CLUB'S 'STARLINE' LAUNCH. BEHIND ARE OTHER EX LATICS' FAVOURITES, DAVID SHAW, BERT LISTER, ERIC GEMMELL, JIM BOWIE, ALAN WILLIAMS, IAN WOOD AND GEORGE HARDWICK — AUG '89

Athletic were hoping their new 'Starline' draw would give manager Royle up to £130,000 a year to spend exclusively on securing extra players, whilst giving supporters the chance of winning cash prizes, but supporters and team alike hit the kind of jackpot this season that neither had dreamed of. Athletic became the underdogs who had so many days. Famous victories over Arsenal, Everton, Aston Villa, Southampton and West Ham United, an historic Wembley appearance against Nottingham Forest, and 19 Cup ties in total.

At the end of the day Athletic finished up with nothing, but gained the respect of every football fan in Britain, not to mention their bank manager. Any regrets? ''Of course'', said Royle, ''I would have swapped all the Cup games for promotion to the First Division. It would be easy to sit back and say we were this, we were that, everyone loved us and we only missed out because we ran out of steam, played too many games. But the bottom line is we were not good enough. We had a few 'paper tigers' away from home''.

Joe Royle the realist never allowed himself to be carried away on the magic carpet ride, not even when bigger and better carpets came along. Manchester City offered him the manager's chair before Christmas. Other clubs of substance and reputation sounded him out during the summer, and the F.A. invited him to be interviewed for the England job. Royle was deeply flattered by every approach and polite in his refusals. He told the F.A., ''Thank-you, but I am not ready to be manager of England. I haven't won anything yet, I haven't managed in the First Division, and I couldn't do without the day-to-day involvement at club level''. Royle was proud that the man who landed the England job, Graham Taylor, had invited him to take charge of the Under-21 Team against Hungary in September, he was ready for that.

ANDY RITCHIE SLAMS IN ATHLETIC'S EQUALISER IN THE 2-1 WIN OVER LEEDS IN THE LITTLEWOODS CUP 2ND ROUND, 1ST LEG — SEPT '89

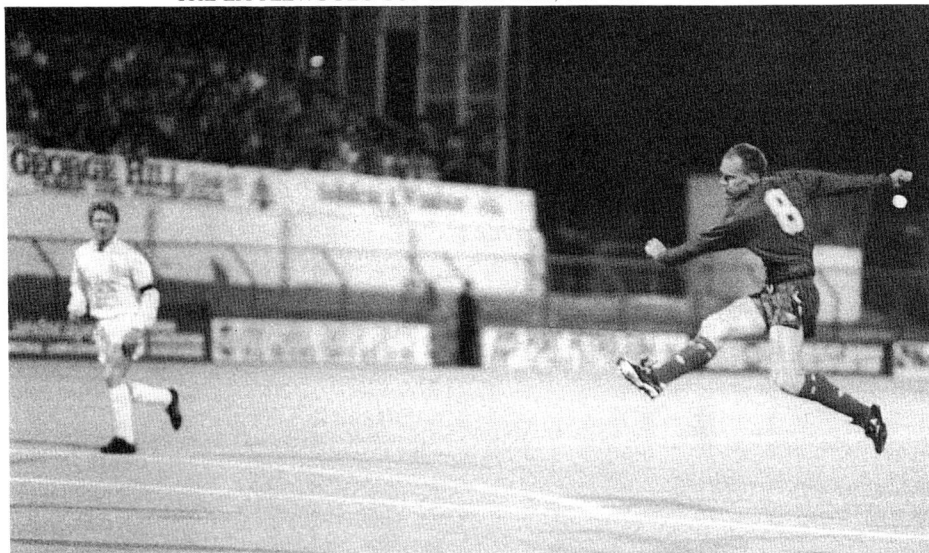

Royle for England

JOE ROYLE has been invited to take charge of the England under-21 team to play Hungary at Southampton on September 11.

New England manager Graham Taylor has asked the Athletic boss to supervise the friendly international on this occasion.

Taylor, who recently took the Athletic squad for a coaching session at Boundary Park, has appointed former Southampton boss Lawrie McMenemy as his right-hand man.

They will be responsible for tactics and coaching, etc., with selected managers, like Royle, being asked to become involved from time to time.

Royle said: "I'm honoured to be asked to play a part."

By courtesy of the Daily Express

EVERTON GOALKEEPER SOUTHALL BEING 'TURNED OVER' BY ATHLETIC'S ROGER PALMER
IN THE F.A. CUP 5TH ROUND 2-2 DRAW AT BOUNDARY PARK

A GOAL WORTH A MILLION ££'S AS ANDY RITCHIE (ON GROUND) HITS ATHLETIC'S EQUALISER IN INJURY TIME, v. SOUTHAMPTON, LITTLEWOODS CUP QUARTER FINAL AT THE DELL — JANUARY '90

Athletic did enough this season to demonstrate they did not have to rely on their 'flexible friend' for results. "I never realised the extent of the feeling we aroused until I was a guest at the Manager of the Year luncheon and ITV commentator Brian Moore started talking about 'the team that warmed the whole country during the winter months'; judging by the letters, Oldham Athletic made friends all over the world", recalled Royle. Joe concluded, "Of course it will be a hard act to follow. Expectations here are higher than ever before, and things might turn sour if we fall short. One way or another, we have to win promotion".

Athletic's injury problems this season were largely overlooked as a tidal wave of emotion and excitement swept them through the second half of the campaign. There was hardly a time when manager Royle could call on a fully fit squad, which was a tribute in itself to the strength of the players who maintained their bid for honours right up to the last week of a hectic season. In the end, the mental and physical strain proved just too much, which made Earl Barrett's 100 per cent appearance record all the more remarkable.

The brilliant Barrett was the only man to appear in all 65 senior matches, but Rick Holden (64), Andy Barlow (61), Denis Irwin (60), and skipper Mike Milligan (60) ran him close. Andy Ritchie topped Athletic's goalscoring charts with an impressive haul of 28 League and Cup goals, the best of his career. However, Roger Palmer once again led the way in terms of League goals, his 16 for the season extending his all-time record to 129.

Crowd figures at Boundary Park were at their highest for more than ten years, as Athletic's magnificent Cup run captured the public imagination and had a knock-on effect on League attendances. In total, Athletic had 370,919 spectators at their 33 home games in League and Cup, producing an average crowd of 11,240.

"WE'RE THERE"... OLDHAM SKIPPER MIKE MILLIGAN, JON HALLWORTH AND NICK HENRY SHOW THEIR RELIEF AND JOY AS LATICS, AFTER A LIFETIMES WAIT, FINALLY MAKE IT TO WEMBLEY FOLLOWING THE LITTLEWOODS CUP SEMI-FINAL 2ND LEG AT WEST HAM'S UPTON PARK

OLDHAM ATHLETIC PHOTO-CALL · PRI

LITTLEWOODS CUP FINAL — APRIL 1990

ANDY RITCHIE HEADS ATHLETIC'S THIRD GOAL, AND WHEELS AWAY IN TRIUMPH v.
ARSENAL, LITTLEWOODS CUP 4th ROUND AT BOUNDARY PARK

CAPTAINS' BRYAN ROBSON AND MIKE MILLIGAN WITH THE MATCH OFFICIALS AND MASCOT BEFORE THE FIRST F.A. CUP
SEMI-FINAL AT MAINE ROAD — APRIL '90

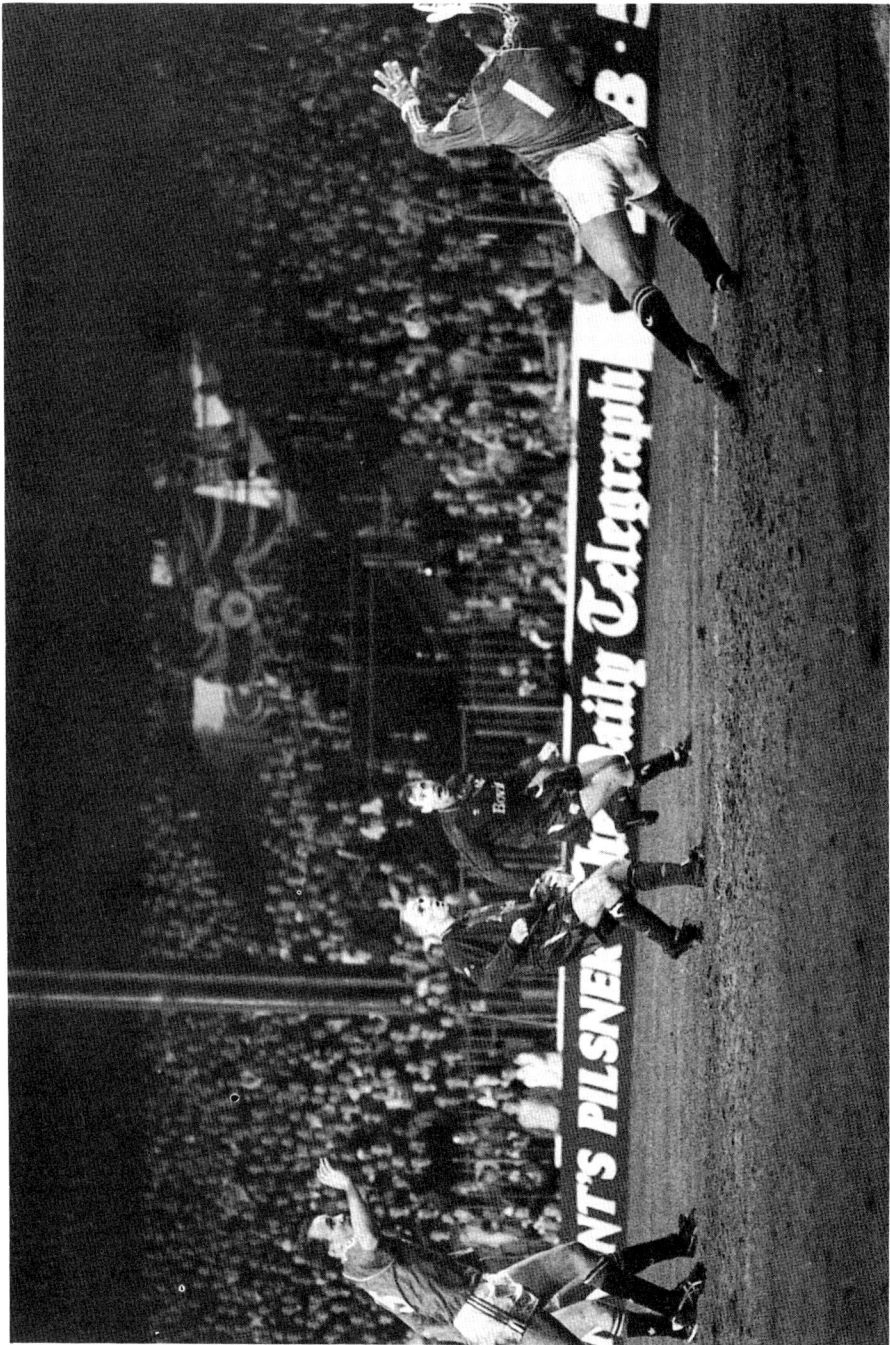

ANDY RITCHIE SLOTS IN ATHLETIC'S DRAMATIC LATE EQUALISER PAST UNITED'S JIM LEIGHTON TO FORCE EXTRA TIME IN THE F.A. CUP SEMI-FINAL REPLAY AT MAINE ROAD — APRIL '90

"Keeping the Dream Alive"

THE FACTS & FIGURES OF THE 'PINCH ME SEASON'

				LATICS SCORE SHOWN FIRST	
AUGUST					
19	Blackburn Rovers	A	0-1		9,939
22	Watford	H	1-1	(R Holden)	6,230
26	Swindon Town	H	2-2	(Palmer 2)	5,531
SEPTEMBER					
2	Newcastle United	A	1-2	(R Holden)	20,804
9	Plymouth Argyle	H	3-2	(Palmer, Ritchie, R Holden)	4,940
16	Stoke City	A	2-1	(Palmer, Ritchie)	10,673
19	Leeds United (Litt. Cup)	H	2-1	(Ritchie, R Holden)	8,415
23	West Bromwich Albion	H	2-1	(Ritchie 2)	6,907
26	Sheffield United	A	1-2	(Bunn)	14,314
30	Leicester City	H	1-0	(Morgan o.g.)	6,407
OCTOBER					
3	Leeds United (Litt. Cup)	A	2-1	(Bunn, Ritchie)	18,092
7	Barnsley	H	2-0	(Bunn, Milligan)	6,769
14	AFC Bournemouth	A	0-2		6,500
17	Hull City	A	0-0		5,109
21	Middlesbrough	H	2-0	(Ritchie 2)	6,835
25	Scarborough(Litt. Cup 3)	H	7-0	(Bunn 6, Ritchie)	7,713
28	Wolverhampton W	A	1-1	(Milligan)	15,278
31	Bradford City	H	2-2	(Barlow, Ritchie pen)	7,772
NOVEMBER					
4	Sunderland	H	2-1	(Ritchie, Warhurst)	8,829
11	Oxford United	H	1-0	(Ritchie)	4,480
18	Brighton & H Albion	H	1-1	(Milligan)	7,066
22	Arsenal (Litt. Cup 4)	H	3-1	(Ritchie 2, Henry)	14,924
25	Ipswich Town	A	1-1	(Yallop o.g.)	12,304
DECEMBER					
2	Blackburn Rovers	H	2-0	(R Holden, Ritchie)	10,635
9	Watford	A	0-3		9,399
16	West Ham United	A	2-0	(Milligan, Foster o.g.)	14,960
26	Port Vale	H	2-1	(Adams, Barrett)	11,274
30	Portsmouth	H	3-3	(Milligan 2, Palmer)	8,815
JANUARY					
1	Leeds United	A	1-1	(Palmer)	30,217
6	Birmingham (FA Cup 3)	A	1-1	(Bunn)	13,131
10	Birmingham (FA 3 replay)	H	1-0	(R Holden)	9,982
13	Swindon Town	H	2-3	(McGarvey, Adams)	7,785
20	Newcastle United	H	1-1	(Ritchie)	11,190
24	Southampton (LC 5)	A	2-2	(Ritchie 2)	21,026
27	Brighton (FA Cup 4)	H	2-1	(Ritchie, McGarvey)	11,034
31	Southampton (LC 5 R)	H	2-0	(Ritchie, Milligan)	18,862
FEBRUARY					
3	West Bromwich Albion	A	2-2	(Ritchie pen, Palmer)	12,237
10	Stoke City	H	2-0	(Palmer, Ritchie)	10,028
14	West Ham (LC Semi 1)	H	6-0	(Ritchie 2, Palmer, R Holden, Adams, Barrett)	19,263
17	Everton (FA 5)	H	2-2	(Ritchie pen, Palmer)	19,320
21	Everton (FA 5 rply)	A	1-1	(Marshall)	36,663
24	Ipswich Town	H	4-1	(Marshall 2, Palmer, Irwin)	10,193
MARCH					
3	Brighton & H Albion	A	1-1	(Adams)	8,229
7	West Ham (Litt Cup Semi 2)	A	0-3		15,431
10	Everton (FA 5)	H	2-1	(Palmer, Marshall pen)	19,346
14	Aston Villa (FA 6)	H	3-0	(Redfearn, Holden, Price o.g.)	19,490
17	Barnsley	A	0-1		10,598
20	AFC Bournemouth	H	4-0	(Palmer 2, Redfearn, Milligan)	10,109
24	Hull City	H	3-2	(Palmer 2, Marshall)	11,472
28	Sheffield United (7.30 p.m.)	H	0-2		14,160
31	Middlesbrough	A	0-1		17,238
APRIL					
3	Leicester C (7.45 p.m.)	A	0-3		10,368
8	Man Utd (FA semi 3.30 p.m.)...Maine Rd		3-3	(Barrett, Marshall, Palmer)	44,026
11	Man Utd (FA Semi replay) ..Maine Rd		1-2	(Ritchie)	35,005
16	Leeds U (Noon)	H	3-1	(R Holden 2, Bunn)	16,262
16	Port Vale	A	0-2		11,451
18	Plymouth Argyle (7.30 p.m.)	A	0-2		8,146
21	West Ham United	H	3-0	(Bunn 2, Ritchie)	12,190
24	Portsmouth (7.30 p.m.)	A	1-2	(Barrett)	9,601
29	Nottm F (Litt. C final)	Wembley	0-1		74,343
MAY					
1	Oxford (7.30 p.m.)	H	4-1	(R Holden 3, Palmer)	12,616
3	Wolves (7.30 p.m.)	H	1-1	(Palmer)	17,468
5	Sunderland	A	3-2	(Ritchie, Palmer, Adams)	22,223
7	Bradford	A	1-1	(Redfearn)	6,798

The full list of appearances (substitutes in brackets) was:

Barrett	65
R Holden	64
Barlow	61 (2)
Irwin	60
Milligan	60
Henry	58 (2)
Ritchie	50 (1)
Palmer	44 (18)
Marshall	37 (3)
Rhodes	36 (1)
Warhurst	36 (10)
Bunn	34 (1)
Adams	30 (18)
Hallworth	29
Redfearn	20
Donachie	8
A. Holden	8
McGarvey	6 (12)
Moulden	5
Williams	2 (25)
Heseltine	1 (5)
Blundell	1
Kelly	(1)
Mooney	(1)
Makin	(1)

ATHLETIC, 12-1 AGAINST WINNING THE 2ND DIVISION CHAMPIONSHIP — AUGUST '90

IAN MARSHALL COMPLETES HIS HAT-TRICK WITH A STUNNING DRIVE IN ATHLETIC'S 3-2
WIN AT WOLVERHAMPTON — AUG '90

1990-91

Athletic's inability to hold onto Denis Irwin and Mike Milligan served to pinpoint the problems a successful Second Division club like Athletic faced. "I didn't want to sell Irwin or Milligan but life goes on and there were going to be changes anyway," said Royle. Irwin's £625,000 transfer to Manchester United made him one of the most expensive right-backs in British football, and not many players move from a Second Division club to the First Division for £1 million, as did Mike Milligan to Everton. Obviously the days of Athletic giving players away were over. Athletic set out their stall to make this season the one when promotion was finally achieved, and manager Royle set his side a target of eight away wins, coupled with a good home record to win promotion. Athletic were unlikely to enjoy another season as remarkable as the last one, but confidence was high that this season would be memorable in its own right. Athletic had 5,000 season ticket holders, twice as many as the previous season, and could boast 10,000 supporters who were either season ticket holders, or members of the club.

Richard Jobson signed for a club record £460,000 in late August, to help compensate for the early season injury to Andy Holden. This transfer took Athletic's summer outlay to £1,150,000 and was the third time the club had smashed its transfer record during August. Royle's other signings were John Keeley, a £240,000 recruit from Brighton, regarded as one of the best goalkeepers in the Second Division, and David Currie, a £450,000 signing from Nottingham Forest who had been included to add extra punch to the forward line. A lack of goals in away matches, only 20 in 23 League games, was considered the main reason for Athletic's failure to secure a play-off spot last season. Royle said, "The supporters put a lot of money into the club last season, and pre-season ticket sales have been marvellous. We are trying to repay their loyalty by recruiting top players".

The season got off to a perfect start with an excellent 3-2 win at Wolverhampton Wanderers, Ian Marshall, a defender converted to striker recording a superb hat-trick. The first home game of the campaign against Leicester City, also saw Marshall on target, along with Andy Ritchie, as Athletic won 2-0. Sadly club captain Andy Holden suffered a serious knee injury during this game, and played no further part in Athletic's season. There was no stopping Athletic as they secured top spot in the Second Division with a 3-1 home win over Portsmouth, a hard fought 1-0 success at Barnsley, and a resounding 3-0 victory over Oxford United at Boundary Park. Ian Marshall sat proudly on top of the Second Division's list of leading goalscorers with six in five matches convinced that his dual target of 20 goals and promotion could be realised. It was already clear that Joe Royle's team meant business and the record of five straight wins at the start of a season equalled Athletic's best opening to a League campaign, set in 1930.

Underrated Charlton denied Athletic a record sixth successive win, but the Londoners' manager, Lennie Lawrence, reckoned happier days were ahead for Athletic. After seeing his own side deservedly collect their first point of the season, and stop Athletic's 100 per cent charge to the top of the table, he said, "I fancy Oldham will win promotion this time. Not many teams will leave here with a point. In fact some of them are beaten before they step on the artificial pitch". Athletic travelled to Middlesbrough the following Saturday, when a Roger Palmer special made it six wins out of seven.

ROGER PALMER (INSET) GETS HIS 150TH GOAL FOR ATHLETIC IN THE 2-2 DRAW AT SWINDON — MARCH '91

The League Cup, now sponsored by Rumbelows, opened in controversial fashion at Notts County as Athletic were beaten for the first time in 12 matches, and had defender Paul Warhurst sent off. Athletic were on the end of a harsh penalty decision which resulted in County having a slender advantage to take to Boundary Park for the second leg. Athletic recovered their composure to earn a goalless League draw at West Bromwich Albion and retain top spot, although they faced a Football League fine for their late arrival for the match.

Early October saw Athletic maintain their unbeaten League record with a narrow victory over fellow promotion contenders, Swindon Town. Neil Redfearn's late penalty pinched the points, but few would have complained if the visitors had shared the spoils. Old rivals Blackburn Rovers grabbed a last second equaliser in a wind-spoiled encounter at Boundary Park with Paul Moulden on target for Athletic for only the second time since his £225,000 signing from Bournemouth in March. That took Athletic into the return leg of the League Cup tie against Notts County and, after extra time, they stormed through to the next round by 5-2, after being 3-1 down on aggregate with only ten minutes of normal time remaining.

Athletic had established a reputation for resilience, and the away fixture at Hull City's Boothferry Park underlined the point. Two goals down just after half-time, and playing badly, they fought back to earn a point with goals from Nick Henry and a thunderbolt from Neil Redfearn. A run of three succesive victories, at Bristol City, Ipswich and Notts County at Boundary Park consolidated Athletic's position as League leaders, before they ran out of League Cup luck at Leeds United, losing 2-0, and bringing to an end the Indian sign they seemed to hold over their rivals from Elland Road.

PAUL WARHURST SCORES IN THE 3-1 VICTORY OVER PORTSMOUTH, SEPT '90

ATHLETIC'S NEW RECRUITS GUNNAR HALLE AND PAUL KANE — JAN '91

WHILE THE GROUND STAFF BATTLED TO CLEAR DEEP SNOW, THE PLAYERS TRAINED AS
USUAL — FEB '91

In early November, 34,845 spectators, the biggest crowd to attend a Second Division game all season, saw Sheffield Wednesday and Athletic draw 2-2 in one of the most entertaining matches of this campaign. By this time, Athletic had re-written the club's records by remaining unbeaten in 14 League games from the start of the season, the previous record being 13 in 1953. They progressed to 16 matches, as Watford were beaten 4-1 at Boundary Park prompting Athletic to make Joe Royle the highest-paid official in the history of the Boundary Park club by rewarding him with a lucrative new three-year contract, which he happily signed.

Athletic suffered their first League defeat of the season, losing 1-0 at Port Vale, coinciding with the popular Roger Palmer launching his testimonial year. Loan signing Derek Brazil from Manchester United, made his League debut for Athletic on the tiny non-League ground of Bath City, used this season by Bristol Rovers. Athletic turned in their worst performance of the season in losing 2-0, and surrendering top spot to West Ham. Athletic players faced a test of character against Brighton for the first match in December, and bounced back from their two defeats to record their biggest victory of the season by 6-1.

In a light-hearted diversion from the pressures of League football, Athletic faced Baltimore Blast in a six-a-side soccer challenge at Manchester's G-Mex Centre, the American team showing Athletic what it was like to finish on the wrong end of a 6-1 scoreline. The next day saw Athletic's ambitious plans for a 8,500 seat stand shelved following a Trustees' decision not to allow the redevelopment of Clayton Playing Fields. Chairman, Ian Stott, said that Athletic had the blueprint for a 20,000 all-seater stadium but, without the Clayton Playing Fields money to put with grants, they would have to revise their plans.

ATHLETIC'S GOALKEEPER JON HALLWORTH RECEIVES HIS COMMEMORATIVE MEDAL FROM SIR MATT BUSBY, G-MEX, DECEMBER '90

ANDY RITCHIE HELPS ARTIST WALTER KERSHAW PUT THE FINISHING TOUCHES TO THE GIANT MURAL IN THE CANTEEN AT THE BRIAR MILL. SHAW — MAY '91

EQUALISER! ANDY RITCHIE (IN HEADBAND) TURNS AFTER SCORING IN THE 1-1 DRAW WITH MILLWALL — APRIL '91

After a ten day lay-off because of adverse weather, Athletic travelled to Sheffield United for a Zenith Data Systems Cup tie and hung their heads in shame after a 7-2 defeat. Luckily, they wasted no time in returning to true form as they completed their first League double by defeating Wolverhampton Wanderers 4-1 at Boundary Park, quickly followed by a 5-3 home win over Plymouth Argyle, which took them back to the top of the Division. That set up the big promotion clash with close rivals West Ham United at Upton Park on Boxing Day, and Athletic slipped to only their third defeat in 23 League games, by 2-0. Three days later, they found themselves in East London again, this time at Millwall, and earned a difficult 0-0 draw.

The New Year greeted Oldham with a slice of good fortune. Just 13 seconds away from only their second defeat in 56 matches on the artificial pitch, Newcastle full back Mark Stimson's own goal gave Athletic a dramatic 1-1 draw. They also lived dangerously in the 3rd round F.A. Cup tie with Brentford at Boundary Park before winning 3-1, Neil Redfearn's two penalty strikes being decisive. Athletic followed that with one of their best away displays of the season as they hammered Portsmouth 4-1 at Fratton Park, Ian Marshall returning after injury to score twice.

Boundary Park was expecting the biggest crowd of the season for the visit of Yorkshire rivals Barnsley, who returned over the M62 on the wrong end of a 2-0 scoreline. Notts County gained ample revenge for their Rumbelows Cup defeat by sending Athletic packing from this years' F.A.Cup 2-0 at Meadow Lane.

The signings of Gunnar Halle and Paul Kane for a combined total of £630,000 was evidence that the club really meant business in the promotion stakes. The team were now free to concentrate on the League programme, but Oxford United caught them in a benevolent mood in February, as they put five goals into Athletic's net with only one in reply, the club's heaviest defeat of the season. Even so, they were the top goalscorers in the entire Football League with 55 to their credit, plus a further ten in Cup competitions.

Bad weather again disrupted the fixtures as the games against Middlesbrough and Charlton were postponed before Athletic returned to action with a 2-0 home win over Port Vale. That was followed by a 1-1 draw at Watford, as Joe Royle's men headed for the last third of the season in a strong position.

The visit to Brighton was blessed with a marvellous second goal from Andy Ritchie in the 2-1 win, and was a worthy contender for Goal of the Season, and when Athletic went on to beat Bristol Rovers 2-0 at home, they found themselves back at the top of the table. A 2-2 draw at Swindon Town brought another milestone in the career of long-serving Roger Palmer. The club's all-time record marksman could not have picked a better time to score his 150th goal for Athletic as they were staring defeat in the face in a League game for only the fifth time this season. West Bromwich Albion came to Boundary Park and put up the shutters, but Roger Palmer's second goal of the game, in the fourth minute of injury time, brought three vital points.

In a week which saw Ian Marshall face a make-or-break battle for fitness, Hull City visited Boundary Park, and manager Joe Royle warned, ''We know there are no easy games, and these matches against teams fighting against relegation are probably the toughest of the lot''. Hull's 2-1 win inflicted Athletic's first home defeat for a year. When Athletic lost 2-0 at Blackburn only 3 days later, supporters were getting decidedly nervous, even though it was only the second time all season they had lost two League games in a row.

Good Friday brought close rivals, West Ham United, to Oldham for a match billed as the Second Division's 'Match-of-the-season'. From the first incredible save by West Ham's world-class keeper Ludek Miklosko, to Andy Ritchie's dramatic last-gasp penalty point-saver, this contest crackled with thrills, tension and football of the highest quality. Andy Ritchie continued his goalscoring exploits, as he and Neil Adams were on target in a hard fought 2-1 victory at Home Park, Plymouth, on Easter Monday, and he scored again in the home draw against promotion rivals Millwall. That 1-1 scoreline enabled West Ham to take over as the Division leaders, but it was becoming increasingly evident that only a collapse of Titanic proportions was likely to prevent Oldham and the Hammers going up.

IAN MARSHALL HEADS ATHLETIC INTO THE LEAD IN THE DECISIVE 2-1 WIN AT IPSWICH TOWN — APRIL '91

THE DRAMATIC MOMENT WHEN ATHLETIC BECAME 2ND DIVISION CHAMPIONS. NEIL REDFEARN'S INJURY TIME PENALTY GIVING LATICS A 3-2 VICTORY OVER SHEFFIELD WEDNESDAY — MAY '91

DIVISION
JOE ROYLE AND EAR
Back: IAN LIVERSEDGE (Physio) · DAVID CURRIE · BILLY URMSON (Coach) · MIKE FILLERY ·
PAUL KANE · ROGER PALMER · NICK HENRY · FRANKIE B
Front: IAN THOMPSTONE · RICHARD JOBSON · PAUL MOULDEN · PAU

VE COME...
SMILE PROUDLY WITH
IIE · ANDY HOLDEN · JOHN KEELEY · JON HALLWORTH · IAN MARSHALL · NEIL REDFEARN
E DONACHIE (Player/Coach) · RONNIE EVANS (Kit Manager)
T · WAYNE HESELTINE · ANDY BARLOW · RICK HOLDEN · NEIL ADAMS

SKIPPER EARL BARRETT AND CHAIRMAN IAN STOTT RECEIVE THE BARCLAY'S EAGLE
TROPHY FROM THE BANK'S REGIONAL DIRECTOR KEN ATKINSON
(INSET) OOOPS!...WEST HAM 2ND DIVISION CHAMPIONS???

BARCLAYS OFFICIALLY PRESENT EARL BARRETT WITH THE 2ND DIVISION
CHAMPIONSHIP TROPHY BEFORE THE ROGER PALMER TESTIMONIAL MATCH

A sequence of three away games in eight days began with a trip to Leicester, where home goalkeeper and ex-Latic loan player, Martin Hodge, stood between Athletic and a cricket score. His agility earned his side a goalless draw. Then on to Newcastle, under new manager Ossie Ardiles, whose new side caught Royle's boys on a bad day, winning 3-2. However, Athletic bounced back to earn a 1-1 draw at bogy side, Charlton, despite having Paul Warhurst sent off for a professional foul.

Manager Royle had always maintained that eighty points would be enough to see his side clinch an automatic promotion place, and following those three away fixtures, they now had 76. Exactly one year after stepping out for their first ever Wembley appearance, Athletic headed for Ipswich knowing a victory would secure a return to the First Division for the first time in sixty eight years. Almost 3,000 supporters made the long trip to East Anglia to see Ian Marshall fittingly end the journey he began with that hat-trick at Wolves on the opening day, with two wonderful goals, as Athletic won 2-1 to guarantee First Division football at Boundary Park next season. Joe Royle said,"I won't say it's an anti-climax, but I thought early on that the top three were the best sides. Eighty points will always get you up. The players are elated, but it isn't as if someone scored the winner in the last ten minutes of the last game. Promotion seems to have been with us for a long time".

With promotion assured, Athletic set off in pursuit of the Championship, but their hopes took a knock when they lost for the third time at Notts County in League and Cup. They returned to winning ways when beating play-off hopefuls Middlesbrough by 2-0 at an odd-looking Boundary Park. Work had started on removing the roof on the 'Chaddy End' in preparation for the changeover to a 3,200 all-seater stand.

The last day of the season saw second-placed Athletic take on third-placed Sheffield Wednesday, while leaders, West Ham, were also at home to fourth-placed Notts County. Steven Spielberg could not have dreamed up the amazing climax to this season. West Ham, possibly thinking they had done the hard work, lost 2-1 to County, but as news filtered through of Athletic being two goals down to Wednesday, the Championship looked destined for Upton Park. Even a 2-2 scoreline at Boundary Park would see West Ham triumphant, but after 92 minutes of tremendous action came the unbelievable. Referee Vic Callow awarded Athletic a penalty, and Neil Redfearn struck it home to give Athletic a 3-2 victory and the Second Division Championship. "I just closed my mind to everything else going on," he said, "all I was concerned with was deciding where to place the shot and making sure of a good strike. I never thought I would miss, but it was a relief and a great feeling when it went in".

The Second Division Championship trophy arrived at Boundary Park with West Ham United's name engraved on it. The trophy had been hastily dispatched to Boundary Park by special courier before embarrassed League officials realised their big mistake. A club spokesman said, "We were a bit taken aback when we received the trophy and discovered West Ham's name engraved on it. Fortunately we have a trophy centre as part of the commercial set-up at Boundary Park, and we were able to correct the mistake in time for the official presentation".

ATHLETIC'S TITLE WINNERS CELEBRATE WITH THE MAYOR, COUNCILLOR SID JACOBS AT
THE CIVIC RECEPTION — MAY '91

THE CHAMPIONS WITH THEIR TROPHY, BEFORE THE ROGER PALMER
TESTIMONIAL MATCH — MAY '91

There was a carnival atmosphere as the Champions took an open-top bus ride from the ground to the Civic Centre for an official reception on Sunday 12th May. More than 15,000 jubilant fans packed the streets to congratulate Athletic, who proudly displayed the silver Championship trophy. As the team held the trophy aloft from the Civic Centre balcony, and rain clouds began to threaten, Councillor Jacobs spoke for the thousands of fans, young and old, when he said, ''Well done Joe, Champion just Champion''.

Injuries were again a problem for Athletic this season, but the strength-in-depth of the squad, evident for the first time, saw them through to the First Division. Three players appeared in all 52 League and Cup matches, goalkeeper Jon Hallworth, defender Andy Barlow and captain Earl Barrett, who capped this season literally, winning his first full England cap on a summer tour of S. E. Asia, Australia and New Zealand. Striker Ian Marshall topped Athletic's goalscoring charts with an impressive total of 18 League and Cup goals in only 27 starts and one outing as substitute. Neil Redfearn's name would go down in the club's history books for that penalty strike, but he made a telling contribution of 17 goals to finish a close second.

Athletic's average League attendance showed another huge increase to 13,234, and the level and quality of Athletic's away support was a feature of a memorable season.

ATHLETIC'S PLAYERS TOURED OLDHAM ON ROUTE FOR A CIVIC RECEPTION IN AN
OPEN-TOP-BUS — MAY '91

ATHLETIC'S PROMOTION SEASON IN DETAIL

AUGUST
LATICS SCORE SHOWN FIRST

25 Wolverhampton Wanderers.................A 3-2 (Marshall 3)...............................20,864
28 Leicester City.....................................H 2-0 (Marshall, Ritchie)....................13,099

SEPTEMBER
1 Portsmouth...H 3-1 (R Holden, Kuhl o.g.
Warhurst)...............................11,657
8 Barnsley...A 1-0 (Marshall)...............................11,257
15 Oxford United....................................H 3-0 (Marshall, Barrett,
Redfearn)...............................12,492
18 Charlton Athletic...............................H 1-1 (Redfearn)..............................13,176
22 Middlesbrough...................................A 1-0 (Palmer).................................19,363
25 Notts County (Rumbelows Cup
round 2 — 7.45 p.m.)........................A 0-1 7,089
29 West Bromwich Albion.......................A 0-0 13,782

OCTOBER
2 Swindon Town....................................H 3-2 (Moulden, R Holden,
Redfearn pen)..........................12,575
6 Blackburn Rovers...............................H 1-1 (Moulden)..............................12,093
9 Notts County (Rumbelows Cup
round 2...H 5-2 (Currie 2, Redfearn pen,
Moulden, R Holden)................10,757
13 Hull City..A 2-2 (Henry, Redfearn).....................8,676
20 Bristol City...A 2-1 (Adams 2)...............................14,031
23 Ipswich Town......................................H 2-0 (Moulden, Currie)....................13,170
27 Notts County.......................................H 2-1 (Redfearn, Ritchie)...................12,940
31 Leeds United (Rumbelows Cup
round 3)..A 0-2 26,327

NOVEMBER
3 Sheffield Wednesday...........................A 2-2 (Henry, Currie).........................34,845
10 Watford..H 4-1 (Ritchie 2 (1 pen), Redfearn,
Henry)...................................12,410
17 Port Vale..A 0-1 11,384
24 Bristol Rovers.....................................A 0-2 6,542

DECEMBER
1 Brighton...H 6-1 (Marshall 2, Henry, Adams,
Redfearn, Ritchie)...................11,426
11 Sheffield United (ZDSC round 2)........A 2-7 (Palmer, Marshall)......................3,144
15 Wolverhampton Wanderers.................H 4-1 (Barrett, Ritchie, Palmer 2)........11,587
21 Plymouth Argyle (7.30 p.m.)..............H 5-3 (Palmer 2, Redfearn 2, Barrett)....11.296
26 West Ham United (noon)....................A 0-2 24,950
29 Millwall...A 0-0 10,010

JANUARY
1 Newcastle United (1 p.m.)..................H 1-1 (Stimson o.g.).........................14,550
5 Brentford (FA Cup round 3)...............H 3-1 (Redfearn 2 pens, Adams)..........12,588
12 Portsmouth...A 4-1 (Marshall 2, R Holden,
Palmer).................................10,840
19 Barnsley...H 2-0 (Marshall, Ritchie)...................13,849
26 Notts County (FA Cup round 4)...........A 0-2 14,002

FEBRUARY
2 Oxford United....................................A 1-5 (Adams)..................................5,411
16 Port Vale..H 2-0 (Redfearn, Jobson)...................12,630
23 Watford..A 1-1 (Redfearn)...............................8,320

MARCH
2 Brighton...A 2-1 (Ritchie 2)...............................9,496
9 Bristol Rovers.....................................H 2-0 (Ritchie, Redfearn)...................12,775
12 Swindon Town....................................A 2-2 (Ritchie, Palmer)......................8,193
16 West Bromwich Albion.......................H 2-1 (Palmer 2)..............................12,584
19 Hull City..H 1-2 (Ritchie pen)..........................12,626
23 Blackburn Rovers...............................A 0-2 12,175
29 West Ham United (3 p.m.)...................H 1-1 (Ritchie pen)..........................16,932

APRIL
1 Plymouth Argyle (2.30 p.m.)..............A 2-1 (Ritchie, Adams).......................8,852
6 Millwall...H 1-1 (Ritchie).................................13,434
10 Leicester City (7.45 p.m.)...................A 0-0 11,846
13 Newcastle United................................A 2-3 (Marshall, R Holden)................16,615
16 Charlton Athletic (7.45 p.m.)..............H 1-1 (Adams)..................................5,367
20 Bristol City...H 2-1 (Marshall, Redfearn pen)...........14,086
27 Ipswich Town......................................A 2-1 (Marshall 2)............................12,332

MAY
4 Notts County.......................................A 0-2 12,311
7 Middlesbrough (7.30 p.m.)..................H 2-0 (Marshall, R Holden)................14,213
11 Sheffield Wednesday...........................H 3-2 (Marshall, Bernard,
Redfearn pen)..........................18,809

The full list of appearances (substitutes in brackets) was:

Barlow 52
Barrett 52
Hallworth 52
Henry 49
Jobson 49 (1)
R Holden 48
Redfearn 47 (4)
Warhurst 35 (2)
Ritchie 30 (2)
Marshall 27 (1)
Palmer ......,..... 24 (10)
Adams 20 (12)
Currie 20 (12)
Halle 17
Moulden 13 (14)
Donachie 13 (7)
Kane 13 (5)
Bernard 2
A Holden 2
Fillery 1 (1)
Brazil (loan).......... 1
Williams .... (3)

Chairman, Mr.Ian Stott, stated that Athletic would reluctantly resign from the Football League and join the F.A.'s breakaway 'Super League' for the '92-93 season. It was understood that every club who was in the First Division this season, bar one, had moved into the F.A.'s corner. Mr. Stott said,"I am not happy at being forced into this position, but I cannot now see anything to prevent the F.A. from implementing their proposals. We have waited 68 years to regain our place in the top flight, so my personal feelings don't come into it. We simply cannot afford to be left behind, and if nothing happens to alter the situation, we will tell the F.A. before the August deadline that we wish to be included".

Athletic's summer transfer outlay amounted to £1.6 million, as the club's record was broken with £600,000, Mike Milligan returning to Boundary Park from Everton, Graeme Sharp arriving, also from Everton for £500,000, Coventry City's ex-captain, Brian Kilcline, signing for £400,000, and youngster Craig Fleming coming with high recommendations, for £80,000 from Halifax Town.

While the players were enjoying a summer break, then a six-game tour of Sweden, the face of Boundary Park was changing fast. Gone was the artificial pitch which had served Athletic so well for five years, replaced by a new grass surface which had made remarkable progress in a short space of time. Gone too, was the popular standing accommodation in the Chadderton End, and in its place was a new all-seater stand, complete with refurbished roof. Also new to Boundary Park was the extra hospitality suite on the main stand side of the ground.

The dream finally became reality on Saturday August 17th 1991, when Athletic stepped out at Anfield for a First Division match for the first time in 68 years.

THE 'CHADDY ROAD END' UNDER RE-DEVELOPMENT — JULY '91

A SOCCER GHOST STORY

A biting wind whistled around the vast, black emptiness of Boundary Park. No moon, no stars, no rain... just a desolate moan rushing eerily in every nook and cranny. Somewhere a door flapped aimlessly open and shut. The goalposts stood stark and cold...

As I stood silent and alone, there seemed to come, from the caverns of the Chadderton End, a jumble of noises born out of the wind itself. I listened intently as familiar sounds filled the air. As they did, so vague shapes appeared out of the gloom, flitting effortlessly in pools of brilliant light. There was Holden, with a delicate chip into the crowded goal mouth, as the massed voices roared their approval; Redfearn's cracking shot blistering the paintwork, Barratt's magnificent tackles; and there, Ritchie with a flashing header, arms aloft to the delirious rapture of the Crowd. To the cocky chant of 'Zigga Zagga' man after man combined to astound the struggling opposition... over with the centre... Marshall running in... 'Hit it, lad''...!

As suddenly as they had come the apparitions dissolved, the wind howled unceasingly in the inky blackness, and the glories of the 1990's had fled, for ever.

ANON